The Second Messiah

To my wife and our three children.

R.L.

To my wife Susan and our daughters
Kathryn, Lucy and Sophie.

C.K.

THE SECOND MESSIAH

TEMPLARS, THE TURIN SHROUD AND THE GREAT SECRET OF FREEMASONRY

Christopher Knight and Robert Lomas

FAIR WINDS
PRESS
GLOUCESTER, MASSACHUSETTS

First published in the UK by Century Books Limited 1997

' Christopher Knight and Robert Lomas 1997

This paperback edition published in the USA by
Fair Winds Press 2001

Library of Congress Cataloging-in-Publication data
Knight, Christopher. 1950-
The Second Messiah: Templars, the turin shroud, and the great
secret of Freemasonry / Christopher Knight and Robert Lomas
p. cm.
Includes bibliographical references and index.
1. Freemasonry History. 2. Templars History. 3. Holy Shroud
I. Lomas, Robert. 1947-- II. Title.
H5403. K553 1998   9/--26609
366¢.1 dc21   CIP

ISBN 1-931412-76-6

Printed in Canada

ACKNOWLEDGEMENTS

The authors would like to thank the following people for their help and support during the writing of this book.

W. Bro Alan Atkins, W. Bro John Barlow, Russell Barnes, Dr Frank Bartells, Baron St Clair Bonde, Mark Booth, Robert Brydon, The Right Revd Gerrard Crane, Revd Mrs Pam Crane, Greg Clark, Prof Philip Davies, Judy Fisken, W. Bro Edgar Harborne, Jacques Huyghebaert, W. Bro Arthur Issat, Revd Hugh Lawrance, Dr Jack Miller, Dr Alan Mills, Dr Graham Phillips, Barbara Pickard, Tessa Ransford, Liz Rowlinson, Dr Neil Sellors, Iain Sinclair, Niven Sinclair, Robert Temple, Tony Thorne, Roy Vickery, Bridget de Villiers, John Wade, Dr Tim Wallace-Murphy, the staff of the Library of the Grand Lodge of Antient Free and Accepted Masons of Scotland, the staff at Rosslyn Chapel, the Trustees of Rosslyn Chapel, the Scottish Poetry Museum, the National Museum of Natural History.

We would also especially like to single out for thanks our agent Mr Bill Hamilton of A. M. Heath Ltd for his invaluable guidance and encouragement during the writing of this book.

PHOTO CREDITS – PLATE SECTION

Wine is strong,
a king is stronger,
women are even stronger.
But truth will conquer all.

The Book of Esdras

Contents

Introduction

In our previous book, *The Hiram Key*, we uncovered the early origins of Freemasonry which showed how modern Masonic rituals have developed from those once used by the Jerusalem Church and later adopted by the famous crusader order of the Knights Templar. These warrior monks had a very strange history that started with a nine-year-long excavation of the ruins of Herod's Temple following the First Crusade and ended, nearly two hundred years later, with them being arrested as heretics.

Our findings were controversial, but they were warmly received by many biblical, Templar and Masonic scholars, as well as several Catholic priests.

Over the months following publication we met hundreds of Freemasons of every rank, all over England, Scotland and Wales, and we received nothing but support and congratulations from them.

The notable exception to this reception was that of the United Grand Lodge of England, which did not even acknowledge the pre-publication copy of the book we sent. It appeared to consider that, as Freemasons, we had committed the sin of conducting independent research past the golden year of 1717. We had not contravened any rule of the Order, but we soon became aware of a letter sent out from Grand Lodge to the provincial grand lodges of England and Wales, giving a short and extremely disingenuous account of our findings.

Shortly afterwards the worshipful master of a famous Masonic lodge attended one of our bookshop talks with the intention of gathering evidence against us, but at the end he congratulated us, bought a copy of our book and asked us to sign it for him. A constant stream of letters continued to arrive from people all over the world, many providing us with yet more supportive evidence. Some very senior Freemasons were extremely complimentary: for instance, David Sinclair Bouschor, Past Grand Master of Minnesota, was kind enough to say:

The Hiram Key *could spark the beginning of a reformation in Christian thinking and a reconsideration of 'the facts' which we have so blindly accepted and perpetuated for generations. This book is a must for freethinkers.*

Another American, a Doctor of Divinity, who we perhaps should not name, wrote to us saying:

I am a 32 degree Scottish Rite Mason, Master of my lodge 3 times, Past Wise Master of Rose Croix, a member of The Order of Amaranth and a Shiner, in addition I am an ordained minister in the Reformed Baptist Church. All this experience and education did not prepare me for the material contained in your book. If I had not been searching for our ancient origins and had the courage to look outside the dogmas of the establishments, perhaps I would not have finished reading The Hiram Key, *however, I was, I did and I too find your data totally acceptable to what I have found. This has led me to believe that perhaps there is some truth to the accusations levelled against Masonry that 'only the top (HIGH) degrees know the truth'.*

This last comment was particularly fascinating because, as far as we know, there is only one degree higher than the 32 degree to which this gentleman belongs. Could there be a secret so great that only a handful of Freemasons know it? Perhaps, we thought, this great secret has been lost and now needs to be rediscovered.

The situation was far too intriguing to ignore. We knew for certain that Freemasonry had developed the rituals used by the Jerusalem Church and the Knights Templar and it seemed likely that the United Grand Lodge of England had either lost contact with its own origins or it was deliberately concealing something very big indeed – even from its own officers. Its determination to prevent discussion about anything outside of its official doctrine was very different from every other grand lodge that we know of, and we decided that our researches must continue.

When we set out on our quest, six key questions lay before us:

1. Have some Masonic rituals been deliberately changed or suppressed?

2. Is there a great secret of Freemasonry that has become lost, or has been deliberately hidden?
3. Who was behind the formation of the Knights Templar?
4. Why did the Templars decide to excavate beneath the ruins of Herod's Temple?
5. What were the beliefs which led to the destruction of the Templars as heretics?
6. Can the deeper rituals of Freemasonry shed further new light on the origins of Christianity?

We knew that the answers would not be easy to find, but as our researches progressed we found the answer to one very important question that we had not posed ourselves: what is the definitive origin of the Shroud of Turin?

We had previously speculated that there could have been a Templar connection with this unique relic, but we were not prepared for the magnitude of its role in history and the importance of the man whose image it bears.

Chapter One

THE DEATH OF A NATION

Who controls the past controls the future. Who controls the present controls the past.

George Orwell: *1984*

A NEW LIGHT ON OLD BELIEFS

It is said that more information has been produced in the last thirty years than over all the previous five thousand. Thanks to modern techniques of investigation and the advent of powerful data storage and retrieval systems, we all can have rapid access to huge amounts of information. We can now understand more about the world we live in, its past and its potential future, than was ever dreamed possible, even just a generation ago.

Ordinary people have had to acclimatise themselves to the idea of a never-ending innovation avalanche; everything, from toothpaste to motor-cars, gets smarter year on year. Most of us now believe that newer means better, but whilst new things may change outlooks, old ideas still die hard and the 'truths' that were placed in our minds as children remain unchallenged. How do we know that Columbus discovered America? Why do we think that Jesus turned water into wine? We believe we know the answers to both questions because someone told us that it was so and we have never had occasion to challenge these, culturally accepted, assertions.

History it seems is not so much a record of past events, more a catalogue of preferred beliefs expounded by people who have a vested interest. As George Orwell observed in his novel *1984*, history is always written by the

1

victors and whoever controls the writing of history books controls the past. Without doubt, the most consistently powerful force in the western world over the last two thousand years has been the Roman Catholic Church and consequently history has often been what it wanted it to be.

The Church has always been the provider of western cultural 'truths', but, as more and more hard evidence emerges, it has had to concede that the papacy is not as infallible as it once claimed. For instance, Galileo was sentenced to life imprisonment and his work burned when he argued that the Earth moved through space, and it was not until 1992 that a papal commission acknowledged the Vatican's error in opposing him. In the nineteenth century, Charles Darwin's theory of evolution was viciously attacked by the Church, but in 1996 the Vatican once again had to admit that it had been wrong.

In times past the Church provided answers to life's puzzles when no one had a better solution, but as science has advanced, the need for myths has receded. However, whilst the Vatican moves slowly and cautiously when it comes to rethinking mankind's role in creation, it hardly moves at all concerning its interpretation of events described in the New Testament, despite considerable amounts of new historical evidence.

A good illustration of this history-power occurred in November 1996 when Pope John Paul II met the Archbishop of Canterbury, the head of the Church of England. At this meeting between the two Church leaders, the pope felt it necessary to remind the Englishman of his absolute superiority by reaffirming his historical status as the direct successor to St Peter, to whom, it is said, Christ had entrusted his Church.[1]

This claim of power based on a direct inheritance from Jesus Christ himself, known as 'Apostolic Succession', is based on a Roman Catholic version of history that has become widely discredited as modern scholars re-examine the circumstances of the Jerusalem Church. The weight of evidence now strongly indicates that Jesus led an entirely Jewish sect and that he was succeeded not by Peter but by his younger brother James, the first Bishop of Jerusalem.

The role of James, the brother of Jesus, has always been seen as a threat by the Roman Catholic Church, and from its earliest times the Church has controlled history by removing information about this highly important figure. As recently as 1996, Pope John Paul II issued a statement declaring that

[1] *The Times* (London) 28 November 1996

2

Jesus was Mary's only child and that therefore James was not his brother after all.[2] The Pontiff made this strange and completely unsubstantiated statement despite biblical evidence and much scholarly opinion to the contrary.

The weight of evidence that now exists shows that whilst Peter may well have been leader of the Christian movement in Rome from AD 42 to 67, he was certainly not the leader of the Church. The supreme leader of the entire Church in those days was James, the brother of Jesus, the Bishop of Jerusalem. We know of no serious biblical scholar who doubts this fact and S.G.F. Brandon put it most clearly when he said:

> . . . the fact of the supremacy of the Jerusalem Church and its
> essentially Jewish outlook emerges clear of serious doubt, and so
> also does the unique leadership of James, the brother of the Lord.[3]

James was a fine successor to his crucified brother and provided strong leadership for the community that we call the Jerusalem Church, and the Jews of the Diaspora (the dispersion into the Greco-Roman world) such as the communities in Ephesus in Turkey, Alexandria and Rome itself.

Some three years after the death of Jesus, Paul, a Diaspora Jew from the southern Turkish city of Tarsus, arrived in Israel. Due to the false 'history' given out today, many people believe that this man was called 'Saul' when he persecuted the Christians and changed it to 'Paul' when he suddenly became a Christian after being struck blind on the road to Damascus.

The reality is quite different. For a start there were no Christians at that time; the Jerusalem Church was Jewish and the cult called Christianity did not begin until many years later as an entirely Roman idea. The man who gave rise to this new religion had changed his name from the Hebrew 'Saul' to the Roman 'Paul' when he became a Roman citizen as a young man, as he wanted a name that sounded similar to his original one.

We are told that Paul had a zeal for the Jewish Law and this led him to persecute the Jerusalem Church, holding it to be a Jewish sect that was untrue to the Law, and therefore should be destroyed. He is even said to have been involved in the stoning of St Stephen, the first Christian martyr. This, however, can only be viewed as a Jewish sectarian issue when the Jerusalem

---

[2] *The Times* (London) 30 August 1996
[3] S.G.F. Brandon: *The Fall of Jerusalem and the Christian Church*

Church led by James was entirely Jewish and there was no suggestion at this time that Jesus was anything other than a Jewish martyr who had died in an attempt to establish home rule for his people.

At some point Paul became fascinated by the idea of the sacrificial nature of Jesus's death and he opposed James for not accepting that his brother was a god. In his Galatian Epistle he is at great pains to point out that, during the period of his conversion, he was completely independent of the Jerusalem Church or any other human agency and he puts his colourful ideas down to the direct intervention of God. Paul says:

> It was the good pleasure of God . . . to reveal his Son in me, that I might preach it to the gentiles.[4]

The ideas that Paul generated, and that subsequent gospel writers built upon, came largely out of his imagination. Christian scholar S G F Brandon wrote:

> The phrase 'to reveal his Son in me' is admittedly a curious one, but it clearly has a high significance for our understanding of Paul's own interpretation of God's purpose for him . . . When carefully considered as a statement of fact, the words really constitute a tremendous, indeed a preposterous, claim for any man to make, and more especially a man of Paul's antecedents. They mean literally that in the person of Paul God had revealed his Son to the end that Paul might 'evangelise' him among the Gentiles . . . What Paul's statement implied, was a new unveiling of His Son, so that there was afforded an apprehension of Jesus which was hitherto unknown in the Church . . . The position which we reach then is that Paul is the exponent of an interpretation of the Christian faith which he himself regards as differing essentially from the interpretation which may be best described as the traditional or historical one.[5]

If the account given by Paul and his followers is a distortion of the true beliefs of the Jerusalem Church, the question remains: what were its original ideas?

---

[4] Galatians 1:15,16
[5] G.F. Brandon: *The Fall of Jerusalem and the Christian Church*

In our last book we made a complex but, we hope, well-reasoned argument that the Jerusalem Church used 'living resurrection' ceremonies to initiate people into its higher level of membership. In these ceremonies the candidate underwent a symbolic death and was wrapped in a shroud before being resurrected, just as Freemasons are today. It is known from contemporary documents, including the Dead Sea Scrolls, that it was normal practice at that time for Jews to call people inside their sect 'the living' and those outside it 'the dead'.

After studying the terminology used by the people of first-century Jerusalem, we came to the conclusion that there is absolutely no requirement to apply supernatural meaning to the actions of Jesus Christ. His supposed miracles, including 'raising the dead', can be seen to be simple misunderstandings of much more mundane events, by later individuals who had a very different mindset from the Jews. Other misunderstood phrases include terms such as 'turning water into wine' which simply meant elevating ordinary people to a higher station in life. Today, Freemasons still use a stylised resurrection ritual to raise a candidate from his 'grave' in order to make him a fully fledged Master Mason. This is done in darkness, in front of Boaz and Jachin, the two eastward-facing pillars that stood at the entrance to the Jerusalem Temple.

After Paul became convinced that he had a new interpretation of the death of Jesus (based on his misunderstanding of the terminology of Jerusalem), he knew that he would have problems with James, the head of the Jerusalem Church. His embarrassment when explaining his new gospel to James is apparent in the second chapter of his Epistle to the Galatians, where he says:

> And I went up by revelation, and communicated unto them that gospel which I preach among the gentiles . . .
>
> But contrariwise, when they saw that the gospel of the uncircumcision was committed unto me, as the gospel of the uncircumcision was unto Peter.
>
> (For he that wrought effectually in Peter to the apostleship of the circumcision, the same was mighty in me toward the Gentiles:)
>
> And when James, Cephas, and John, who seemed to be pillars, perceived the grace that was given unto me, they gave to me and Barnabas the right hands of fellowship: that we should go unto the heathen, and they unto the circumcision.

Some Christian observers have tried to claim that Paul's 'gospel of the uncircumcision' was merely a geographical agreement where Paul took responsibility for preaching to the gentiles outside the Jewish homeland, but this is a hollow argument. In his Second Epistle to the Corinthians, Paul clearly warns about others who are preaching of 'another Jesus' and 'another spirit', whilst warning his audience not to heed any explanation but his own.[6] Whilst we are sure that James did not approve of the gospel preached by Paul, New Testament scholars have shown evidence that some rabbis in Palestine did accept that it was necessary to present Judaism in a different form which could be appreciated by those nurtured in the traditions of Greco-Roman culture.[7]

Not many people take the trouble to read the findings of biblical scholars and they therefore remain open to standard Catholic Church dogma which holds Paul's vision to be real, despite the fact that it has no basis in the original Jerusalem Church. One such scholar summed up the situation as follows:

> *The value that can be attached to the Christian evidence turns on the reasons why this literature came into being and the circumstances which gave it birth. Initially, however, it is suspect because it sets out to prove as facts assertions which are now known to be impossible. The Gospels demonstrate a belief or assert a claim that Jesus was a semi-divine being who was born contrary to the laws of nature and who conquered death. This was not the belief of the original followers of Jesus, nor did he himself make such claims.*
>
> *The letters of Paul are the earliest documents, Christian or otherwise, relating to the origins of Christianity that have survived; yet they are the least useful in establishing facts about Jesus . . . It is significant that they show a marked lack of interest in both Jesus the historical man and the proverbial founder of the faith.*[8]

Paul invented an heretical creed that is essentially un-Jewish and flies in the face of a theological structure that has always placed an absolute gulf between God and man, and Paul's strange gospel, designed for gentiles, is

---

[6] Corinthians 11:4
[7] W.L. Knox: *Some Hellenistic Elements in Primitive Christianity*
[8] R. Furneaux: *The Other Side of the Story*

completely without parallel in all extant records of Jewish thought.[9] If we are right that the Jesus of Paul's teachings was completely at odds with those of James and the Church at Jerusalem, the question we need to answer is: why did this heretical form survive and the real Church die out?

To pursue this question it is necessary to try and understand the outlook of James, the brother of Jesus, who was known as 'the Just'. It is clear from surviving accounts that the Jews of the Jerusalem Church had a considerable mistrust of the Jews of the Diaspora and that they had little or no interest in the conversion of gentiles.

James the Just was Bishop of Jerusalem and had been established as an official high priest by the Zealots in direct opposition to the pro-Roman Boethusean and Sadducean high priests.[10]

We are told in an account given in chapters 66 to 70 of the *Clementine Recognitions*[11] that James undertook a public lecture in the Temple regarding the true doctrine of his brother Jesus, with the famous rabbis Gamaliel and Caiaphas putting questions to him. The eloquence and logic of James were gaining the full support of the invited audience when an enemy (believed by many scholars to be Paul)[12] caused a major disturbance which resulted in James being thrown down a flight of stairs and injured.

Eusebius, the third-century Church historian, gives an account of the death of James which provides a much more comprehensive version than the brief account recorded by Josephus.[13] James is depicted as an ascetic of huge popularity who possesses some curious religious practices and is detained in the Temple by Ananus, who convenes a Sanhedrin and has James charged with breaking the Law. Here he is asked a strange question which no scholar has ever understood:

> *Oh Just One, whom we all are obliged to trust announce unto us what is the gate of salvation. (Sha'ar ha-yeshu 'ah)*[14]

This makes perfect sense if Ananus had heard rumours of the twin pillar paradigm that was so important to the Nasoreans, who were the senior

---

[9] Guignebert: *Le Monde Juif vers le Temps de Jesus*

[10] R. Eisler: *The Messiah Jesus and John the Baptist*

[11] Translated by the Ante-Nicene Christian Library, vol. iii

[12] S.G.F. Brandon: *The Fall of Jerusalem and the Christian Church*

[13] Eusebius: *Ecclesiastical History*

[14] K. Kohler: *Jewish Encyclopaedia*

members of the Jerusalem Church, and was asking James to explain it. The twin pillars of Boaz and Jachin were the ones that stood either side of the entrance to the 'holy of holies' – the inner sanctum of Yahweh's Temple – and they were represented by the kingly and priestly messiahs of Israel. Salvation for the Jewish people could only be achieved when both pillars were in place – and that would require the removal of Roman rule and their puppets, the Sadducees.

James was not about to explain his beliefs to these inferior Jews and he answered with a statement that appeared to his inquisitors to make no sense. They then threw James down from the Temple walls, stoned him and finally dispatched him with a blow to the temple from a fuller's club.

The leadership of the Jerusalem Church was monarchical, rather than ecclesiastical, for following the murder of James, in AD 62, a first cousin of Jesus, Simeon son of Cleophas, became the new leader of the Church.[15] He too was later murdered; executed by the Romans as a pretender to the throne of David.[16] The fact that Jesus assumed the role of full leadership after the killing of his cousin John the Baptist, was followed by his brother James and then the next male member of the family, has led many commentators to observe that the Jerusalem Church was structured as an hereditary monarchy.[17] Just as one would expect of the royal bloodline of David.

It is believed that James and Paul both died violent deaths and some scholars have suggested that Paul may have been executed by Zealots for some part he played in the killing of James. The question remains as to why Paul's religion prospered while that of James died out.

Why has no documentary evidence of the Jerusalem Church survived?

We believe that it has survived right up to today, but, like the Dead Sea Scrolls found at Qumran, the scrolls of the Jerusalem Church have been hidden away to protect them from the contamination of the gentiles. To understand what happened to these important documents we must turn to a terrible period of Jewish history.

THE MISSING YEARS

Christians today read their Bible to find inspiration from the teaching of Jesus and his followers; who sought to establish the kingdom of heaven upon

---

[15] H. Schonfield: *The Passover Plot*
[16] H. Maccabee: *The Mythmaker*
[17] Ibid.

earth almost two thousand years ago. According to the King James Bible, the stories told in the four Gospels all conclude with the crucifixion and resurrection in the year AD 33, although AD 36 is also accepted as a probable date. The New Testament then picks up the story in the Book of Acts from that point to go on as far as AD 62. Other books such as Timothy and the Epistles of Peter refer to years up to AD 66, but from then onwards nothing is mentioned until the First Epistle of John, which is dated at AD 90.

Although the four gospels of the New Testament deal exclusively with the period of the life of Jesus, the earliest of them, that of Mark, is widely accepted as being compiled by an otherwise unknown early Christian, who drew on a variety of traditions, during the period AD 70 to 80.[18] Although no one knows for sure, Paul is believed to have been executed in Rome in AD 65.

Most Christians will almost certainly have never bothered about this little gap in Christian chronology of some ten to fifteen years between the contemporary writings of Paul and the retrospective ones of Mark and the other gospel writers, yet these missing years are of unparalleled importance.

The kingdom of heaven did not arrive as the Jerusalem Church expected – but the kingdom of hell certainly did.

By AD 65, much was wrong with the country. Taxation from Rome was heavy, officials were increasingly corrupt, and in Jerusalem eighteen thousand men were thrown out of work as the Temple was finally completed. Malcontents – some patriots, some no more than brigands – levied their own toll on the local population in what amounted to 'protection racketeering'. Unrest grew almost daily and the historian Josephus tells us that although he has little sympathy with the politico-religious fanaticism of the Zealots and their willingness to draw their nation into a hopeless war with Rome, he believes that the Romans were totally insensitive to Jewish culture. One of the most inflammatory examples of this insensitivity was carried out by the homicidal emperor Caligula who had a statue of himself erected inside the Temple at Jerusalem. Naturally, this caused huge offence to Jews everywhere and might have been a contributory factor in Caligula's assassination soon after.

Not only did the Romans make life difficult; the chief sacerdotal families of Jerusalem also instigated violence against anyone who did not please them.[19] According to Josephus, the beginning of the end occurred at

[18] B. L. Mack: *The Lost Gospel*
[19] J. Klausner: *Jesus of Nazareth*

Caesarea when the procurator Gessius Florus deliberately goaded the Jewish population into insurrection in the hope that his own, recent misdeeds would go unnoticed in Rome due to the ensuing mayhem.[20] The news of large-scale rioting in Caesarea spread rapidly across the whole country and the Zealots of Jerusalem descended upon the Jewish leaders of the city and the Roman garrison, slaughtering everyone that they could lay their hands on. Even the Samaritans, who were never close friends of the Jews, sided with the Zealots as the revolt gained pace.

The news of the destruction of the Roman garrison at Jerusalem had disastrous consequences for the Jews of Caesarea, which was the headquarters of the procurator. Enraged by the loss of friends and family in Jerusalem, the Roman soldiers commenced the systematic massacre of the entire population. As is the nature of war, this in turn outraged the Jews who immediately attacked the gentile cities of Philadelphia, Sebonitis, Gerasa, Pella, Scythopolis, Gadara, Hippos, Kedesa, Ptolemais and Gaba, where huge numbers of gentiles perished as victims of Jewish fanaticism.[21]

The Jews felt that their day had finally arrived, and whilst there seems to have been little central organisation at this time, the intensity of their hatred for the Romans and all gentiles was such that the entire nation appears to have been irresistibly drawn into a frenzy of religious exultation. Josephus records that the battle fever spread outside Palestine, with pogroms breaking out in Tyre, Alexandria and in several Syrian cities including Damascus.

As leaders emerged they must have known that their cause was hopeless, since it was only a matter of time before Rome would send its full might to crush the tiny province. However, the Zealots had not taken up arms because they thought that they were stronger than the Romans; their motivation was the belief that God would provide a miracle to save his chosen people, as he had done before when the Israelites triumphed over the might of the Egyptians.[22] Such was their faith in God's favour that new coins were issued bearing the inscription: '*The first year of the redemption of Israel*'.

The Zealots were uncompromising, killing any members of the priesthood they viewed as being in opposition to them. They dispossessed and imprisoned those who did not show strong enough support for the cause.

The expected attack by the Romans was a long time coming, but when it

---

[20] Josephus: *History of the Jewish War*
[21] Ibid.
[22] D.A. Schlatter: *Geschichte Israels von Alexander dem Grossen bis Hadrian*

arrived it was powerfully delivered. Cestius Gallus entered Palestine with a strong force of legionary and auxiliary troops who experienced little resistance from the disorganised Jews as they marched straight for Jerusalem. The legate succeeded in pushing his attack to the very point of breaching the Temple walls, then, for no obvious reason, he ordered his troops to withdraw from the final assault and to retreat northwards from the city. The Jews, who had expected the Romans to be upon them within hours, were astonished to see their enemies so strangely turn upon their heels in the face of imminent victory. At first they thought it was some trick within the Roman battle strategy, but as they realised that they had simply marched away the Jews were overcome with joy.

At this key point it is necessary to recall a document that must have been in the mind of every Jew who had just defended the Temple of Yahweh.

Called *The Assumption of Moses*, this strange document has an apocalyptic theme and describes imaginary events such as the occasion when the archangel Michael was digging a grave for Moses and the devil appeared to claim the body but was quietly refused. It is believed that the document was started prior to the crucifixion, but it seems to cover a period up to and including the Jewish war. It also refers to a mysterious figure by the name of 'Taxo' who exhorts his sons to die rather than be disloyal to their faith, and from their death we pass to the expected intervention of God in the battle to establish His kingdom. Many scholars have identified the figure of Taxo with the Teacher of Righteousness[23] described in the Dead Sea Scrolls, who we identify as James, the Bishop of Jerusalem.

The Assumption of Moses states that the reign of God will be established through great destruction of men, and nations, but the final triumph will bring an end to the reign of Satan. One passage reads:

And then His kingdom shall appear throughout all His creation
And then Satan shall be no more
And sorrow shall depart with him . . .
For the Heavenly One will arise from His royal throne,
And He will go forth from His Holy habitation

Yahweh's 'Holy habitation' can only refer to the inner sanctum of the Temple that the Jews had been fighting to defend. The passage continues:

[23] *Peake's Commentary on the Bible*

With indignation and wrath on account of His sons . . .
For the Most High will arise, the Eternal God alone,
And He will appear to punish the Gentiles,
And He will destroy all idols
And thou, Israel, shall be happy

This document records that the Jews fighting this battle were required to bury their most precious scrolls and treasures as close to the Holy of Holies as they could get, where they would be in God's safe keeping. We can be sure that these items were secreted beneath the temple because the 'Copper Scroll' (so called because of the metal from which it was made) confirms that these instructions were carried out.

A section of the Copper Scroll script that tells of hidden scrolls under the Temple

This metal record states that at least twenty-four scrolls were secreted below the Temple, including another copper scroll which contains the same information as the Qumran scroll – and more besides. A total of sixty-one coded locations are given where precious items were concealed, the last entry saying:

> In the Pit adjoining on the north in a hole opening northwards, and buried at its mouth: a copy of this document, with an explanation and their measurements, and an inventory of each thing, and other things.[24]

John Allegro, who carefully analysed the scroll, said of its purpose:

> The Copper scroll and its copy (or copies) were intended to tell the Jewish survivors of the war then raging where this sacred material lay buried, so that if any should be found, it would never be desecrated by profane use. It would also act as a guide to the recovery of the treasure, should it be needed to carry on the war.[25]

The Jerusalem Church had decided to hide its documents, and consign its treasures to God's keeping, in the spring of AD 68, but by June of that year Qumran was destroyed by the Romans. The Jews had just enough time before they arrived to cut up most of their scrolls to prevent the gentiles from reading them. It was this action that made the reconstruction of the Dead Sea Scrolls so difficult for modern scholars. The most holy scrolls escaped such treatment because they were placed beneath the Temple to be defended to the last.

The jubilant defenders of Jerusalem believed, when the Romans had earlier retreated, that the miracle of the escape from the Egyptians had been repeated and Yahweh in some mysterious way had saved His holy sanctuary from the enemy of His people. Filled with the conviction that divine intervention had won the day, the Jews pursued the Romans and Josephus records that they managed to kill no fewer than six thousand soldiers in the retreating columns before the legion escaped beyond the boundaries of Palestine.

This defeat, when viewed alongside similar losses in Britain and Armenia, seriously undermined imperial prestige and the Jews probably considered the war to be won. Then, in the spring of AD 67, a new opponent by the name of Vespasian entered Palestine with three legions and a large body of auxil-

---

[24] J.M. Allegro: The Treasure of the Copper Scroll
[25] Ibid.

iary troops intent upon laying waste the provincial areas of the Jewish homeland before attacking Jerusalem itself. This proved to be a harder task than
expected because the Jews retreated to their fortified cities where they fought
with a fanatical courage that matched the discipline and military science of
the Romans. They caused the Romans huge losses, but city after city
inevitably fell and the vengeful attackers massacred the population that survived the battle.[26] By the end of the first year Gabara, Jotapata, Japha,
Tarichaea, Gischala, Gamala and Joppa were ghost towns and the Romans
had control of Galilee, Samaria and the seaboard west of Judea. In the following year Vespasian continued his strategy and the cities of Antipatris,
Lydda, Emmaus, Jericho and Adida fell, leaving the strongholds of
Herodium, Machaerus, Masada and Jerusalem itself to be dealt with.

The war suddenly stopped at this point as Vespasian was proclaimed
emperor and once again the Jews saw this change of fortunes as an act of
divine intervention. However, just days before the Passover in the spring of
AD 70, Titus, the son of the emperor, assembled his forces outside the walls
of Jerusalem in preparation for a final attack. His army was far stronger than
anything the Jews had seen before, with four legions and a huge number of
auxiliaries.

The siege that followed has been described as one of the most terrible in
history. The joint Jewish commanders, John of Gischala and Simon
ben-Gorias, led their forces with great skill, as did Titus and his men. The
city could not be taken in a single action because it was subdivided with three
separate defensible locations, namely the fortress of Antonia, the Herodian
palace and the Temple itself. This meant that once the outer walls were
breached, the fighting continued in restricted spaces, which was a type of
conflict that suited the guerrilla tactics of the Jews far more than it did the
Roman battle formations. Inevitably, the Jews were driven back until only
the Temple remained, being the embodiment of all that the Jews held dear.
They believed that the outer court of the Temple may indeed be trodden
under the foot of the gentiles, but that their sanctuary could never be touched
because Yahweh would never suffer the heathen to desecrate His Holy Place.

We can sense something of the expectation of the Jews, as they defended
their holy city, from passages in the apocryphal Second Book of Esdras
which was written just before the fall of the Temple.[27] The words tell of a
vision of the expected messianic intervention:

[26] S.G.F. Brandon: *The Fall of Jerusalem and the Christian Church*
[27] A.L. Williams: *The Hebrew-Christian Messiah*

*And they were all mixed together; the blast of fire, the flaming
breath, and the great tempest; and fell with violence upon the
multitude which was prepared to fight, and burned them up
everyone, so that upon a sudden of an innumerable multitude
nothing was perceived, but only dust and smell of smoke: when I
saw I was afraid.*[28]

*Hear, O ye my beloved, saith the Lord: behold, the days of trouble
are at hand, but I will deliver you from the same.*[29]

Knowing in their hearts that the intervention of Yahweh was near they
realised that the action they had taken in withdrawing their most precious
scrolls and treasures to within the Temple had been God's will. The great
secrets of the Jews would be saved by Yahweh Himself as He rose to smite
His enemies at the twin-pillared entrance to His sacred chamber.

But Yahweh slept.

After a battle lasting one hundred and thirty-nine days, the heathens
stormed the Temple and polluted its inner sanctuary. They set fire to
Yahweh's house, but still He did not answer the call of His people, and His
messiah did not descend, as many expected, to blast the impious invader
with his holy breath.

The sight of the burning Temple caused the remaining Jews to lose heart
and they were quickly dispatched by the ferocious legionaries. The city lay in
ruins, its inhabitants dead. The Romans then proceeded to destroy the three
remaining strongholds of Herodium, Machaerus and Masada. The population of Masada held out for three years until all hope was gone and then they
committed mass suicide.

However, even after the Temple had been fully destroyed, Josephus tells
us that the underground maze of tunnels provided hiding places for some of
the Jewish fighters:

*This Simon (bar Giora), during the siege of Jerusalem, had occupied
the upper town; but when the Roman army entered within the walls
and were sacking the whole city, he, accompanied by his most
faithful friends, along with some stone-cutters, bringing the tools*

[28] 2 Esdras 13:11
[29] Ibid. 16:74

15

required for their craft and provisions sufficient for many days, let
himself down with all his party into one of the secret passages. So
far as the old excavation extended, they followed it; but when solid
earth met them, they began mining, hoping to be able to proceed
further, emerge in safety and so escape. But experience of the task
proved this hope delusive; for the miners advanced slowly and with
difficulty, and the provisions, though husbanded, were nearly
exhausted. Thereupon, Simon, imagining that he could cheat the
Romans by creating a scare, dressed himself in white tunics and
buckling over them a purple mantle arose out of the ground at the
very spot whereon the Temple formerly stood. The spectators were
at first aghast and remained motionless; but afterwards they
approached nearer and enquired who he was. This Simon declined
to tell them, but bade them summon a general. Accordingly, they
promptly ran to fetch him, and Terentius Rufus, who had been left
in command of the force, appeared. He, after hearing from Simon
the whole truth, kept him in chains and informed Caesar of the
manner of his capture . . . His emergence from the ground led,
moreover, to the discovery during those days of a large number of
other rebels in subterranean passages. On the return of Caesar to
Caesarea-on-sea, Simon was brought to him in chains, and he
ordered the prisoner to be kept for the triumph which he was
preparing to celebrate in Rome.[30]

This story interested us for a number of reasons. It certainly provided a
vivid impression of the scale of the labyrinth that must still exist under the
Temple ruins and we had to ask ourselves what these warriors were doing
with white tunics and a purple mantle in circumstances where they had
lowered themselves into these subterranean chambers to escape impending
death.

The only explanation for the presence of white tunics is that these last
surviving fighters were Essenes who always wore white, and who we equate
fully with the Nazarenes and the Jerusalem Church. The wearing of white
was considered a symbol of having undergone resurrection.[31] The fact that
they had a purple mantle with them is of considerable interest because such

[30] Josephus: *The Jewish War*
[31] *Peake's Commentary on the Bible*

a robe could only indicate a royal connection and would seem to suggest that the king of the Jews, in the form of Simeon, son of Cleophas, had been involved in the defence of the Temple. If he was, he certainly escaped because it is recorded that he was crucified at a later date by the Romans.[32]

When the war finished, the nation of the Jews had ceased to exist and only a religion remained: a faith that had lost God's house and its original *raison d'être*. Judaism found a new bond of union in the study of the Law and the worship of the synagogue; the Talmud took the place of the Temple and, in time, became the shining symbol of the spirit of Israel's race.[33] The surviving Jews, mostly the ones from the Diaspora (many being gentile converts), reinvented themselves with a highly diluted version of their faith because the radical Jews of Jerusalem were gone.

Between AD 66 and 70, a huge proportion of the population of Palestine had been put to the sword. According to calculations made from the various reports of Josephus, over 1,350,000 men, women and children had been slaughtered[34] – yet the New Testament fails to give even a passing mention to the genocide inflicted upon the people that are at the heart of the Christian story, many of whom must have been eye-witnesses to the baptism, to the sermons and to the crucifixion of Jesus!

Why?

Because the gentile Christians of the Diaspora had been taught Paul's strange interpretations of the life and death of Jesus, there was no longer anyone left to correct their erroneous understanding. They rejected circumcision and soon they ceased to think of themselves as a Jewish sect at all. Having acquired the history of 'God's chosen people' as their own heritage, they turned their backs on the nation of the Jews, even falsely holding them responsible for the murder of their own Davidic messiah.

The only detailed records of the Jewish war come from Josephus, a man who started the war as a Jewish military leader and ended it by fighting on the other side as a Roman soldier. No written accounts of the war from the Jerusalem Church's standpoint have ever been known to exist; indeed all of its records have disappeared. Many Christian scholars have considered it highly significant that the gentile Church so instantly lost all knowledge of its forebears in Jerusalem:

---

[32] H. Schonfield: *The Passover Plot*
[33] W.O.E. Oesterley and G.H. Box: *A Short History of the Literature of Rabbinical and Mediaeval Judaism*
[34] Milman: *History of the Jews*

The fact that Christian tradition has preserved no other account of the fortunes of the Mother Church of Jerusalem than that, obviously inaccurate, given by Eusebius and Epiphanius must surely mean that in whatever was known of the passing of that famous Church there was found nothing which could be conveniently utilised in the growing taste for hagiography [worship of saints]. Such silence, in view of the former unique authority and prestige of the Jerusalem Church, is significant, and, when it is seen in its context with the knowledge which we have reached of the nature and outlook of Jewish Christianity, the conclusion appears in every way reasonable and necessary that the Jerusalem Church fell together with the Jewish nation in the catastrophe of AD 70 . . .

Thus in so short a space of time this flourishing Jewish Christian Church, with its revered company of original disciples and witnesses at Jerusalem and its sturdy peasant members in the country districts, was so fatally shattered by the blast of war that it fades almost completely out of the life of the Catholic Church.[35]

There is, we believe, one reference to the fall of Jerusalem in the New Testament that usually goes unrecognised. The Book of Revelations contains impenetrable apocalyptic visions that appear to be a memory of the destruction of Jerusalem. It was written by an unknown Jewish-minded Christian around forty years after the fall of the Temple and it describes the creation of a New Jerusalem. In chapter twenty, the visionary author describes how those martyrs who had died defending Jerusalem from the *beast* (the Romans) would be with Christ for a thousand years after which time they would be resurrected. At the end of the first millennium, he tells us, the reign of Christ and his 'beloved city' would be attacked by heathen nations, led by Gog and Magog.

Jerusalem had been razed by the Romans in AD 70; one thousand years and a few months later, Seljuk Turks arrived and devastated the city.

We have to believe that this accurate fulfilment of the prophecy is just a strange coincidence but, as we will show, the rulers of medieval Europe certainly took it most seriously.

[35] S.G.F. Brandon: *The Fall of Jerusalem and the Christian Church*

CONCLUSION

The role of James, the brother of Jesus, was deliberately played down by the Roman Catholic Church and the importance of Peter and Paul was emphasised to ensure that the Roman popes were seen to have a direct line of authority back to Christ himself.

Paul had arrived in Jerusalem and claimed that he had experienced a special message from God that gave him a unique gospel that was quite different from the one preached by James and others who had known Jesus personally. He then travelled outside Israel and Judah to convert gentiles to his 'revealed' version of events that included supernatural occurrences. Paul was never accepted by the Jerusalem Church. He misunderstood their Jewish theology and turned it into a cult suitable for Roman citizens.

Paul misunderstood the Jerusalem Church's use of 'living resurrection' and he and his Pauline followers erroneously believed that Jesus made dead people return to life.

Following the murder of James, the Jews entered into a war with Rome that resulted in the destruction of the Temple and a large proportion of the Jewish nation, including almost everyone connected with the original Jerusalem Church. By this time, Paul was also dead and the new breed of gentile Christians was free to develop a cult that had little in common with the teachings of its founders.

Before the Temple was destroyed, the most precious scrolls and treasures of the Jerusalem Church were buried beneath the ruins of Herod's Temple. The truth about Jesus and his secret rituals lay dormant, but it was not lost: the Templars would eventually recover the lost secrets.

Our next task is to consider how the events of AD 70 in Jerusalem could be connected to Freemasonry. For this we needed to look more closely at Rosslyn, the medieval reconstruction of the Jerusalem Temple built by the descendants of the Knights Templar.

Chapter Two

THE SECRETS OF ROSSLYN

THE NINE KNIGHTS

The small village of Roslin lies about ten miles south of Edinburgh off the road to Penicuik. It is known for three things: a government-run experimental farm which has produced a pair of genetically identical cloned sheep; the ruins of a castle that was destroyed by the Roundhead army when the English Civil War spread into Scotland; and a very unusual medieval chapel. Rosslyn Chapel was begun in 1440 and it has shown itself to be the earliest monument that has clear connections with both modern Freemasonry, the Knights Templar and first-century Jerusalem.

To understand Rosslyn we had to understand the Knights Templar who are, without doubt, the most famous order of Christian warriors to come out of the medieval, or any other, period. These fighting monks had an improbable conception, a controversial existence and a spectacular demise; all of which has ensured that they have found their way into many a legend. Extraordinary claims of Templar deeds have been made by all kinds of romantics and charlatans over the centuries and many serious scholars tend to be immediately sceptical of any theory that as much as mentions them by name.

Whilst it is completely true that there has been much nonsense written about the Templars, it would be absurd to assume that they were just an ordinary order that happened to catch the imagination of a number of esoteric types. Quite simply, the Templars were anything but ordinary.

According to the accepted account, this hugely successful order appears

20

to have come into being almost by accident in 1118, just after the death of the first Christian king of Jerusalem, Baldwin I, and the succession of his cousin Baldwin II. It is said that this new king was approached by nine French knights who apparently informed him that they wanted to volunteer themselves as a crack defence force to protect pilgrims from robbers and murderers on the highways of the Holy Land. The story goes that the recently appointed king immediately gave them lodgings on the site of the Temple of Solomon and paid for their upkeep for nine full years. In 1128, despite the fact that the group had never ventured far from Temple Mount, they were elevated to the status of a Holy Order by the pope for their sterling work in protecting pilgrims for a full decade. It was at this point that they formally adopted the name of *The Order of the Poor Soldiers of Christ and the Temple of Solomon*, or more simply 'the Knights Templar'. This tiny band of middle-aged men was suddenly positioned as the official defence arm of the Roman Church in the Holy Land. The Saracen hordes must have been quaking in their boots!

Things changed quickly. Within a very few years, the ragamuffin gang that had camped on the broken Temple of the Jews was miraculously transformed into a splendid and fabulously wealthy Order that went on to become bankers to the kings of Europe.

We strongly felt that the history-book account of the rise of the Knights Templar was really very silly and we needed to find out what really happened in the second decade following the First Crusade.

In our last book, we came to the conclusion that the Templars had not protected any pilgrims because they had spent all of their time excavating below the ruined Temple, looking for something, possibly Solomon's treasure.[1] Indeed, others had come to similar conclusions before us:

> *The real task of the nine knights was to carry out research in the area in order to obtain certain relics and manuscripts which contain the essence of the secret traditions of Judaism and ancient Egypt, some of which probably went back to the days of Moses.*[2]

In 1894, almost eight hundred years after the Templars had begun digging under the ruined Temple of Jerusalem, its secret depths were probed

[1] C. Knight & R. Lomas: *The Hiram Key*
[2] G. Delaforge: *The Templar Tradition in the Age of Aquarius*

21

again, this time by a British army contingent led by Lieutenant Charles Wilson of the Royal Engineers. They found nothing of the treasures concealed by the Jerusalem Church, but in the tunnels cut centuries earlier they found part of a Templar sword, a spur, the remains of a lance and a small Templar cross. All of these artefacts are now in the keeping of Robert Brydon, the Templar archivist for Scotland, whose grandfather was a friend of a certain Captain Parker who took part in this, and other later expeditions to excavate beneath the site of Herod's Temple. In a letter to Robert Brydon's grandfather written in 1912, Parker tells of finding a secret chamber beneath Temple Mount with a passage which emerged out in the Mosque of Omer. On breaking through into the mosque, the British army officer had to run for his life from irate priests and worshippers.[3]

There can be no doubt that the Templars did indeed conduct major excavations in Jerusalem, and the only questions that we needed to consider were: what prompted them to undertake such a huge project and what precisely did they find? At the time of writing our last book, although we became convinced that we knew what they had found, we could only speculate that the motivation for the whole venture must have been opportunistic treasure-hunting.

We returned to consider the mutual oath of allegiance that the nine knights established at the outset of their excavations, ten years before they were established as the Order of the Knights Templar. Most books about the Templars usually state that the vow was a promise of 'chastity, obedience and poverty' – which sounds more like a vow for monks than a small independent group of knights. However, when the vow is looked at in its original Latin, it actually translates to 'chastity, obedience and *to hold all property in common*'.[4]

There is clearly a vast difference between swearing to have nothing and swearing to share in each other's wealth – and wealth is precisely what they acquired in a very short time!

We remained intrigued, however, by the very religious nature of this mutual vow. Other observers have glossed over this because they know with hindsight that the Templars did become an order of warrior monks, but how did these nine knights know what was going to happen ten years later? Several questions needed answers:

[3] R. Brydon: private communication
[4] L. Charpentier: *The Mysteries of Chartres Cathedral*

1. Why did they need to embrace 'chastity' at a time when even Roman Catholic priests did not?
2. Why did an entirely independent small group of men need to swear an oath of obedience, and to whom were they planning to be obedient?
3. If they were simply treasure-hunters, why did they want to share all property in common when the normal method would be to share out the spoils?

To answer these questions properly we would need to know a lot more about the circumstances of this small band of knights that assembled in Jerusalem in 1118. We felt certain that something was wrong here, and our main fear was that the truth may have been lost over the centuries and we would never unravel the motivations of these men.

We felt that we could reasonably conclude about question two that the need for 'obedience' strongly suggested that other people must have been involved and there must have been a broader plan than simple treasure-hunting. The three vows put together were those of priests not knights. We were strongly reminded of the lifestyle of the men of the Essene community described in the Dead Sea Scrolls: an ascetic existence that equally applied to the leaders of the original Jerusalem Church who had originally buried the scrolls and treasures that the Templars found.

From our previous researches, we believe that the scrolls removed by the Templars now reside beneath Rosslyn Chapel in Scotland.

A TEMPLAR SHRINE

Rosslyn Chapel is tucked away down a small side road that can go almost unnoticed as one navigates a tight bend through Roslin village, passing between two excellent inns. It is difficult to see much of the building at first as it is obscured by trees and the high wall that runs the length of the north side, but the strangely proportioned west wall looms up with its two empty pillar bases at the summit.

Entry is made through a tiny cottage where souvenirs can be purchased and tea and biscuits are served. As one passes out of the rear door of the cottage, the splendour of this curious and unique little chapel is immediately obvious, and it takes only minutes to realise that this is nothing less than a medieval text written in stone.

William St Clair's feat of craftsmanship is unlike anything that we have seen before or since and we never fail to be spellbound by the aura that is generated by the heavily carved interior and exterior. As a piece of architecture it is not particularly graceful, nor is its size physically imposing, yet one instinctively feels that this is a very special place.

We found nothing Christian about this so-called 'chapel', an observation that has been upheld by many observers known to us since then. There is a statue of Mary with an infant Jesus, a baptistery with a font, and many stained-glass windows of Christian imagery, but all are Victorian intrusions that occurred when the chapel was consecrated for the first time. These acts of vandalism were well meant but ill-conceived, yet they cannot take away from the utter magnificence of the heavily carved original building.

This carefully planned construction was not only built without a baptistery, it has no room for an altar in the east and a wooden table now serves that purpose near to the centre of the single hall. History records that it was not consecrated until Queen Victoria paid a visit and suggested that it should become a church.

Built between 1440 and 1490, the structure is covered in is a combination of Celtic and Templar motifs with elements that are instantly recognisable to modern Freemasons. Armed with a detailed awareness of the ancient origins of Freemasonry, we began to realise that there are precise secret clues built into the fabric of the building that establish an unambiguous link between Herod's Temple and this medieval wonder.

There are just two rooms: the main hall, and a crypt accessed via a staircase down in the east. The hall has fourteen free-standing pillars, twelve of which are matching, but the ones in the southeast and northeast are each unique, both being most splendidly carved to quite different designs. It has long been said that these pillars represent the ones that stood at the inner porchway of the Temple in Jerusalem called Boaz and Jachin, which are now of great importance to Freemasons.

Closer examination revealed to us that the west wall and the entire floor-plan had been designed as a copy of the ruins of Herod's Temple and the superstructure above ground level and forward of the west wall was an interpretation of the prophet Ezekiel's vision of the heavenly Jerusalem.

The principal pillars of Boaz and Jachin are positioned in Rosslyn in precisely the same way as they were in Jerusalem. We knew that the ritual of the Masonic degree known as the Holy Royal Arch describes the excavation of the ruins of Herod's Temple and it clearly states that there should be two splendid pillars in the east and twelve more of normal design – exactly as we found in Rosslyn.

We then realised that the layout of the pillars formed a perfect triple Tau (three interlocking 'T' shapes), exactly as described in the Masonic ritual. Furthermore, according to the Holy Royal Arch degree, there should also be a 'Seal of Solomon' (the same as the star of David) attached to the triple Tau and further inspection revealed that the whole geometry of the building was indeed constructed around this design.

When he built Rosslyn, William St Clair had inserted these clues and he placed the means of decoding them within the then secret ritual of the Holy Royal Arch degree. Through Masonic ritual he explains down the years precisely what he was trying to say:

> The Triple Tau, signifying, among other occult things, Templum
> Hierosolyma – **the Temple of Jerusalem**. It also means Clavis ad
> Thesaurum – **A key to a treasure** – and Theca ubi res pretiosa
> deponitur – **A place where a precious thing is concealed**, or Res ipsa
> pretiosa – **The precious thing itself**.

This was a huge confirmation of our thesis that Rosslyn was a reconstruction of Herod's Temple. We immediately wondered whether this ritual of Freemasonry contained these words for the sole purpose of unlocking the meaning of Rosslyn, or was it that Rosslyn had been designed in this format to conform with older knowledge? At that time it did not matter because it was clear to us that William St Clair was the man who had been involved with both. The Masonic definition of the 'Seal of Solomon' went further:

> The Companion's Jewel of the Royal Arch is a double triangle,
> sometimes called the Seal of Solomon, within a circle of gold; at the
> bottom is a scroll bearing the words, Nil nisi clavis deest – **Nothing
> is wanting but the Key**, and on the circle appears the legend, Si tatlia
> jungere possis sit tibi scire posse – **If thou canst comprehend these
> things, thou knowest enough**.

William St Clair had carefully hidden his cipher within the rituals of Freemasonry, which must have been in existence prior to 1440. At this point, we knew that it was certain that the architect of this Scottish 'Temple of Yahweh' had put his own definitions to these ancient symbols so that someone in the distant future could 'turn the key' and discover the secrets of Rosslyn.

Plan of Rosslyn

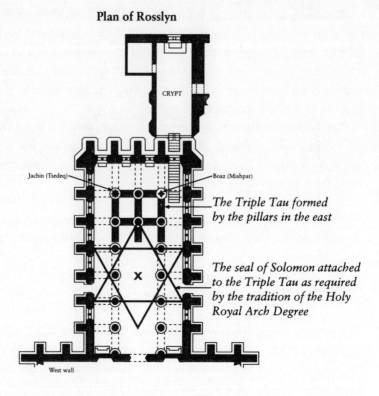

Jachin (Tsedeq)

Boaz (Mishpat)

CRYPT

The Triple Tau formed by the pillars in the east

The seal of Solomon attached to the Triple Tau as required by the tradition of the Holy Royal Arch Degree

West wall

The original nine knights who dug beneath the rubble of Herod's Temple carefully mapped out the foundations below ground, but they had no way of knowing what the main superstructure looked like, except for a section of the west wall which was still standing at that time. The main walls of Rosslyn match exactly with the line of the walls of Herod's Temple found by the British army expedition led by Lieutenant Wilson and Lieutenant Warren of the Royal Engineers.

Wilson began a survey of the whole city of Jerusalem to Ordnance Survey standards in 1865 and, in February 1867, Lieutenant Warren arrived to undertake an excavation into the vaults beneath the Temple area.[5] One of the many diagrams produced by Warren illustrates the type of difficulties they faced and begins to explain why the Knights Templar had taken nine years to conduct their excavations.

Most of the Rosslyn building was designed as an interpretation of Ezekiel's vision of the rebuilt or 'heavenly' Jerusalem with its many towers

[5] K.M. Kenyon: *Digging up Jerusalem*

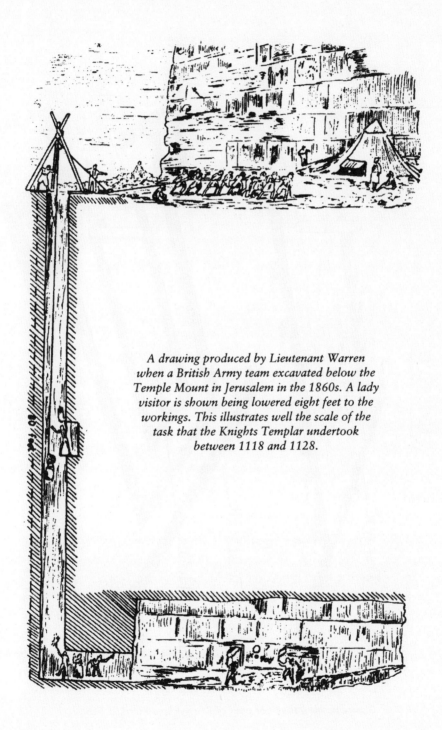

A drawing produced by Lieutenant Warren when a British Army team excavated below the Temple Mount in Jerusalem in the 1860s. A lady visitor is shown being lowered eight feet to the workings. This illustrates well the scale of the task that the Knights Templar undertook between 1118 and 1128.

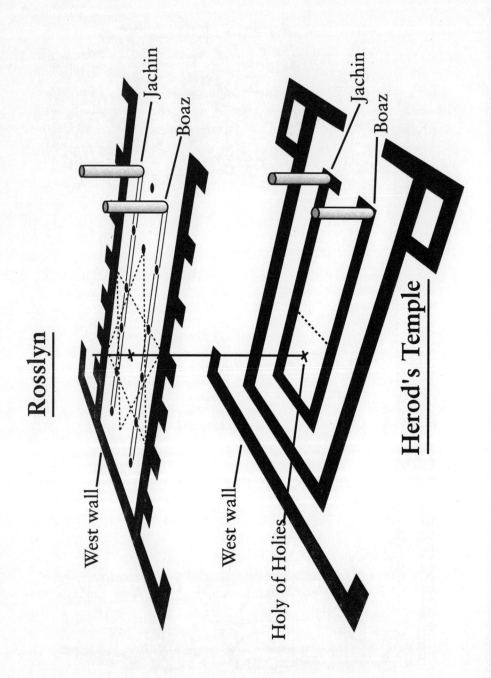

Comparison of the floor plan of Rosslyn and Herod's Temple

and spires. The one part of the building that is clearly different is the west wall which is built to larger proportions. The official explanation for this larger scale is that the 'chapel' itself was only intended as the lady chapel of a far grander collegiate church. The current guardians of Rosslyn admit that this explanation is an assumption, as there is no evidence at all that this was William St Clair's plan. Clearly, any wall that stands alone could be part of a building that was intended to be finished, or it could be part of a building that has been mostly demolished. In this case there is a third option: that the wall is a replica of a mostly demolished building, so there never was any other part – either actual or intended.

At first it seemed as though it would be impossible to conclusively settle the debate.

After the publication of our previous book we were contacted by a great number of people, many of whom had information for us or were in a position to offer assistance. Amongst these people was Edgar Harborne who is a very senior Freemason, being a Past Assistant Grand Director of Ceremonies of the United Grand Lodge of England. Edgar is also a statistician and held a senior research fellowship at Cambridge University, where he was sponsored by the Ministry of Defence to analyse battlefield breakpoint and surrender. He was able to confirm that our thesis concerning the murder of Seqenenre Tao, the seventeenth-dynasty Ancient Egyptian king, was highly plausible because the injuries were not at all typical of ancient battlefield wounds.[6]

Edgar was keen to visit Rosslyn with his good friend Dr Jack Millar who holds a very rare DSc award from Cambridge and is a director of studies at the famous university. Happily for us, Jack is a geologist of some considerable standing, with over two hundred academic publications to his name.

At the beginning of August 1996, Edgar and Jack flew up to Edinburgh where, late one Friday afternoon, we met them and immediately took them to Rosslyn for a two-day evaluation of the site as a precursor to a full ground-scan investigation. There we were met by Stuart Beattie, the Rosslyn project director, who had kindly opened up the building for us. Edgar and Jack spent a couple of hours taking in the beauty and complexity of the craftsmanship and we then retired to the hotel to discuss our plan of action for the next day. Both men were very excited and we all talked a great deal about what we had seen. However, Jack waited until breakfast the next day

[6] C. Knight and R. Lomas: *The Hiram Key*

to tell us that he had spotted something about the west wall that he thought we would find interesting. When we arrived back at Rosslyn he explained.

'This debate about whether the west wall is a replica of a ruin or an unfinished section of an intended bigger building,' Jack said, pointing to the northwest aspect. 'Well, there is only one possibility – and I can tell you that you are correct. That west wall is a folly.'

We listened intently for the reasoning that could prove our argument. 'There are two reasons why I can be sure it is a folly. Firstly, whilst those buttresses have visual integrity, they have no structural integrity; the stonework is not tied into the main central section at all. Any attempt to build further would have resulted in a collapse . . . and the people that built this "chapel" were no fools. They simply never intended to go any further.' We looked up at where Jack was pointing and we could see that he was absolutely right.

He continued: 'Furthermore, come around here and look at the endstones.' Jack walked around the corner and we followed, so that we were all standing in front of the ragged return walls that had stones protruding in a westerly direction. 'If the builders had stopped work because they had run out of money or just got fed up, they would have left nice square-edged stonework, but these stones have been deliberately worked to appear damaged – just like a ruin. These stones haven't weathered like that . . . they were cut to look like a ruined wall.'

Jack's explanation was brilliantly simple.

Earlier in the year, we had brought Professor Philip Davies, of Sheffield University Biblical Studies Department. and Dr Neil Sellors, a colleague of Chris's, up to Scotland where we were all guests of Baron St Clair Bonde, a direct descendant of William St Clair and one of the trustees of Rosslyn Chapel.

We had driven up to the Baron's incredibly beautiful home in Fife where we were made very welcome by him and his Swedish wife, Christina, and were then entertained to a splendid Swedish meal at which we were introduced to another trustee, Andrew Russell, and his wife, Trish.

The following morning we all went across the Firth of Forth to visit Rosslyn where Professor Davies had arranged to meet his old friend Professor Graham Auld, the Dean of Divinity from Edinburgh University. The two biblical scholars studied the building inside and out and then wandered across the valley to view it from a distance. Both men know Jerusalem very well indeed and they concluded that the masonry was remarkably reminiscent of the Herodian style.

Looking up at the outer north wall, Philip summed up his impression: 'This does not look anything like a place of Christian worship. The overwhelming impression is that it was built to house some great medieval secret.'

Putting together the evidence of these three very senior academics from Cambridge, Sheffield and Edinburgh universities, it seems that we have proven our argument that Rosslyn was designed as a replica of Herod's Temple.

Baron St Clair pointed out that over 50 per cent of the huge number of figures carved into the building are carrying either scrolls or books, and a small frieze ends with a scene that appears to show something like scrolls being placed into wooden boxes with a sentry standing by holding a key with a square end. The square is a primary piece of Masonic symbolism. This and other evidence from the carvings convinced us that the Nasorean scrolls that we knew had been removed from below Herod's Temple by the Knights Templar were here at Rosslyn.

THE LINE OF KNOWLEDGE

It had always struck us as odd that the name of the 'chapel' is spelt as *Rosslyn*, yet the village around it is spelt *Roslin*. Upon enquiring about this difference, we were told that the spelling with the double 's' and the 'y' was only devised in the 1950s as a way of making the place seem more Celtic.

We knew that Celtic places names always have a meaning, in fact some of the longer ones, such as the Welsh village of Llanfairpwllgwyngethgogerwyllyndrobwllllantisiliogogogoch, contain a full description of the location. (It means: Mary's church by the rapid whirlpool near the hollow white hazel tree opposite the red cave of St Silio.) However, we were puzzled by the Gaelic meaning of 'Roslin', which has often been said to mean a waterfall and promontory[7] as this does not describe the location either now or at any time in the past. The common Gaelic words for promontory are *roinn*, *rubha*, *maoil* or *ceanntire* and for waterfall *eas* or *leum-uisge*. An additional meaning for Ross, occurring in Irish place names only, is wooded promontory, so only if the name had Irish connections (or previous researchers had used an Irish Gaelic dictionary by mistake) would that form have been used.

As a Welsh speaker, Robert knew that the phonetic sound 'Roslin' would

[7] A. Sinclair: *The Sword and the Grail*

31

be spelt 'Rhos Llyn' which means 'lake on the moor'. Not surprisingly, however, the Welsh words do not describe the location any more than the Irish do, so we looked up the two syllables in a Scottish Gaelic dictionary which gave us:

Ros: A noun meaning *knowledge*
Linn: A noun meaning *generation*

It seemed that in the Gaelic, Roslinn would translate as *knowledge of the generations*.

We were aware that relying on dictionaries often results in odd translations, so we decided to seek advice from someone who had knowledge of the Gaelic (correctly pronounced *Gal-ic* and never *Gay-lic*).

During a visit to the Grand Lodge of Scotland in 1996, we had been introduced to Tessa Ransford, the director of the Scottish Poetry Library in Edinburgh. We were extremely flattered to discover that she, a noted Scottish poet, had written a poem to celebrate our previous book. One of the main purposes of the Library is to make visible to the public the poetry of Scotland in whatever language it is written; this means that Tessa, who is married to a Gaelic speaker from the Isle of Skye, meets regularly with a large number of people who have a detailed knowledge of the language.

We contacted Tessa and asked if she could have our translation of the name Roslin checked out and she kindly agreed to discuss it with a number of Gaelic speakers. A few days later, she rang to tell us that our translation had missed a significant overtone in the word 'Ros' which more correctly carries an import which makes it specifically '*ancient* knowledge', so the translation she confirmed was precisely: *ancient knowledge passed down the generations*.

Tessa and her colleagues were really excited and we were amazed at this even more powerful translation that appeared to fit the purpose of Rosslyn as a sanctuary of ancient scrolls perfectly.

The next question was: when was the word 'Roslin' or 'Roslinn' (there was no standardisation of spelling in those days) first used? We knew that it long predated the building of William St Clair's 'chapel' which could indicate that the scrolls removed from beneath Herod's Temple had been kept at the castle before the 'chapel' was built.

With a little digging, we soon found that the story of the St Clairs, in Scotland, began with a knight called William de St Clair who was popularly known as William the Seemly. William came from Normandy and his family were noted opponents of King William I, the Norman who conquered England in 1066. William de St Clair considered that he had at least as good a claim to the throne of England via his mother Helena, who was the daughter of the fifth Duke of Normandy, because William the Conqueror was the illegitimate son of Robert, Duke of Normandy and a tanner's daughter called Arletta. The St Clair family still refer to King William I simply as William the Bastard.

William the Seemly was the first St Clair to move to the area from Normandy and naturally he was a French speaker, but his son Henri was brought up under the strongly Celtic rule of Donald Bran[8] and he spoke the Gaelic as well as Norman French (as did all the later St Clairs until the time of Sir William, the builder of the 'chapel'[9]). We found that it was this Henri St Clair who first took the title of Baron of Roslin, directly after he returned from the First Crusade.

This dating was a great disappointment to us as it spoiled our nice theory. Henri would have returned from the Crusade in around 1100, some eighteen years before the Templars started digging, so the name Roslin (*ancient knowledge passed down the generations*) could not be a reference to the scrolls that had not yet been discovered. However, as we sat down and thought it through, we felt certain that we had something new and very important for our quest. We refused to believe that it could be mere coincidence that Henri had used such a meaningful name for his new estate and we dug around, looking for more clues.

We soon found that Henri St Clair had fought in the Crusades and marched into Jerusalem alongside Hugues de Payen, the founder of the Knights Templar! Furthermore, very soon after Henri chose 'Roslin' as his title, Hugues de Payen married Henri's niece and was given lands in Scotland as a dowry. The connections were beyond dispute, but what did they mean? Was Henri, by his choice of title, signalling that he had special knowledge of an old tradition, or was it, perhaps, just a piece of word play for Henri's own amusement? It seemed that our hunch that the nine knights who formed the Templars *knew* what they were looking for was accurate, but we could not imagine *how* they could have known what was buried under Herod's Temple. Perhaps further study of the building would reveal some clue.

[8] J. Marsden: *The Tombs of the Kings*
[9] Baron St Clair Bonde: private communication

THE KNIGHTS OF THE RED CROSS OF THE
BABYLONISH PASS

Our finding that Rosslyn had unarguable connections to modern Masonic degrees caused much interest after the publication of *The Hiram Key* and several researchers contacted us. One of them was a Masonic historian in Belgium by the name of Jacques Huyghebaert. Jacques sent us an e-mail asking about the origins of a Latin inscription carved into an archway at Rosslyn Chapel we had mentioned in our book. Translated into English it reads:

WINE IS STRONG, A KING IS STRONGER, WOMAN ARE EVEN STRONGER. BUT TRUTH WILL CONQUER ALL.

This strange motto is the only original inscription in the whole building, so it was clearly of very great importance to William St Clair in the 1440s.

Jacques' e-mail message read:

Could you provide me with the original Latin version of this inscription which is carved into the Rosslyn Shrine? Have you been able to date it?

. . . are you perhaps familiar with a particular [Masonic] side degree which deals with the relationship between Wine, Kings, Women and Truth?

This degree is called the 'Order of the Knights of the Red Cross of Babylon' or the 'Order of the Babylonish Pass' and in England it is intimately associated with the Royal Arch.

. . . Its ritual is based upon the Book of Esdras and events which occurred during the captivity in Babylon . . . According to the Masonic legend of this degree, Zerubbabel, Prince of Judah, seeks audience at the Palace in Babylon in order to obtain permission to rebuild the Temple of the Most High in Jerusalem.

The King of Persia, while expressing his willingness to grant permission, adds that 'it has been the custom from time immemorial, among the Kings and Sovereigns of this realm, on occasions like this to propose certain questions'. The question which Zerubbabel has to answer is: 'Which is the strongest, the Strength of wine, the Strength of the King or the Strength of Women?'

We were very excited to hear this news and we responded to Jacques, saying that the existence of this inscription in Rosslyn and its central use in a higher degree of Freemasonry must be beyond coincidence. He replied:

> *As you say it must certainly be beyond coincidence. However I would recommend to be cautious . . . could you attempt to verify if this inscription was not carved by a 'clever boy' in the 19th or 20th century, who knew about this degree, and added it discreetly during recent restoration work.*
>
> *If however by chance the Latin inscription in Rosslyn proves to be OLDER than 1700 you have no doubt made a MAJOR DISCOVERY because this would be the first indisputable proof that higher degree rituals were worked in Scotland long before their generally assumed place and period of creation: in France, after Chevalier Ramsay's 'Oration' i.e. from the 1740s onwards.*

We immediately contacted Judy Fisken, who was curator of Rosslyn at that time, to establish the originality of the inscription. Judy informed us that the stone carrying the inscription was an intrinsic part of the fabric of the building and she was certain that the carved words dated from the building of the 'chapel' in the mid-1400s. We were able to write back to Jacques:

> *The chances of the Latin inscription being a later addition are zero. No area of the interior was left uncarved and these words are certainly not overcut on top of something else. The lettering certainly looks fifteenth century. Also until 1835 the Masonic connection of the building was not widely known as someone had plastered over the Jachin pillar, making it look just like all the other pillars, so that the Masonic significance of the twin pillars was hidden.*[10]

One evening we discussed this development with Philip Davies, and the next morning he turned up in Chris's office with a photocopy of both the first and second books of Esdras which are part of the Apocrypha of the Bible. We kept Jacques up to date with our researches:

[10] J. Fisken: private communication

Prof. Philip Davies has just come back to us with a full English translation of the book of Esdras. The section that we are interested in is quite long but very interesting! The original story is believed not to have included 'truth' which was added by a later Jewish author.

The king has asked his bodyguards to say what is the strongest thing and told them that whoever produces the wisest answer will become a kinsman of the king and enjoy great riches. The man that says 'truth is strongest' is made kinsman and then says to the king:

'Remember the vow that you made on the day when you became king, to build Jerusalem, and to send back all the vessels that were taken from Jerusalem which Cyrus set apart when he began to destroy Babylon, and vowed to send them back there. You also vowed to build the temple, which the Edomites burned when Judea was laid waste by the Chaldeans.'

This was important to William St Clair because Rosslyn was his reconstructed Temple on the model of Herod's Temple and Ezekiel's vision of the New Jerusalem.

As you say, all of this cannot be coincidence.

In the meanwhile, we had been asking around our fellow Masons for information about the ritual of the Knights of the Babylonish Pass and we found our first reference to it in a Masonic newsletter.

Red Cross of Babylon: The most profoundly mystical of the Allied Masonic Degrees, this degree is similar to the 15th (Knight of the Sword or the East), 16th (Prince of Jerusalem) and 17th (Knight of the East and West) of the Ancient and Accepted Rite. The three points or parts of the ceremony have descended from three of the degrees of rites worked in the mid-eighteenth century. Part of the ceremony is akin to the 'Passing of the Veils' in the Scottish rites and those of the Camp of Baldwyn . . . To be a member of the Allied Masonic Degrees you have to be both a Royal Arch Mason and a Mark Master Mason.[11]

Now that we knew that the degree existed under the auspices of the Grand Chapter we were soon able to locate the ritual and it was fascinating

[11] Peter Preston: *The Fraternity of Yorkshire West Riding Newsletter*, Autumn 1994

reading. The 'Camp of Baldwyn', we thought at first, seemed to be a reference to the encampment of the Knights Templar on the site of the ruined Temple of Herod under the auspices of King Baldwin of Jerusalem, but we were later to learn it was associated with an early group of Masons in Bristol.

The full title of the degree is *Knight of the Red Cross of Babylon or Babylonish Pass*. It consists of three ritual dramas, or points, which tell of three incidents drawn from Ezra chapters 1–6, 1 Esdras chapters 2–7 and Josephus' *Antiquities of the Jews* Book 11 chapters 1–4.

This degree deals in detail with the motives and purpose of the rebuilding of the Temple of Jerusalem. The leader of the degree, known as the Most Excellent Chief, makes the point right at the opening of the degree when he asks the question:

Excellent Senior Warden, what hour is it?

He receives the formal reply:

The hour of the rebuilding of the Temple.

The ritual goes on to say that Darius agrees to support Zerubbabel, the prince of Judah, and issues a decree which allows the rebuilding of the Temple and *'furthermore, the vessels of gold and silver, which Nebuchadnezzar carried away, are to be restored and put back'*. At this point in the ceremony Darius creates the candidate, acting the part of Zerubbabel, a knight of the East, and gives him a sash of green trimmed with gold which he is told signifies initiation into secret mysteries.

Before Zerubbabel is allowed to leave the court of Darius and return to his task of rebuilding the Temple he, along with two others, is set a riddle by Darius, the correct answering of which carries with it great prestige and honour:

The great King makes known his pleasure through me, that each of you three should give his opinion in answer to the question. Which is the strongest, Wine, the King or Women?

The ritual then calls on three responses to be made to Darius's riddle. The first young man says that wine is strong because it can change the mind and mood of anyone who drinks it; the second young man says that the King is

An outline of the carving at Rosslyn showing a Knight Templar initiating a candidate into Freemasonry (see photograph in the plate section).

stronger because even soldiers must obey him. Now it is the turn of candidate Zerubbabel to speak and the ritual puts the following words into his mouth.

O, Sirs, it is true that wine is strong, men and the King great; but who rules over them? Surely Women. The King is the gift of a woman. Women are the mothers of those who tend the vineyards, that produce the wine. Without women men cannot be. A man does foolish things for the love of a woman, gives her rich gifts and, sometimes, even sells himself into bondage for her sake. A man will leave home, country and kinsmen for her sake.

O, Sirs, are not women strong, seeing they can do this?

Neither Women, the King or Wine are comparable with the mighty force of Truth. As with all other things they are mortal and transient; but Truth alone is unchangeable and everlasting. The benefits we receive from her are not subject to the variations of time and fortune. In her judgements there is no un-righteousness; and she is the wisdom, strength, power and majesty of all ages.

Blessed be the God of Truth.
Great is The Truth and mighty above all things!

In the face of such evidence, no one can deny that William St Clair was familiar with this Masonic degree which, until now, was believed to have first been practised after 1740. It is at least three hundred years older – and we would soon find evidence that would date it far earlier still.

THE SECRET OF THE STONES

Having found indisputable evidence that one of the higher degrees of Freemasonry was known to William St Clair, we started looking more closely than ever at the tiny details of Rosslyn's intricately carved interior and exterior. One small but fantastic find was a carving of two men, side by side. Although this external carving was weather-worn and only around twelve inches in height, we could make out most of the original detail quite well. It showed a blindfolded man in medieval garb kneeling and holding a book with a cross on the front in his right hand, his feet placed unnaturally to form a square. Around this man's neck was a running noose, the end of which was held by the second man who was wearing the robe of a Templar with the distinctive cross shown on his chest.

When we found this little carving we were with Edgar Harborne, an officer of the United Grand Lodge of England. Between the three of us we had over seventy years of Masonic experience, and we all knew exactly what we were looking at. Edgar was as excited and surprised as we were because there was no possible doubt; this was the image of a candidate for Freemasonry in the process of his initiation at the critical point of being obligated. The form of the feet, the cable tow, the blindfold, the volume of the sacred law – this tableau shows a man being made a Freemason over five and a half centuries ago! What is more, this little statue was the first visual representation of a Templar conducting a ceremony that we now consider to be uniquely Masonic.

The fact that it depicts a Templar conducting the candidate implies that the carving was showing an historical event that dated from the Templar period, so it could be showing us a seven-hundred-year-old Masonic ceremony.

Inside the building we studied each little carving. This was difficult because, at some point in the relatively recent past, some helpful soul had covered the entire interior with a gritty cement wash in a misguided attempt to protect the stonework, thus obscuring the fine detail.

On top of two half-pillars built into the south wall, at a height of approximately nine feet, we found tiny tableaux that were extremely interesting. One of them, only a few inches high, shows a group of figures with one person holding up a cloth which has the face of a bearded, long-haired man appearing out of the centre. The figure holding the cloth has its head missing and, given that there is very little that is damaged in the building, it seems as though it was deliberately removed. This caused us to look at the other heads and we were struck by the distinctive features of each one. The faces are not bland and anonymous, as one normally sees in such buildings; they create the impression that they were deliberate likenesses of known individuals – almost like miniature death masks.

We could not help but wonder: does this tiny carving depict someone holding the Shroud of Turin?

There are only two possible explanations for such an image: it is the Shroud of Turin being held up, or it is what is known as a 'Veronica'.

The non-biblical legend of St Veronica tells how a woman (often said to be Mary Magdalen) gave her cloak (in some versions her veil) to Jesus to wipe his face when he was either leaving the Temple or *en route* to Calvary bearing his cross. When he returned the cloth to her, it had the image of his face miraculously imprinted on the fabric. Modern scholars believe that the name 'Veronica' is derived from the Latin *vera* and the Greek *eikon*, meaning 'true image'. The name and the idea are somewhat suspect, indeed the Roman Catholic Church does not recognise a saint called Veronica. Despite this denial of beatification, the 'original cloth' is to be found in St Peter's Basilica in the Vatican City.

Isabel Piczek, an artist who has studied the Shroud of Turin and proved that it could not be a painting, was once unofficially allowed to see the Veronica in St Peter's Basilica. She said of this experience to Shroud investigator Ian Wilson:

> *On it was a head-sized patch of colour, about the same as the*
> *shroud, slightly more brownish. By patch, I do not mean that it was*
> *patched, just a blob of brownish rust colour. It looked almost*
> *uneven, except for some little swirly discolorations . . . Even with*
> *the best imagination, you could not make out any face or features*
> *out of them, not even the slightest hint of it.*[12]

[12] I. Wilson: *Holy Faces, Secret Places*

Awareness of this rather unimpressive 'holy' relic, or the idea behind it, may predate the arrival of the Shroud, but it was certainly not until after the public displays of the Turin Shroud at Lirey that the popularity of an image of the holy face grew. The Christian historian Father Thurston categorically states that the legend of the Veronica, as used in the current Stations of the Cross, dates no further back than the late fourteenth century.[13] Such a dating would mean that the legend emerged only after the Shroud of Turin was first put on public display in 1357.

Christ's head had always been depicted upon icons as having long hair with a central parting and a full beard, and when a cloth turned up with just such imagery it could have sparked off the idea of a 'Veronica'.

The next column in Rosslyn has an equally small scene which shows a person being crucified, but strangely, once again the head has been removed. The only apparently deliberate damage that we know of in the building is to the heads of the person holding the face on the cloth and the crucified person. It is as if someone felt a need to hide the identity behind these images. The other faces in these miniature carvings are certainly very distinctive – as though they are likenesses of real people. We wondered whether the person who disguised the pillar of Jachin with plaster also removed the heads of these key figures.

If this was a simple Veronica and a standard representation of Jesus on the cross, there would be no need to disfigure the main faces.

The crucified figure is not nailed to the normal Christian idea of the cross, where the upright continues up through the crossbeam, but to a cross in the form of a Jewish Tau which is T-shaped. Medieval Christian imagery often shows a second crossbeam representing the sign that mockingly proclaimed Jesus to be the king of the Jews – but it never shows a Tau cross.

'Tau' is the last letter of the Hebrew alphabet and, like the Greek letter 'Omega', it represents the end of something, especially life. It is also true that most Roman crucifixions were conducted upon structures of this shape, but no fifteenth-century stonemason could possibly have known it. It seems that the originator of this little carving was either uniquely well informed about Roman crucifixion methodology, or was deliberately using the Jewish symbolism for death. When researching a previous book we had come to the view that the image on the Shroud of Turin might be that of the Last Grand Master of the Templars and if our suspicion that the Shroud of Turin is the

[13] H. Thurston: *The Stations of the Cross*

image of Jacques de Molay is correct, we would expect William St Clair to be aware of the fact, as his family had been closely involved with the Templars that had escaped to Scotland after the fall of the Order – but why is it displayed in Rosslyn in this way? Perhaps the Shroud would prove to be much more important than we had thought.

The governing body of English and Welsh Freemasonry, the United Grand Lodge of England, is emphatic that nothing is known for sure about the history of the organisation prior to the establishment of the Grand Lodge of London in 1717. It had been very critical of us for suggesting that there is a history to be discovered for those who choose to look, and here, at Rosslyn, we have proof positive that some Masonic rituals are no less than two hundred and seventy-five years older than the official history of Freemasonry as defined by the United Grand Lodge of England.

Our next stage of research was to look closely into how and why English Freemasonry lost contact with its own past, and to establish what, if anything, is being concealed behind a bald refusal to acknowledge any history prior to 1717.

CONCLUSION

It appears that the Knights Templar knew what they were looking for when they began their nine-year excavation, and their vow of obedience strongly suggests that others were involved in the background.

Rosslyn is a deliberate copy of the ruins of Herod's Temple with a design that is inspired by Ezekiel's vision of the new 'heavenly Jerusalem'. The clues to understanding the building were placed into the then secret ritual of the Holy Royal Arch Degree of Freemasonry. William St Clair used this method to tell us that the building is 'the Temple of Jerusalem', 'a key to a treasure' and 'a place where a precious thing is concealed', or 'the precious thing itself'.

The great west wall of Rosslyn can be conclusively shown to be a reconstruction of part of Herod's Temple and the name 'Roslin' has the astounding meaning 'ancient knowledge passed down the generations' when understood in the Gaelic. The reason for this name is not clear, but Henri St Clair of Roslin was exceptionally close to Hugues de Payen, the leader of the original Templar group.

A carving on the exterior clearly shows a candidate being initiated into 'Freemasonry' by a man wearing Templar garb, and an inscription inside the building demonstrates that the builders were familiar with one of the higher degrees of Freemasonry, three hundred years ahead of the previously accepted date of origin.

A carving inside the building seems to show the Turin Shroud being held up and another shows the crucifixion of a headless person on a Jewish Tau cross. Perhaps the Shroud of Turin is directly connected to the story that Rosslyn tells in its stone text.

Chapter Three

THE MISSING HISTORY OF FREEMASONRY

THE SECRETS OF FREEMASONRY

Ask the average man and woman in the street about Freemasonry and one of the first words that will be mentioned will be 'secrecy'. The impression of cultic secrecy has always been the most obvious feature of Freemasonry and it has caused the organisation its greatest problems because human nature makes people suspect the worst when something appears to be withheld from them deliberately.

The wall of silence that used to surround the Order has largely disappeared over recent years, but a public perception of secrecy is still as strong as ever, generating theories where Masonic 'conspirators' are imagined to be acting in their own interests, to the detriment of the general public. The continuing idea that there is some very important secret concealed at the heart of Freemasonry was neatly summed up in 1995 by a leader in the *Daily Telegraph*, published in London:

> *Masonry puts considerable stress on encouraging high standards of morality among its members. But it is hardly surprising that a society which uses secret handshakes, signs and language for the mutual recognition of its members is suspected of being an influence for bad rather than good. Why have such methods, if not to hide the*

truth? Why hide, if there is nothing to hide?

The logic is hard to fault. If there is nothing to hide why have secrets?

For ordinary Freemasons, the aura of secrecy is a wonderful way of not having to discuss the odd-ball rituals that are learnt by rote and enacted for the initiation or advancement of candidates. It is difficult to tell people what you do when you do not understand it yourself. We are now certain that many Masons are victims of their own mythology, believing that most or all of what they do is a sworn secret, but the Grand Lodge of England is very clear that only the means of recognition are to be withheld from the world at large. These signals of recognition are not used in business situations to form brotherly bonds with complete strangers, as some people suspect. They are simply a means of restricting attendance at lodge meetings to qualified people alone; like a membership card or a coded door entry system.

The big question that is asked by many concerns the possible existence of some huge, dark secret at the very heart of Freemasonry that is concealed from all but the highest Masons. This type of speculation could be dismissed as being due to the paranoia of anti-Masons, but when the question is raised by very senior Masons themselves, the possibility cannot be ignored. One such person is the Doctor of Divinity who, as we reported in the introduction to this book, is a 32 degree Mason who has come to believe that, perhaps, there is some truth in the accusations that only those at the top of Freemasonry know the real truth.

If such a huge secret exists we were determined to find it. Our suspicions that there was something to hide had certainly been raised by the quietly obstructive reaction that our previous researches had unexpectedly generated from the United Grand Lodge of England. Our previous work had been warmly welcomed by other Grand Lodges and by Masonic researchers world-wide, yet we received no acknowledgement or direct response to the copy of our book that we sent to the English Masonic headquarters. However, we certainly became aware of their negative attitude from their actions elsewhere. We do not believe for a second that the United Grand Lodge would do anything underhand, but it is possible that certain individuals may have taken the negative vibes from it, and acted dishonestly in 'defence' of their gentlemen's club.

We had bookshop talks arranged all around the country – and strangely those in London were cancelled at the last minute. Lodges everywhere were extremely interested in our work and many asked us to present our findings to their members, but then several lectures were cancelled due to pressure brought to bear from above. Even our mail, addressed to lodge secretaries, was illegally intercepted on a number of occasions before it could get to the named recipient.

One person managed to intercept nine letters before they reached the addressees and proudly stamped the lodge name thirty-eight times all over them before returning them to us. We wrote to this lodge (we shall not name it) to ask if there were any suggestions as to how the tarnished name of their lodge could be restored, but we received no reply.

A number of people seemed determined that we should be denied our right to be heard.

THE POWER AND THE GLORY

It is estimated that there are at least five million male Freemasons in the world today and an unknown, but far smaller, number of female Freemasons. The United Grand Lodge of England currently presides over some three hundred and sixty thousand members in England and Wales and it is universally acknowledged to be the premier Masonic authority in the world.

According to the current constitutions of this regulatory body, the Grand Master must always be a prince of royal blood, and the current holder of this office is His Royal Highness, the Duke of Kent. To avoid any commoner rising too far above his station in life, the second most senior post, that of the Pro Grand Master, can only be held by a peer of the realm.

This ruling in favour of the aristocracy seemed to us to be at odds with the history of Freemasonry which was originally a highly democratic and republican organisation. Despite the impressive-sounding rule, it was sixty-five years before English Freemasonry had its first Grand Master of royal blood, in the Duke of Cumberland.

We looked into how the organisation is structured today and discovered that this pre-eminent governing body of Freemasonry is a private limited company, nominally valued at £6.6 million, with four directors including the Grand Secretary, who is effectively the 'managing director'. The headquarters in Great Queen Street in London houses a considerable business which spends some £2.7 million annually on direct staff costs alone. We were unable to establish the ownership of this private company.

There are seventy-nine ranks of officers within the membership of English Grand Lodge and thousands of men hold these highly regarded titles. New officers are chosen from the Craft lodges of England and Wales, but, unlike the Scottish system, these elevations are made by appointment rather than by election. This unpredictable and unchallengeable process of selection creates an environment where all who aspire to high office have to conform to the edicts and dogmas of the Grand Lodge for fear that they will fall out of favour. It is generally understood that anyone who has expressed a Masonically heretical thought too strongly is highly unlikely to be invited to join Grand Lodge no matter how great their contribution to Freemasonry.

Potential debate of Grand Lodge's role is further headed off by requiring every Worshipful Master (the officer who leads a lodge for a twelve-month period) to swear his personal allegiance to this governing body. This small, and at first view innocuous, requirement actually changes the face of Freemasonry quite dramatically. The original system had been to have individual cells called lodges that operated independently, sharing a heritage with the Celtic Church which acknowledged that all of its priests had equal and direct access to God. English Freemasonry is now structured more like the Roman Catholic Church with an unelected hierarchical pyramid that channels unquestioned authority upwards through the bishops and the cardinals and finally to a single man.

It seems to us that the purpose of Freemasonry has been subsumed by its own bureaucracy.

Following the publication of our previous book, the Grand Librarian of the United Grand Lodge of England said of our work (and the Grand Secretary repeated in a letter published in our local newspaper) that: 'Masonic historians will be saddened by the authors' cavalier attitude to Masonic research over the last hundred years.' We could not understand why it is 'cavalier' to investigate and publish new evidence and to question a standard dogma that is patently wrong. However, despite the impression that Grand Lodge has tried to create, we are far from alone in questioning its official history of Freemasonry. Many other Masonic researchers over the last hundred years have also found that asking questions incurred the wrath of the unelected powers in Great Queen Street.

> . . . if Freemasonry be older than the Grand Lodge of London,
> surely the origin of our ritual must be sought further back . . . Alas,
> even now there are men, some of them prominent in the field of
> Masonic Research, who are so mystified that they refuse to see the
> daylight, and actually use their influence to obstruct those who can
> see a little further than themselves. They present a pathetic spectacle

*turning over and over the relics of the Mason Craft but without
finding what they are looking for, the real esoteric Freemasonry of
the past.*[1]

So wrote the respected Masonic historian, the Reverend Castells, in 1931.
Like ourselves, and scores of other researchers, who preferred to investigate
truths rather than simply repeat the required dogma of English Grand Lodge,
the Reverend Castells was attacked by Grand Secretaries. We had to smile at
the similarity to our own thoughts when we read his appeal that common
sense should prevail:

*It is no good being vindictive towards brethren who quite
disinterestedly and absolutely unaided are trying to reconstruct
Masonic history. Let us be honest and confess that in 1717 the
Grand Lodge of London had not a monopoly of wisdom and that in
Ireland, as in England, it had been preceded by a far more
intellectual movement.*

He is absolutely right. By the time the Grand Lodge of London was established, the great achievements of Freemasonry in England were complete and
all it really formalised was a gentlemen's dining club that built its credibility
on the reputations of the many famous men who had gone before.

The reaction of this governing body of English Freemasonry to investigation seems pretty consistent. While we were talking to a senior Mason about
our observations of United Grand Lodge's undue distaste for discussing early
Freemasonry, he commented that over twenty years ago he had approached
United Grand Lodge Library staff to request access to copies of old rituals.
They asked why he wanted them, and when he replied that he intended to
put on a demonstration of a typical eighteenth-century lodge meeting he was
refused access to the material. They told him that United Grand Lodge of
England did not want to encourage the study of rituals which had been
replaced by more 'suitable' material.

The governing body of English Craft Freemasonry (the basic three
degrees) even changed its own history to accommodate the preferred idea
that Freemasonry appeared out of the ether in London in 1717. *The Masonic
Year Book*, published by the United Grand Lodge of England, used to record

---

[1] F.P. Castells: *English Freemasonry*

that Sir Christopher Wren, the architect of St Paul's Cathedral, had been a Grand Master before 1717, but in 1914 this record quietly disappeared. In his day Wren had been a famous and respected Freemason[2] and there is a considerable amount of evidence in existence to prove it, including contemporary newspaper reports and the Grand Lodge's own *Book of Constitutions* created by its official historian, Dr Anderson, who wrote in 1738:

> *Wren continued as Grand Master until 1708, when his neglect of the office caused the Lodges to be more and more disused*[3]

It seems that these 'Orwellian' manipulators of history had no place for him or anyone else prior to their chosen magic year. We hope that the current Grand Librarian of the United Grand Lodge of England will not once again accuse us of another 'error' in repeating this well-documented observation.

Whether or not Wren was a Freemason is unimportant to our work, but it serves to illustrate the strange cover-up that appears to have been going on in London for some considerable time.

When we were passing the headquarters of the United Grand Lodge of England in Great Queen Street, London, in 1996, we found that there was a public exhibition dealing with the history of English Freemasonry. As we entered the first room we read a notice which, once again, stated that nothing is known of the origins of Freemasonry prior to the magic year of 1717.

They may have just as well named 1817 or 1917, or any other arbitrary date; if an organisation chooses to ignore well-documented, contemporary historical evidence because it predates its own existence it will inevitably conclude that it came first. Whilst Freemasonry in Scotland was not established under a Grand Lodge until 1736, there is abundant evidence that Masonry had been in Scotland for a very long time indeed. Even putting aside our new evidence from Rosslyn, there are minutes still in existence of Scottish lodge meetings dating back to 1598 and there are records of James VI of Scotland (James I of England) being initiated into the Lodge of Perth and Scoon (Scone) in 1601, just two years before he went to live in London.

Whilst the United Grand Lodge of England says it does not know its own history, it contradicts itself by making a very clear statement about which

---

[2] F.P. Castells: *English Freemasonry*
[3] Dr Anderson: *The Book of Constitutions of the Grand Lodge of London 1738*

degrees are and are not of ancient origin. Today, when every English Freemason receives the agenda of his next lodge meeting, he will find the following footnote taken from the *Book of Constitutions* established by the United Grand Lodge of England:

> *Pure Antient Masonry consists of three degrees and no more, viz.*
> *those of the Entered Apprentice, the Fellow Craft, and the Master*
> *Mason including the Supreme Order of the Holy Royal Arch.*

This statement is unambiguous. It is stating that all other degrees of Freemasonry are not 'pure ancient degrees'; by implication they are either more recent inventions or they have been adulterated in some way. Given that Grand Lodge claims to know nothing of its own origin before 1717, we have to assume that people either know more than they are admitting or the early eighteenth century is now to be considered 'Antient'.

What of the fifteenth-century inscription in Rosslyn that demonstrates the use of the degree of the 'Order of the Knights of the Red Cross of Babylon'? Why, we wondered, does English Grand Lodge not accept that other degrees predate it by centuries? We needed to look closely at how Freemasonry started in England and see if there have been changes to the rituals since that time.

The claim by the English to be the premier Masonic organisation in the world is based on the claim that the Grand Lodge of London was the first body officially to declare itself to be representative of a small group of lodges. However, a body which eventually called itself the 'Grand Lodge of All England' was formed in the City of York twelve years before London established itself. The United Grand Lodge of England did not exist until 1 December 1813, following the amalgamation of two strongly opposed Grand Lodges, both based in London, both led by a royal prince and both claiming to be the true upholders of Masonic tradition.

The official line that English Freemasonry started as a London gentlemen's club cannot be correct because we know that the first documented initiation of a Freemason on English soil was that of Sir Robert Moray in Newcastle in 1641.[4] There are records of Elias Ashmole being made a Mason in Warrington, England, in 1646[5] and of Abram Moses being made

---

[4] R. F. Gould: *History of Freemasonry*
[5] E. Ashmole: diary entry

a Mason at a lodge in Rhode Island, in the American colonies, in 1656.[6] The important pioneering work in the study of nature and science by Freemasons such as Sir Robert Moray and Elias Ashmole resulted in the creation of the Royal Society for the Advancement of Science which started the new age of technological discovery.

At a time when these far-sighted Freemasons were encouraging experimental science, the Inquisition was placing Galileo under house arrest for daring to observe that the heavens might not be constructed in the way that the Church believed. The right to think and to publish is hard won and easily lost and Freemasonry was the champion of democratic and scientific freedoms in the seventeenth century.

As Freemasons ourselves, initiated into just five degrees, we are aware that there are many more degrees in Masonry which are likely to contain additional material which could help us to understand the development of modern Freemasonry. Why, we wondered, are these higher degrees, many of which are of Scottish origin, deliberately downplayed by the United Grand Lodge of England?

THE EARLY YEARS

The denial of virtually all Masonic history prior to Grand Lodge of London in 1717 started to make sense as we began to look closely at the political circumstances of the period. The year in question was in the middle of a turbulent time in British history concerning the relationship between the kingdoms of Scotland and England. The two Crowns had been combined in 1603 when the Freemason king, James VI of Scotland, succeeded Queen Elizabeth to become James I of England.

By this time, both countries were officially Protestant, but the Scots were predominantly Presbyterian (they did not accept the authority of bishops or archbishops) whilst the English followed the Episcopalian tradition of the Church of England. The Scots considered Episcopalianism to be too close to the teachings of the Roman Catholic Church for their tastes and wanted nothing to do with a system of patronage through bishops and archbishops which was so alien to the Scottish tradition that had been established by the Celtic Church.

The relationship between the two countries continued in a strained manner until, during the reign of Charles I, a charter was drawn up and signed

[6] Hugh & Stilson: *History of Freemasonry*

at Greyfriars' Kirkyard in Edinburgh by the Presbyterians. This document, known simply as 'the Covenant', was signed by all those assembled 'to defend the worship of their forefathers against the king'.

Initially, these Scottish Covenanters twice marched south against the king and it was on the second of these incursions that Sir Robert Moray was initiated into Freemasonry by the leading Covenanters acting on the Authority of the Lodge of Edinburgh St Mary's. Eventually, King Charles came to Edinburgh to make his peace with the Scots and to try to form an alliance against his new opponent Oliver Cromwell, and the English Parliament.

After Charles I had lost both the war and his head, the Scots offered the crown of Scotland to his son, also called Charles, on the condition that he sign the Covenant, which he reluctantly did on 21 May 1650. Oliver Cromwell responded by taking his army to Scotland to punish the Covenanters and their king. With the support of Generals Monk and Wade, Cromwell took Scotland and razed the castles of the supporters of the Covenant, including Roslin Castle. It was at this time that he visited Rosslyn Chapel, but, as a Freemason himself, he did not damage it.

Following the death of Cromwell, Monk offered Charles the throne of England and Charles became king of Scotland, Ireland and England. The Scots then sent the Reverend Sharp, a Presbyterian minister, down to London to remind the king that he had signed the Covenant. However, the minister returned to Scotland as Archbishop Sharp of St Andrews and, filled with the zeal of his newly won power, he appointed bishops to enforce Episcopalian practices on the dismayed Presbyterian Covenanters. In 1679, twelve Covenanters murdered Sharp for his treachery and the Scots once again marched against the English. After winning the Battle of Loudon Hill, they were defeated by the Duke of Monmouth at Bothwell Bridge and for five months a thousand Covenanters were held prisoner by the English in Greyfriars' Kirkyard where the Covenant had been signed. The conditions were appalling and many died. Others were sold into slavery in America.

When Charles II died in 1685, he was succeeded by his brother James VII (II of England), a Roman Catholic who attempted to force both the Scots and the English to convert to Roman Catholicism. This caused outrage in England, and in July 1688 the English Parliament invited the Stadtholder of the Netherlands, William of Orange, and his wife Mary to take the throne of England. They accepted and signed the Declaration of Rights drawn up by the English Parliament on 22 January 1689 which curbed the monarch's powers over the state religion and ensured a Protestant succession. The

Scottish Parliament accepted them as rulers of Scotland, but Roman Catholic Ireland had to be subdued by force at the Battle of the Boyne, which is still celebrated by the Marches of the Orange Order of Ulster.

When William died, the crown passed to Anne, the daughter of James VI, who married a German prince of Hanover. Then in 1706, there was a move to combine the Parliaments of Scotland and England and the Presbyterians were again afraid that the Episcopalians would try to impose their beliefs on the Scots. The following year, the English forced the amalgamation and Scotland sent forty-five members to sit in the House of Commons and sixteen to the House of Lords. This concession to combine the two Parliaments was agreed on the firm understanding that Scotland was to retain its ancient laws and Presbyterian worship.

Ironically, with the Covenant now guaranteed by both Parliaments, the last remaining reservation about a return of the Stuart line had been removed for many Scots. This was to become an important factor when the English had a German king in London.

Although James VII had died in France, his son James VIII was still living there when Queen Anne died and George I (the son of Sophia, granddaughter of James VI) became king. The supporters of James VIII were known as Jacobites and did not like the idea of having a German king who did not even speak English. They called George Hanover 'the Wee German Lairdie' and planned for the return of the 'king over the water', as James VIII was known. Their discontent came to a head when the Earl of Mar set up a meeting in Braemar where he invited the nobles of Scotland to take up arms for 'James VIII of Scotland'.

On 6 September 1715, they unfurled their banner and marched against the English to restore the kingdom of Scotland to a Scottish king and free it from the rule of the Hanoverian king of England. The first battle, at Sheriffmuir in Perthshire, was inconclusive, but James VIII was no hero and he retreated to France where he remained for the rest of his life.

Freemasonry had first come to London at least as early as 1603 with James VI. Whilst it may have had contact with operative stone masons in London, it retained its strong Scottish, Jacobite flavour, but after the major battle with the Scots in 1715, the Freemasons of London were worried. There was a climate of witch-hunting following the crushing of the Scottish army of James VII and anybody with Jacobite sympathies was suspected of disloyalty to the Hanoverian King George I, who had no Masonic connections. Alarmed by the danger of being known to be a Freemason in

Hanoverian London, many Masons deserted the Order and it became clear that if Freemasonry wanted to continue, its members would have to ensure that they purged the movement of its dangerous Jacobite associations.

Another entry in the first *Book of Constitutions*, written by Dr James Anderson in 1738, points to the embarrassment that the 1715 Jacobite campaign had caused Freemasons at the time, even to the extent that their previous Grand Master was keeping away:

King George I enter'd London most magnificently on 20th Sept. 1724. And after the rebellion was over – A.D. 1716 – the few Lodges at London, finding themselves neglected by Christopher Wren, thought fit to cement under a Grand Master as the centre of union and harmony, viz. the Lodges that met

1. At the Goose and Gridiron Ale-house in St. Paul's Churchyard;
2. At the Crown Ale-house in Parker's Lane, near Drury Lane;
3. At the Appletree Tavern in Charles-Street, Covent Garden;
4. At the Rummer and Grape Tavern in Channel-Row, Westminster.

They and some other old Brothers met at the said Apple-Tree, and having put into the chair the oldest Master Mason, they constituted themselves a Grand Lodge pro Tempore in Due Form, and forthwith revived the quarterly Communication of the Officers of Lodges (call'd the GRAND LODGE), resolv'd to hold the Annual Assembly and Feast, and then to chuse a Grand Master from among themselves, till they should have the Honour of a Noble Brother at their Head.

The wording of Dr Anderson's report very clearly suggests that the Jacobite campaign had brought Freemasonry in London to its knees and this meeting was an attempt to re-establish themselves as loyal subjects of their Hanoverian king. The usage of words such as 'revived' in reference to the quarterly communication makes it certain that these things had been normal once before but had waned. Their stated aspiration, that they looked forward to a time when they would have a 'noble brother' at their head, seems to imply that this had once been the norm, which we know to be the case – James I had been their head over a hundred years earlier.

It is interesting to note that two London lodges declined to join this breakaway Hanoverian system, for an old book called *Multa Paucis* (which historian J.S.M. Ward found and reproduced) says that there were six lodges at this meeting not four.[7] This is another fact that the Grand Lodge of England prefers not to discuss.

These London lodges did not invent Freemasonry and they, and their precursors, had to have taken their ritual from somewhere. Prior to 1646 the only bodies to issue warrants to form lodges were the Scottish lodges taking their authority from the Schaw Statutes of 1602 (ordered by James VI of Scotland prior to his becoming James I of England). If the four surviving London lodges were legitimate Freemasonic Lodges, they must have been acting according to warrants issued by the Scottish Schaw Lodges, the only legitimate source of Masonic authority. It therefore seems that the United Grand Lodge of England should be considered to be junior to the Grand Lodge of Scotland, which now represents the Schaw Lodges.

For Hanoverians this must have been an incredibly disturbing thing to have to acknowledge. They would have known that for many years prior to the 1715 Jacobite campaign, the Scottish lodges had kept a fund to which all candidates contributed to provide for the purchase of weapons that were used against the English – '*keeped and reserved for the defence of the true Protestant religion, king and country and for the defence of the ancient cittie and their privileges therein*' – and they were obligated to '*adventure their lives and fortunes in defence of one and all*'.[8]

London Freemasons would not wish to be associated with these sentiments, which would have been treated as treasonable by the Hanoverian authorities, but they had the problem that their authority to act as Freemasons stemmed from the obviously Jacobite Schaw Lodges of Scotland. Their solution was novel and, arguably, Masonically illegitimate. They needed an alternative source of authority for their activities, which they engineered by bringing together four of the remaining lodges of London to form a Hanoverian Grand Lodge which immediately denied its Scottish origin.

This instant abandonment of their true history for political reasons left them the problem of explaining where they had come from. Their solution was simply to say, 'No one knows' – which brings us back to the current stance of the United Grand Lodge of England.

---

[7] J.S.M. Ward: *Freemasonry and the Ancient Gods*
[8] Minutes of the Lodge of Edinburgh (St Mary's) (Metropolitan) No. 1, 23 March 1684

Having altered the history books to remove all memory of their true origins, the English attempted to match the regal heritage of Scottish Freemasonry by courting the Hanoverian Royal Family, encouraging them to join and eventually lead London Freemasonry. Within four years they had a noble duke as their Grand Master, within sixty-five years they would have a number of Hanoverian princes at their head. The price to be paid for this acceptance was the erasure of all trace of their Scottish roots and therefore their understanding of the original purpose behind Freemasonry.

The decision by this small group of London gentlemen Masons to set themselves up unilaterally as the ruling body for the whole of Freemasonry in 1717 was not generally accepted and soon led to a response from other groups of Masons who refused to acknowledge their self-appointed authority. Soon after the formation of a Grand Lodge of London in 1717, Grand Lodges were publicly revealed in York and in Ireland in 1725, although they were probably in existence long before this date.

The Hanoverians had good reason to worry about the Stuart line. Although James VIII had shown himself to be a weak leader, his son was made of stronger mettle and Charles Edward Stuart, Charles III, known as 'Bonnie Prince Charlie', was ready to risk all to regain his rightful crown from George II.

To prevent Wales forming its own uncontrolled national Grand Lodge, the London Grand Lodge persuaded a Mason by the name of Hugh Warburton to establish his country as a 'province' of England in return for being made the first Provincial Grand Master of North Wales (a strange arrangement which is still resented by many Welsh Freemasons).

A system of control and patronage was quickly being developed to ensure all lodges complied with the edicts of the gentlemen Freemasons of London. In 1734, the Grand Master of London Freemasonry was a Scottish Mason, the Earl of Crawford, and it was very likely that he would be asked to become the first Provincial Grand Master of Scotland, thereby reducing a second Celtic country to the status of a 'province' of England.

The lodges of Kilwinning and Scoon and Perth did not think this was a serious threat, but the Edinburgh lodges took it seriously enough to come up with a solution. They proposed to elect their own Grand Lodge to administer their affairs, issue warrants and protect their interests. To carry out this plan they needed a Grand Master Mason, in which matter the Schaw Statutes left them no choice.

THE FIRST GRAND MASTER MASON OF SCOTLAND

English Freemasonry is very different from the Freemasonry which developed and still exists in Scotland. When the Scottish lodges decided to elect a Grand Lodge to administer them, they went back to their traditional loyalty and agreed that Sir William Sinclair of Roslin was their hereditary Grand Master. He was a direct male line descendant of the Lord William St Clair who had built Rosslyn.

The only snag with this plan was that Sir William Sinclair was not a Freemason! Before he could become Grand Master Mason of Scotland, he had to be initiated, and between May and December 1736 he was progressed rapidly through the minimum five degrees which are part of the Craft in Scotland. Once appointed, his very first act was to renounce and resign in writing his hereditary rights of patronage, and institute the system of election of officers of the new Grand Lodge which still protects the rights and privileges of Scottish Freemasons today.[9] Interestingly, he sold off Roslin Castle and the Chapel as soon as he had been made a Mason; perhaps he felt that his ancestors' wishes had just been fulfilled. Even Gould the master of English Masonic dogma, begrudgingly commented:

> . . . *the opportune resignation of William St Clair was . . . calculated to give the whole affair a sort of legality which was wanting in the institution of the Grand Lodge of England.*[10]

There were soon major disagreements within the new Freemasonry of England. Following the formation of the Grand Lodge of London, two groups of Masons known as 'the Antients' and 'the Moderns' emerged. These groups disagreed about the nature and form of the rituals, and the Antients, who were also known as the Atholl Grand Lodge because of the Scottish origins of their leader the Duke of Atholl, accused the Moderns of making changes to the rituals which they were not entitled to do. Their differences would become so great that eventually English Freemasons would split into two separate Grand Lodges under two different Grand Masters, and for a long period neither side would recognise the other's rituals as valid.

The divide found focus when Lawrence Dermott, a Mason brought up in

[9] Records of the Grand Lodge of Antient Free and Accepted Masons of Scotland
[10] R. F. Gould: *History of Freemasonry*

the Irish tradition moved to London in 1748 and joined a London lodge. He was so appalled at the changes this self-appointed Grand Lodge had unilaterally made to the rituals of Freemasonry that he set about doing something about it, eventually becoming the first Grand Secretary of the 'Antients'. It was said of him:

> As a polemic he was sarcastic, bitter, uncompromising and not altogether sincere or veracious. But in intellectual attainments he was inferior to none of his adversaries and, in a philosophical appreciation of the character of the Masonic Institution, he was in advance of the spirit of his age.[11]

He spoke Hebrew and Latin and, being a keen student of Masonic history, he had quickly detected that London Freemasonry had moved away from its ancient roots in its attempts to distance itself from its Jacobite origins.

The Hanoverian supporters of the Grand Lodge of London were unhappy with the success of the Antients in preserving the Jacobite heritage and they were concerned about the threat that it posed to royal support from the House of Hanover. Their solution was to apply 'the carrot' of Royal Patronage to encourage the merging of the two traditions and 'the stick' of an Act of Parliament which threatened to ban Antient Freemasonry as a subversive society. The Prince of Wales was already the Grand Master of the Moderns when, in 1799, the Unlawful Societies Act was brought in by William Pitt for the 'more effective suppression of Societies established for Seditious and Treasonable purposes'.[12] The stalking horse was Prince Edward, Duke of Kent, who had previously joined both Grand Lodges. Without the support of the Royal Family of England the Antients were in danger of being declared illegal. The final clause which excepted all lodges of Freemasons, both Antient and Modern, was eventually agreed, but the price was paid soon afterwards.

The Antients accepted the terms of the surrender and, on 8 November 1813, the Duke of Atholl resigned in favour of the Duke of Kent. At the time, leading Masonic writers from other traditions warned of the dangers in the *Freemason's Quarterly*:

[11] Mackey: *Encylopaedia of Freemasonry*
[12] *Hansard* 1799

Neither the English writer nor the English reader can keep clear
from the egotistical insular tendency to look upon England as the
central point of the whole system of events in this wide world.

To avoid embarrassment to the Crown during the process of threatening the Antients with abolition by Act of Parliament, the Prince of Wales had appointed the Earl of Moira as Acting Grand Master. The Masonic historian Gould commented:

The Freemasons of England owe a deep debt of gratitude to the
Royal Family of their country. Their immunity from the Secret
Societies Act of 1799 was due, in great measure, to the circumstance
of the heir to the throne being at the head of the Grand Lodge of
London [the Moderns] and later, when under the combined
influence of two Princes of the Blood, discrepant opinions had been
made to blend into harmonious compromise.[13]

The Prince of Wales and his brother, the Duke of Kent, had forced the Antients back into Modern's control but the task of rewriting the history of Masonic origins was left to another royal brother, the Duke of Sussex.

The following year, the two constitutions were combined and the present United Grand Lodge of England was formed under the Grand Mastership of the Duke of Sussex. The Moderns had won the battle over the ritual, and their view could no longer be challenged by English Freemasons because they also introduced into their accepted ritual of installation of the Worshipful Master of any Lodge that, before becoming Master, he must declare in open lodge that he will fully and completely accept all orders and edicts of United Grand Lodge without question. As an additional safeguard, to avoid difficult questions, all Officers of United Grand Lodge were to be appointed, not elected. With its system of patronage firmly in place, the United Grand Lodge of England has survived unquestioned until the present day.

The United Grand Lodge denied the history of higher Masonic degrees and so a Supreme Council for England had to be formed to administer the degrees of the Scottish Rite which were widely practised by the Freemasons of the day. It was established in 1819 and, from its formation, it had strong links with the newly formed United Grand Lodge of England, from whose

[13] R. F. Gould: *History of Freemasonry*

Officers it drew all its members. Under the new arrangement, the Duke of Sussex was amongst the first to be initiated into these higher degrees by Admiral Sir William Smyth and he was so offended by what they contained that he did his best to prevent others taking them.[14] He was so strongly opposed to their working that he set about using his influence as Grand Master of the United Grand Lodge of England to completely erase whole sections of their contents from Masonic memory.

The Duke's problem appears to have been the Christian content that had been introduced to the original rituals that were distinctly non-Christian. As a Christian and a Freemason he felt that the older 'pagan' parts were in collision with the new Christian elements and he decided to neutralise the situation by removing all Christian teachings and all aspects that he considered 'strange'. In this way, he neutered Freemasonry by cutting away anything that appeared to have either reference to, or conflict with, Church teachings.

This step removed any chance of understanding the original meaning of Freemasonry, but it did have the benefit of opening up the organisation to men of other monotheistic faiths.

THE HIDDEN DEGREES

William St Clair built Rosslyn to establish a New Jerusalem in Scotland's green and pleasant land, so that it could house the scrolls that had been recovered from Temple Mount.[15] The more we looked the more we found that the rituals of Freemasonry were linked to this building and perhaps, we thought, there may be even more to be found amongst the discarded rituals.

The traditions of Freemasonry mean that members of the various degrees do not talk to other brothers about the content of their rituals unless they are also members of that particular degree. It is probably true to say that the vast majority of Freemasons have no idea of the structures that exist within Freemasonry, let alone understand what they are about.

If the early Freemasons had indeed inherited special knowledge passed down from the original Jerusalem Church, then the originators of the order were very wise to protect that knowledge with a complex system of secret cells, each with its own oaths of secrecy. William St Clair had the foresight and caution to preserve his message in stone and Masonic ritual until the time came when the power of suppression by the Roman Church became limited.

[14] Jeremiah How: *The Freemasons' Manual* (1862)
[15] C. Knight & R. Lomas: *The Hiram Key*

When the English blithely set about changing Masonic ritual for political reasons they threw away the whole purpose of the organisation. We were increasingly certain that they had rendered the whole thing down to a meaningless ritual that was a mere parody of the original. Some background work quickly told us what all of the degrees of Freemasonry were called, but getting to know what they once contained was going to be a difficult if not impossible task after so many years of oblivion.

The first three degrees of all Freemasonry are:

- Entered Apprentice (the first initiation into Freemasonry)
- Fellow Craft
- Master Mason (the standard rank which Freemasons normally attain)

There is a set of degrees which have a distinctly Christian character and seem to be very recent creations:

- Knight Templar (no connection with the original Knights Templar)
- Knight of the Mediterranean Pass
- Knight of St John of Malta
- The Rosy Cross of the Royal Order of Scotland
- Harodim of the Royal Order of Scotland
- Brother of St Lawrence the Martyr
- The Red Cross of Constantine
- Knight of the Holy Sepulchre
- Knight of St John
- The Nine Degrees of the Rosicrucian Society
- Knight of Constantinople.
- Rose Croix

Some recent degrees are:

- The Secret Monitor
- The Seven Grades of the Scarlet Cord
- The Illustrious Order of Light
- The Ancient and Accepted Rite of Scotland

The most interesting of the sets of degrees for us are the original ones known as the Ancient and Accepted (Scottish) Rite, ruled by the Supreme

Council of the 33 degree in Edinburgh. It is to the 16th degree of this system that the inscription in Rosslyn refers. This system starts with the same three degrees as all Freemasonry:

1. Entered Apprentice
2. Fellow Craft
3. Master Mason
4. Secret Master
5. Perfect Master
6. Intimate Secretary
7. Provost and Judge
8. Intendant of Buildings
9. Elect of Nine
10. Elect of Fifteen
11. Sublime Elect
12. Grand Master Architect
13. Royal Arch (of Enoch)
14. Scotch Knight of Perfection
15. Knight of the Sword or of the East
16. Prince of Jerusalem
17. Knight of the East and West
18. Knight of the Pelican and Eagle, and Sovereign Prince Rose Croix
19. Grand Pontiff
20. Venerable Grand Master
21. Patriarch Noachite
22. Prince of Libanus
23. Chief of the Tabernacle
24. Prince of the Tabernacle
25. Knight of the Brazen Serpent
26. Prince of Mercy
27. Commander of the Temple
28. Knight of the Sun
29. Knight of St Andrew
30. Grand Elected Knight of the Black and White Eagle
31. Grand Inspector, Inquisitor Commander
32. Sublime Prince of the Royal Secret
33. Grand Inspector-General

We found that the earliest recorded references to these Scottish degrees occurred in France during the thirty-year period between the two Jacobite campaigns of 1715 and 1745, when the Scots twice invaded England. In France, the Masons who used these degrees were known as 'Maitres Ecossais' (Scottish Masons).[16] These higher degrees were known as Scottish degrees and were associated with Chevalier Ramsey who was born in Ayr in 1686. He is said to have promoted the degrees of the Scottish Rite in France whilst he was tutor to the two sons of James VIII of Scotland, who was living in exile in France.[17]

One of these sons was the young Bonnie Prince Charlie who would lead an expedition to regain the throne of Scotland twenty-one years later. In 1730, Ramsey visited England, by permission of George II, and was made a Fellow of the Royal Society by Isaac Newton who was then president. He had no obvious scientific qualifications, but was known to be a Freemason in France and whilst in England he joined the Horn Lodge (now known as the Royal Somerset House and Inverness Lodge No. 4). In 1737, he published an oration in *L'Almanach de Cocus* which told of a Union between Freemasonry and the Knights of St John of Jerusalem which dated back to the time of the Crusades. He also described a lodge at Kilwinning of which James, Lord Steward of Scotland, was Master in 1286.

Ramsey was a Jacobite to the extent that he was tutor to Bonnie Prince Charlie and he may well have belonged to the lodge which was founded in France in 1725 by the Earl of Derwentwater, who had fled to France with James VII. This lodge, known as the Lodge of St Thomas, met at Hure's tavern, Rue des Boucheries, Paris.[18]

In 1761, the Grand Lodge of France issued a patent to Stephen Morin to spread the Scottish Rite in America. He was made Grand Inspector of the New World and authorised to create inspectors in all places where these degrees were not already established, suggesting that the Scottish Rite may already have existed in America. By 31 May 1801, he had established 'The Supreme Council of the Thirty-third degree for the United States of America', in Charleston, South Carolina. The following year, this Supreme Council issued a circular to all the Grand Lodges of the World, dating the

---

[16] R. F. Gould: *History of Freemasonry*
[17] Thory: *Histoire de la Foundation de Grand Orient* (1812)
[18] A. Whitaker: *The Origin and Progress of the Supreme Council of the 33rd degree of the Ancient and Accepted (Scottish) Rite for England, Wales, The Dominions and the Dependencies of the British Crown* (1933)

origin of Freemasonry to the beginning of the world and, after describing its development up to its own formation, declared itself keeper of Secret Constitutions which have existed from Time Immemorial.[19]

In 1857, the Supreme Council of England proudly announced that the 30th degree had been awarded 'without the aid of the Ritual'. The following year the Supreme Council of England decided to cease alliance with the Supreme Council of Scotland, and all subordinate bodies were ordered to hold no communication with members of subordinate bodies under the Scottish Supreme Council.

We found that today in England the first degree given after the 4th is the 18th, those from the 5th to the 17th being awarded in name only, with no requirement to enact ritual. Similarly the degrees from the 19th to the 29th are given by name only before the 30th degree is conferred.

So, Freemasons who achieve the 30th degree may know nothing of the content of twenty-four of the degrees that they are supposed to understand!

Whatever it was in these degrees which had offended the Duke of Sussex, his system of controlled patronage and deliberate denial had succeeded in almost destroying these rituals. The then leading American Freemason Albert Pike, speaking to the Supreme Grand Council of the Southern Jurisdiction (USA), unashamed of his appalling ignorance and arrogance said in 1878:

The truth is that the Rite was nothing, and the Rituals are almost nought, for the most part a lot of worthless trash, until 1855.[20]

It seems Pike considered the rituals a heterogeneous and chaotic mass. His total failure to understand them caused him to dismiss them, describing them as *'incoherent nonsense and jargon; in some of the degrees of absolute nothingness – as having been purposely constructed to conceal their meaning'.*[21] Pike then proved himself a worthy successor to the Duke of Sussex when he set about assisting the Supreme Council of England in its work of ritual suppression. He wrote:

The Supreme Council for the Southern Jurisdiction of the United

---

[19] Ibid.
[20] *Official Bulletin of the Southern Jurisdiction* (1878)
[21] *Supreme Council History* (1831)

States at length undertook the indispensable and long-delayed task of revising and reforming the work and Ritual of the thirty degrees under its jurisdiction. Retaining the essentials of the degrees and all the means by which the members recognise one another, it has sought out and developed the leading idea of each degree, rejected the puerilities and absurdities with which many of them were disfigured, and made of them a connected system of moral, religious and philosophical instruction. Sectarian of no creed, it has yet thought it not improper to use the old allegories, based on occurrences detailed in the Hebrew and Christian books, and drawn from the Ancient Mysteries of Egypt, Persia, Greece, India, the Druids and the Essenes, as vehicles to communicate the Great Masonic Truths; as it has used the legends of the Crusades and the Ceremonies of the Orders of Knighthood.[22]

However, the work of destruction was not yet complete, for Reverend Whitaker was still not satisfied with the changes. He commented about other alterations which he was not prepared to specify:

A parenthesis in the prayer in the black room is the very antithesis of the teaching of Christ; some portions of the ritual are meaningless. It would be a great thing if a small committee of theological experts undertook the revision of the ritual. The larger part of it is so beautiful that it is a pity to let blemishes remain which wound the feelings of all who pause and think.[23]

It was clear from this study of the history of the Scottish Rite of the 33 degrees that whatever the ritual had been, it had been deliberately altered to suit the personal prejudices of the Duke of Sussex, First Grand Master of the United Grand Lodge of England and Sovereign Grand Inspector-General Albert Pike of the Supreme Council of the Southern Jurisdiction of the USA. We could only wonder what had been in those Jacobite Scottish degrees which so offended these senior Freemasons that they decided to ignore their own

---

[22] A. Pike: *Morals and Dogma*
[23] A. Whitaker: *The Origin and Progress of the Supreme Council of the 33rd degree of the Ancient and Accepted (Scottish) Rite for England, Wales, The Dominions and the Dependencies of the British Crown* (1933)

responsibilities to Freemasonry which told them that it is not in the power of any man or body of men to bring about changes to the ritual of Freemasonry.

In the proceedings of the Supreme Council of England in April 1909, the set of degrees which had been called the Scottish Rite was changed to the Ancient and Accepted Rite. The minutes record: '*it was decided to omit the word Scottish from all certificates etc.*'

The reporter for the *Masonic News* at the time commented that this was a foolish resolution to pass as: '*The Rite had been called the Scottish Rite since the formation of the first Supreme Council in 1801 and had been known as such in every corner of the world. To have made the change showed a complete ignorance of Masonic history.*'

We could not help but observe that the ritual had been known as the Scottish Rite before the formation of United Grand Lodge and its self-appointing membership. We also knew that, by 1908, only Masons who held Grand Rank in United Grand Lodge were allowed to become members of this Supreme Council of England.[24] Looking at the history of the 33 degrees, we were about to find an appalling story of deliberate destruction of a verbal heritage that dated back to the Templars.

Having found that there is a hidden history and deliberately concealed rituals behind English Freemasonry, we had to try and find out what these degrees are and what has been removed from the rituals. It seemed to us that they must contain something very important to have been suppressed so completely.

We had established that the ancient secrets that we were looking for had been cut away by the founders of the United Grand Lodge of England when it was formed; now we wondered whether the resistance that we had experienced from the current paid servants of the order was to dissuade investigation or just the result of bruised egos.

On balance, we doubt very much that they know of any secrets being withheld from other Freemasons, and they almost certainly know little or nothing of the missing rituals. On the other hand, it is likely that a cultural tradition of stonewalling freethinking researchers has been perpetuated ever since 1813 and the present incumbents are simply responding in the only way they know how.

[24] A. Whitaker: *The Origin and Progress of the Supreme Council of the 33rd degree of the Ancient and Accepted (Scottish) Rite for England, Wales, The Dominions and the Dependencies of the British Crown* (1933)

As much as self-appointed censors and reformers can conceal material they cannot hide everything. It is interesting to note that the United Grand Lodge of England was established on St John's Day in 1813. There are two St John's days each year, which are both very important days for Freemasonry, and whilst this may appear to be a Christian observation it is actually a throwback to ancient (possibly Egyptian) sun worship. These holy days are the midsummer and midwinter festivals of a solar cult that have been absorbed into the Christian calendar. That both are of great significance to Freemasonry points to an origin that has long been lost to memory.

Without doubt, Freemasonry is guilty of concealing some great secret. Unfortunately, there may be no one alive today who knows what it is!

From this point we felt that we needed to go back to the circumstances leading to the formation of the Templars to try and understand what and who was behind their mission and what secrets were passed on to Freemasonry before they were lost.

Perhaps by studying this forbidden history from both ends we might meet the long-lost truth in the middle.

CONCLUSION

The world's premier Grand Lodge was set up in London in 1717 as a Hanoverian attempt to deny Scottish origins which were far too Jacobite for English tastes. From the start it denied its own history and when the United Grand Lodge of England was formed in 1813, the rituals of the Order were almost destroyed. Even today, it makes the claim that nothing before 1717 can be known for sure.

From the writings of other researchers and from our own experience, we know that it is Grand Lodge policy to stifle any investigation into Freemasonry before this date. This strongly suggests that something is being hidden, even from Freemasons.

The Grand Lodge of London set about changing ritual to make it more innocuous, but it was opposed by traditionalists, which led to a major rift between two opposing Grand Lodges known as 'the Antients' and 'the Moderns'.

The Moderns had the support of the Hanoverian crown and Parliament and they abused their powers to force an amalgamation of English Freemasonry on their own terms. In 1813, the United Grand Lodge of England was formed and the wholesale destruction of Masonic ritual was carried out. When the Duke of Sussex became the first Grand Master of the

United Grand Lodge of England, he was initiated into all of the 33 degrees of the Ancient Scottish Rite and he was so outraged by their contents that he decided that they should be changed without delay.

The rituals of these degrees were heavily amended and, worse, twenty-four of the thirty-three degrees are now bestowed in England without any ritual being given.

These changes, inflicted by men who understood nothing of the original meaning of Freemasonry, have removed the secret messages that were so carefully implanted into the original Scottish ritual by William St Clair and other descendants of the Knights Templar.

Chapter Four

THE RETURN OF THE KINGS OF GOD

A THOUSAND YEARS OF DARKNESS

We now had the answer to one of our initial key questions: the rituals of Freemasonry have been both changed and suppressed in order to conceal some early material that became too difficult or dangerous to be allowed to remain. Despite the centuries of denial by the United Grand Lodge of England, we have been able to establish that the core of modern Freemasonry developed in Scotland following the demise of the Knights Templar, who had based their own beliefs on the teachings of the original Jerusalem Church. All of the evidence pointed to a Templar unearthing of secret scrolls buried by the Jews in the months before they and their Temple were destroyed by the Romans in AD 70.

We now needed to find out who was behind the development of the Knights Templar before we could progress to try and reconstruct the missing secrets of Freemasonry.

The fact that the Knights Templar had sworn themselves to 'chastity, obedience and to hold all wealth in common', before they started digging, had struck us as very odd and posed questions that we still needed to answer. The requirement for 'obedience' was particularly interesting because this strongly suggested the involvement of some higher controlling authority.

Another tantalising question that had emerged from our investigation was the naming of Roslin by the crusader Henri St Clair. The meaning of 'Ros linn' – *ancient knowledge passed down the generations* – predated the earliest possible finding of the Temple scrolls by at least eighteen years, which seemed to suggest that Henri St Clair was fully involved with the Templars and that they knew what they were looking for from the outset. We now needed to try to understand the motivation for the Crusades, and then reconstruct what really went on at the beginning of the twelfth century in Jerusalem.

In the aftermath of the Roman destruction of Jerusalem, the few Jewish survivors who escaped the wrath of the invaders following the final battle for the city found themselves sold into slavery. It seems unlikely, however, that many of the Nasoreans would have allowed themselves to be taken alive. So, as the bones of the Jewish Christians turned to dust, their precious artefacts remained undisturbed and forgotten beneath the tumbled ruins of Herod's Temple.

In AD 135, Emperor Hadrian rebuilt the city, which he called Aelia Capitolina, and he renamed the province Syria-Palestina. To be certain that the national fervour of the Jews was constrained, he banned them from entering their holy city and there was no permanent Jewish community in Jerusalem for five centuries after its fall.[1]

In Rome, the gentile Christians merged the myths of their old gods into the cult conceived by Paul to create a hybrid religion that had great appeal to the maximum number of people. On 20 May in AD 325, the non-Christian emperor Constantine convened the Council of Nicaea and a vote was taken as to whether, or not, Jesus was a deity. The debates were vigorous, but at the end of the day it was decided that the first-century Jewish leader was, indeed, a god.

The establishment of the Romanised Christian era marked the beginning of the Dark Ages: the period of Western history when the lights went out on all learning, and superstition replaced knowledge. It lasted until the power of the Roman Church was undermined by the Reformation.

The pursuit of ignorance grew to become highly structured and in one day Christians, under Bishop Theophilius, burned down the world's greatest library of human knowledge, at Alexandria. The patriarch of Constantinople at the time, St John Chrysostom (his name ironically meaning 'golden mouthed'), commented on the 'great achievement' of the destruction of old ideas:

---

[1] M. Friedman: *City of the Great King*

Every trace of the old philosophy and literature of the ancient world has vanished from the face of the earth.[2]

Intellectual and moral progress quickly ground to a halt and Western civilisation regressed into a state of crude barbarism.[3] The Church banned education on the basis that 'the spread of knowledge' could only serve to encourage heresy.[4] The new Church knew that it was a palace built on sand and it feared that permitting freedom of thought could only serve to reveal its lack of foundations and cause it to be swept away in a tide of reasoned thinking. Literacy rates across the Roman Empire quickly fell to almost zero, science gave way to superstition and the engineering advances of the early empire were forgotten. Everything that was good and proper was despised and all branches of human achievement were ignored in the name of Jesus Christ. Art, philosophy, secular literature, astronomy, mathematics, medicine and even sex became taboo subjects.

Sex, the Church decreed, was for procreation only, claiming that a women could not conceive if she enjoyed the sexual act[5] and that a man who tried to give pleasure to a women whilst copulating was 'loving Satan'.[6]

The strange alien ideas of the gentiles changed, beyond all recognition, the cult that had been born out of the death of a Jewish messianic leader. Major additions were still happening as recently as the thirteenth century when the theologian Thomas Aquinas pronounced that the consecrated Eucharistic bread and wine undergoes a miraculous transformation into the actual flesh and blood of Christ at the point of consumption by the congregation. This cannibalistic concept of 'transubstantiation', as it is euphemistically called, is based on an idea that can be traced back to Aristotle's analysis of the nature of matter. We are certain that any member of the original Jerusalem Church would have been utterly disgusted by the suggestion that God would allow such a cannibalistic miracle to be performed at all, let alone millions of times a day. Belief in the physical reality of 'transubstantiation' has remained the official teaching of the Roman Catholic Church since the Middle Ages.[7]

[2] T.W. Doane: *Bible Myths and Their Parallels in Other Religions*
[3] J. Campbell: *The Masks of God – Oriental Mythology*
[4] E. Mâle: *The Gothic Image*
[5] G.L. Simons: *Sex and Superstition*
[6] R. Briffault: *The Mothers*
[7] Microsoft: *Encarta 96 Encyclopaedia*

Six hundred years after the destruction of the Temple, the story of a new prophet was establishing itself across the Middle East, and Jerusalem became a holy city for a third great religion. Mohammed had risen to heaven over the very rock that Abraham used when he prepared to sacrifice his son, Isaac – the stone that sits at the centre of the Holy of Holies that had been the innermost sanctum of the Temple of Jerusalem. In AD 691, the Muslims erected the beautiful building known as 'the Dome of the Rock' on top of the site of the Temple of the Jews.

In 1071, the city was taken by Seljuk Turks who devastated it. Twenty-eight years later, on Friday, 15 July 1099, the holy city saw a new devil dancing down its streets. The Christian army of 'Crusaders' captured Jerusalem and, with an efficiency not seen since Roman times, massacred every man, woman and child of the Jewish and Muslim populations in the name of their God.

The idea for a holy Crusade had originated with Pope Urban II who, we are told, had become concerned at the treatment of Christian pilgrims in the Holy Land. On Tuesday, 27 November 1095, in a field just outside the walls of the French city of Clermont-Ferrand, he called to arms the clergy attending a church council. He suggested a plan whereby Christian knights would form a huge army that would secure the Holy Land as a Christian kingdom. The response was positive, and overwhelming, and the bishops at the council returned to their homes to enlist others in this great Crusade. The great lords of Europe were enticed with the offer of salvation and the opportunity to loot what they found, as their reward for assisting in God's work.

Soon Pope Urban had the support he needed and he outlined his strategy.

Individual groups of Crusaders were to begin the journey in August 1096. Each group was expected to be self-financing and responsible to its own leader as they made their separate ways to the Byzantine capital of Constantinople, where they would be assembled into a combined fighting force. From there, they would launch an attack against the Seljuk conquerors of Anatolia, along with the Byzantine emperor and his army. Once that region was under Christian control, the Crusaders would campaign against the Muslims in Syria and Palestine, with Jerusalem as their ultimate goal.

The armies of the crusading nobles duly arrived at Constantinople in November 1096, and in the following May, they attacked their first major target: the Anatolian Turkish capital at Nicea – the very city where Christianity had been formalised. The Crusaders enjoyed rapid success and soon found that they met little resistance during the rest of their campaign in

Asia Minor. The next major obstacle was the city of Antioch in northern Syria which they besieged for almost eight months until its fall on 3 June 1098. By May 1099, the Crusaders had reached the northern borders of Palestine; on the evening of 7 June they camped within sight of the walls of the holy city of Jerusalem.

With the aid of reinforcements from Genoa and newly constructed siege machines, they stormed Jerusalem and joyously conducted their systematic massacre of every inhabitant. The Crusaders were happy that the city had been purified by the blood of the defeated enemies of Christ.

A week later, the Crusaders elected Godfrey of Bouillon, Duke of Lower Lorraine, to rule the newly won city as a governor. Under his leadership, the army then fought its last campaign, defeating an Egyptian army at Ascalon. With God's work largely completed the great majority of the Crusaders returned to Europe, leaving Godfrey with a small remnant of the original force to maintain law and order. Strangely, the 39-year-old Godfrey appears to have died at this precise moment of triumph, because his brother was crowned king of Jerusalem, under the title of Baldwin I, in the year 1100.

THE MOTIVE UNCOVERED

The nine Knights who took the mutual vow of 'chastity, obedience and to hold all property in common' (page 22) had been in Jerusalem when Baldwin I became the first Christian king. We needed to comb through the facts that remain concerning these men and carefully study the events of the time. The original Templars were:

Hugues de Payen – a vassal lord to Hugh of Champagne
Geoffrey de St Omer – son of Hugh of St Omer
André de Montbard – a vassal lord to Hugh of Champagne and uncle of Bernard of Clairvaux
Payen de Montdidier – related to the rulers of Flanders
Achambaud de St-Amand – related to the rulers of Flanders
Gondemare – no details known
Rosal – no details known
Godefroy – no details known
Geoffroy Bisol – no details known

The knights of whom little is known are believed to have been representatives of the ruling families of Champagne, Anjou, Gisors and Flanders.[8]

The leader of the Templars was Hugues de Payen, a middle-ranking noble-man in Champagne who married Catherine St Clair, the niece of his crusading partner Baron Henri St Clair of Roslin, in 1101. Three years later, Hugues left his wife and infant son, Theobald, to travel to Jerusalem with Hugh of Champagne, for reasons unknown. It is also recorded that he returned to Jerusalem once again in 1114, and on the death of Baldwin I in 1118 he formed his full band of nine knights and made his approach to the new king, Baldwin II.

We started to map out the movements of people and put events into a time sequence to see what kind of pattern would emerge. The first person we considered was Pope Urban II who had first called for the Crusade in 1095 and died just as the holy city of Jerusalem was taken.

It struck us as a strange coincidence that the two key figures of the First Crusade both died the very instant that Jerusalem was secured. Had the warrior chief, Godfrey de Bouillon, and the spiritual leader, Urban II, served their purpose, and been quietly dispatched? If so, who had planned such a thing and why?

Urban II had been born Odo of Lagery in France and studied at Reims before he entered the Benedictine monastery of Cluny, of which he became prior in 1073. In 1078, he was created cardinal bishop of Ostia by Pope Gregory VII, who he eventually succeeded.

The Benedictine Order, which Odo joined, had been established in the sixth century and we were interested to find that, whilst they have used black habits for several centuries, they originally wore a long full gown and hood of pure white, just as the Essenes and the Jerusalem Church leaders had.

Another important Church figure in the post-Crusade period was Bernard of Clairvaux, the young man who was personally responsible for obtaining a papal 'rule' for the Templars in 1128. He was of the Cistercian Order rather than a Benedictine, so we looked up the histories of the two orders to see if there was any connection between them. There was.

Curiously, we found that the Cistercian Order had been founded in 1098 by a group of Benedictine monks from the abbey of Molesme, just months before the taking of Jerusalem and the death of Urban II. Too many strange things seemed to be happening all at once to be ignored as mere chance.

The founding Cistercian monks stated that they wanted to get back to the

---

[8] L. Charpentier: *The Mysteries of Chartres Cathedral*

purer and original teachings of St Benedict who had founded the Benedictine order in the early sixth century and became known as the father of Western monasticism. This saint, who the Cistercians so admired, had been born into a distinguished family of Nursia in central Italy and, after spending his early years studying in Rome, he went to live in a cavern for three years. Benedict established what he called a rule of life which later became a requirement for all monastic orders. It stressed the importance of communal living and physical labour, forbade members to own property, required meals to be taken in common and unnecessary conversation to be avoided. This whole worldview sounded exactly like that of the Essenes who were required to spend three years in the desert location of the Qumran Community in order to pass through their three degrees of training, concluding with the ceremony of the 'living resurrection'.[9]

Stranger still, the Cistercians were called 'White Monks' because of the white habit they wore under their black scapulars. Add to this the fact that the original mantle of the Knights Templar was also pure white (the famous red cross being added later) and we had to ask ourselves: was some ancient knowledge rising to the surface connected to the Nasorean values and the wearing of white? The Nasoreans who had fought, and died, at the fall of Jerusalem in AD 70 had worn white as a symbol of resurrection, and just over a thousand years later there was a return to Jerusalem and the wearing of white robes suddenly seems to have become very important. Could this be connected with the prophecy of the Book of Revelations that said the martyrs of Jerusalem would be resurrected after a thousand years?

Many strange things appear to have started happening at the same time and we found that the rise of St Bernard was every bit as unusual as the rise of the Templars themselves. He was born near Dijon in 1090, and at the age of twenty-three he announced his decision to become a priest and join the still very new Cistercian Order. His decision met with considerable opposition from his elder brother, the Count of Fontaine, who was horrified at Bernard's decision to become a monk. However, something rather spectacular must have happened to change his mind because within the year, the Count had joined the Cistercian Order himself – along with no fewer than thirty-one other members of the Fontaine family!

Something very, very unusual was happening here, and the more we looked the more we found.

[9] C. Knight & R. Lomas: *The Hiram Key*

First, Bernard is criticised by his family for becoming a Cistercian; months later his family flock to join; then, within the next year, the twenty-five-year-old Bernard is made Abbot of a new abbey at Clairvaux – built especially for him by Hugh of Champagne: the very man who had visited Jerusalem with his vassal, Hugues de Payen.

Now, even a modest abbey must have taken two years to build – so it seems reasonable to conclude that Hugh of Champagne had commissioned the new abbey at the same time as Bernard had joined as a novice. If we are right, Bernard must have been 'placed' into this key position, at a ridiculously early age, as part of some grand plan.

Add to all this the fact that this young Church superstar was the nephew of André de Montbard, one of the original nine Templars, and the 'grand plan' theory starts to look very real indeed. Henri St Clair, Hugh of Champagne and Bernard of Clairvaux were certainly fully involved with Hugues de Payen, Geoffrey de St Omer, André de Montbard and the other founding Templars in a plan to recover the scrolls and treasure from below the Temple. It was also extremely probable that King Baldwin II of Jerusalem was also a member of the outer consortium.

Were Pope Urban and Godfrey de Bouillon pawns who were removed from the board once their usefulness had been outlived? At the time of his mysterious death Bouillon had been a relatively young man who had survived fierce battles, and the pope had been a previously healthy fifty-nine-year-old when he died at his precise moment of victory in 1099.

The question that we could not answer was: how did these people know what to look for? Then we had a breakthrough!

As we were digging up as many facts as we could to try and deduce what might have been going on, Robert telephoned the historian and writer Dr Tim Wallace-Murphy, regarding a point of detail concerning a particular dating. We had met Tim when we were in the final stages of completing *The Hiram Key* and he was interested to hear about our current research. Robert explained how we had built up a picture of a broad-based plan by a group of French noblemen to excavate under the ruins of Herod's Temple, and how we now believed that this group knew exactly what they were looking for.

Tim listened intently and then said: 'I know you're on to something because it fits with a strange piece of information that I have had for quite some time. Just suspend your usual scepticism for a moment and listen as though I'm telling you a story because it is attractive, but, by all normal standards, it's fantastic.'

Robert was all ears.

Tim told how he had just finished delivering a lecture in London some years earlier when a distinguished man of advancing years had walked up to him and introduced himself in French, a language in which Tim is fluent. He claimed that he was a direct descendant of the Templar leader, Hugues de Payen, and that he felt it appropriate to communicate some information that might be helpful. Tim intuitively felt that the man was not a charlatan and decided to listen. His first impressions were confirmed by the gentleman's soft and unassuming style of speech and his clear insight into a subject that few understand in any detail.

Here is the strange story that Tim heard.

When this man reached the age of twenty-one, his father called him to one side and informed him that he was about to share in secret knowledge that he would have to pass on to his own son when he reached the same age. He heard that there exists an ancient verbal tradition that had been passed down from father to chosen son in his family, and certain other families, for thousands of years.

The Frenchman recalled how he had not been surprised because his father managed to make it sound quite natural that the family should have such an ancient lineage. The next part of the story, he did confess, had shocked as well as surprised him.

At the time even before Jesus was born, the priests of the Temple of Jerusalem ran two schools: one for boys and one for girls. The priests were known by titles which were the names of angels, such as Michael, Mazaldek and Gabriel. This was the way in which they preserved the pure lines of Levi and David. When each of the chosen girls had passed through puberty one of the priests would impregnate her with the seed of the holy bloodline and, once pregnant, she would be married off to a respectable man to bring up the child. It was the custom that when these children reached the age of seven years they were handed back to the Temple schools to be educated by the priests.

Thus, stated the Frenchman, was a virgin called Mary visited by the priest known as 'Angel Gabriel' who had her with child. She was then married off to Joseph, who was a far older man.

According to this verbal tradition, Mary found it difficult to enjoy life with Joseph, her first husband, because he was too old for her but, over time, she grew to love him and had another four boys and three girls.

After Jesus was crucified the main pillars of the Jerusalem Church were

James the Just supported by Peter and John, the beloved disciple. (A fact confirmed in Paul's Epistle to the Galatians.) They formed a triumvirate, which was the traditional Essene way of ruling.

When Jesus was killed there was no public outcry because he was not popular with the mass of the people, but when James was killed, the whole city rose up in revolution, starting the terrible Jewish war against the Romans.

The Frenchman retold how James had become a much more important figure than Jesus in the Jerusalem Church. After the killing of James, and before the final destruction of the Temple, some of the Nazarene Priesthood fled first to Greece, then from there they scattered throughout Europe. They had briefly returned to the destroyed city to recover the remains of someone they knew as 'the saviour', and took these to Greece from where in AD 600 they returned the bones to beneath the Temple, the safest place to hide them, as no one was allowed to be buried in the confines of the Temple. Under the ruins of the Temple they say there are many chambers and on the walls of these chambers are written the genealogies of the children of the priests of the Temple, tracing their lineage back to David and Aaron.

The group of survivors took the group designation of 'Rex Deus' (Kings of God) and they survived the persecution of the Jews by adopting the religious practices of the lands in which they settled, provided they were only required to express a belief in the one true God. They believed that they were preserving the bloodlines of the two Messiahs of David and Aaron, who would one day arrive and establish the kingdom of God on Earth.

This then is the story that was told by a man who claimed to be a member of a Rex Deus family. He had been told to pass it on to his chosen son when he became twenty-one, but as he is childless, he was unable to do this. He was also told that he may be contacted by other members of Rex Deus, and he would know them by the genealogies which they all possessed. However, he said that no one had ever approached him concerning Rex Deus.

'That's a fantastic but quite riveting story,' said Robert.

'Yes, I thought you'd like it.'

'Is it written up anywhere?' enquired Robert.

'I will be mentioning it in the new book I'm co-writing.'[10]

Robert thanked Tim and immediately rang Chris to share this amazing news.

[10] T. Wallace-Murphy & M. Hopkins: *Concurrence of the Oracles*

Had we not arrived at the basic facts for ourselves we would never have believed such a strange claim, but the story fitted everything we knew, far too well not to be considered further. This Rex Deus explanation was a sensational breakthrough . . . if it was true.

It seemed to us that the probability of this elderly Frenchman inventing something so odd was unlikely in itself and, because it so precisely fitted the facts that we had pieced together, we had to adopt it as our working hypothesis. If we could find more evidence to support this account, linking events in first-century Jerusalem with the Knights Templar of the twelfth century, we knew we were on to something very big indeed. However, we also realised that we would have to be prepared to drop the idea if it did not check out as we found more evidence.

The picture that was emerging was of a group of European noble families, descended from the Jewish lines of David and Aaron, who had escaped from Jerusalem shortly before, or possibly even just after, the fall of the Temple. They had passed down the knowledge of the artefacts concealed beneath the Temple to a chosen son (not necessarily the eldest) of each family. Some of the families involved were the Counts of Champagne, Lords of Gisors, Lords of Payen, Counts of Fontaine, Counts of Anjou, de Bouillon, St Clairs of Roslin, Brienne, Joinville, Chaumont, St Clair de Gisor, St Clair de Neg and the Hapsburgs.

At first view, this idea seemed similar to the claims made by Michael Baigent, Richard Leigh and Henry Lincoln in their book *The Holy Blood and the Holy Grail*, which claimed to have identified an organisation called the Prieure de Sion. Baigent and his colleagues believed that Jesus had survived the cross and gone to live in France, where he had raised a family, and his bloodline, coming through the Morvingian kings and the Dukes of Lorraine, had been preserved by this shadowy Prieure de Sion. They claim this organisation was created by Godfrey de Bouillon who was a descendant of Jesus, and had preserved his bloodline intact to the modern day.[11]

The Rex Deus hypothesis is rather less neat, with a close connection to Jesus but no known bloodline. From what we have found, Godfrey de Bouillon was dead, perhaps murdered, before the Templars were formed. For reasons detailed in our last book, we also remained convinced that Jesus did die on the cross; the speech given by James after the crucifixion confirms this.[12]

---

[11] M. Baigent, R. Leigh & H. Lincoln: *The Holy Blood and the Holy Grail*
[12] C. Knight & R. Lomas: *The Hiram Key*

If the Rex Deus group did exist, it is easy to see how the First Crusade provided these families with a 'God-given' opportunity to return to their Holy Temple to recover the treasure that was their birthright – and it would be done at exactly the time that the Jewish writer of the Gospel of John the Divine had predicted! The Rex Deus families were at the forefront of the First, and every other Crusade. Medieval scholars have long wondered why it should be that the same families drove all of the Crusades for their entire duration, and now we had a possible answer.

Once the Christian armies had secured Jerusalem, the non-Rex Deus leaders were quickly removed and the families infiltrated the Jerusalem monarchy and the Church, to ensure that they would not be blocked in the holy endeavour of the 'Kings of God' to regain what their ancestors had left for them.

THE REX DEUS HYPOTHESIS

The story of the Rex Deus families explained how the band of Christian knights knew exactly what they were going to find, and the naming of Roslin now made perfect sense. Henri St Clair took the title that displayed his excitement at regaining the *ancient knowledge passed down the generations*.

Following the fall of Jerusalem, a contingent of elders from the Jerusalem Church escaped the carnage and headed for Alexandria, which had, in many ways, become the second city for the Jews. Here, the small group took stock of their position and decided to head for Greece from where they eventually spread out to other European cities. They adopted the religion of their new lands and became absorbed into their adopted communities, taking names that made them sound less foreign. They were highly intelligent people, descended from the aristocracy of the Jews, and most prospered. As each generation came and went, all memory of their origin faded, but one son was chosen and, when he attained the status of full manhood, was told of his strange birthright and the secrets of the Temple. Over time, some of the individual families lost contact with each other, but the chosen sons knew that others existed and how to recognise them if approached.

By 1095, the members of the Rex Deus group were almost certainly fully Christianised, yet each of them must have had at least one male member who held the traditional history of their high-born Jewish roots close to his heart. No doubt they saw themselves as 'super-Christians', descendants of the very first Church, and privy to the greatest secret this side of heaven. They were a silent elite – 'the kings of God'.

They realised that the taking of Jerusalem by the Seljuk Turks was the foretold attack of Gog and Magog and they used their considerable influence to plant the idea of a great Christian crusade into the mind of Pope Urban II. They told him that the prophecy of John the Divine had come true and it would be his great role to lead Christendom to rescue the Holy City from the heathen invaders. Indeed, the history books record that his leadership marked the papacy's assumption of the leadership of Western Christendom.[13]

Naturally, the Rex Deus families were the first to pledge allegiance to the crusading cause, and Pope Urban II must have been very surprised to find himself suddenly become so influential. Until that time, his six years as pontiff had been rather uninspiring and he had been kept out of Rome by the antipope, Clement III. Now, he was 'the man of the moment'.

Developing this scenario, we could imagine the situation in Jerusalem in the early months of 1100. There must have been a small contingent of Rex Deus members present and they surveyed the problem before them. Each of them had a slightly different story passed down to them because time changes things, no matter how hard people try to keep a verbal tradition completely pure. They pooled their knowledge of the secret points of entry from the top of the ruined Temple Mount, but they could not make sense of anything because the Muslim Dome on the Rock was covering the site of the inner Temple. Months of tapping around for hollow sounds had yielded nothing, and now others were becoming very suspicious.

We could image that there might well have been a split in the ranks. Some wanted to set a team of labourers digging immediately, but others saw danger in any public activity; how could they explain away such actions? The Vatican would quickly become most interested in any excavation on this holy site. As the newly crowned king of Jerusalem, Baldwin did not want anything to bring papal suspicion down on himself and he quickly sided with the cautious members, pointing out that they had control of the Temple once again and that was the most important thing. The treasures, he lamented, were buried beneath thousands of tons of rock and, as they had no clue where to start digging, it was better not to rush into anything.

Back in France, the Rex Deus families met to consider their position. They heard descriptions of the problems in Jerusalem and consulted drawings made by visitors. Obviously, things were much more complicated than

[13] Microsoft: *Encarta 96 Encyclopaedia*

they thought and their own people were now barring their access to the treasures of their forefathers.

Various senior members tried to use their influence to persuade Baldwin to allow an excavation, but to no avail; he replied that he was on the spot and that it would be impossible to act in secret, and suicidal to go public with their intentions. In 1104, Hugues de Payen made his first recorded visit to Jerusalem, accompanied by Hugh de Champagne, when they surveyed the site in detail for themselves. They consulted with Baldwin and left for Europe with a carefully documented record of the Temple area which allowed them to develop a plan of action.

The years rolled by and Baldwin still showed no sign of changing his mind. In 1113, however, something happened that created a new opportunity. A group of Christian knights formed themselves into a new order that they called 'The Sovereign Military Order of the Hospital of St John of Jerusalem of Rhodes, and of Malta' or, as they were generally known, the Knights Hospitaller. They established themselves as the protectors of a hospital built in Jerusalem before the First Crusade by Gerard, and the brothers happily swore to assist in the defence of Jerusalem.

This venture planted a new idea into the minds of the Rex Deus group and Hugh de Champagne and Hugues de Payen made a second visit to Jerusalem in 1114, to convey a new plan to Baldwin, which they were confident he would accept. They told him that they wanted to post a small contingent of knights in Jerusalem to carry out some exploratory digging under the pretext of being an order rather like the Hospitallers; their cover story was that they were to be guardians of the highways for pilgrims. They proposed that this new 'order' should be stationed on the site of Herod's stables, where they would be hidden from view, and, as they would be at a lower level, they would have horizontal access to excavate directly into the subterranean vaults where the treasures were located.

Unfortunately, the king was not persuaded and he simply rejected the new plan out of hand. The two lords returned home dejected.

They felt that Baldwin was a hopeless case and so they turned their attention to the cousin of the king who could, one day, become his successor. This potential king, also called Baldwin, had been a prisoner of the Muslims for four years and he had far more radical ideas about what needed to be done. In 1118, Baldwin I died at the age of sixty (presumably from natural causes) and his cousin was rapidly crowned King Baldwin II of Jerusalem.

Within weeks, the nine French knights were camped on the site of

Herod's stables, which was now part of the palace adjoining the former Al-Aqsa Mosque, under the patronage of Baldwin II. The world was told their mission was to save Christian pilgrims from the evil Muslim bandits, but their true mission was to locate and rescue the scrolls and treasures of the Jerusalem Church.

The work must have been extremely hard and the days long.

Cutting a new tunnel through solid rock with hand tools required huge effort and it took many months even to connect with an original passage that then carried them deep under the 'Haram', the gigantic base upon which the Temple had been built. Once inside the labyrinth, progress seemed to accelerate.

First they must have found a small pot of coins, next several gold and silver vessels, then a wooden box containing a scroll and another box with a scroll. The precious metal objects were quickly buffed up to reveal a dazzling splendour, but the scrolls meant nothing to the illiterate group who could not recognise more than a few words of French, let alone these Aramaic and Greek texts.

The team of primitive archaeologists began to feel highly protective of their finds and Geoffrey de St Omer, the second-in-command, was dispatched back to France to have the scrolls translated. He took them to the very learned Lambert of St Omer who was able to understand everything that his unbelieving eyes lighted upon. He asked that the scrolls be left with him and, unbeknown to Geoffrey, he made a hurried copy of one of them, a visual depiction of the Heavenly Jerusalem. We strongly suspect that the aged cleric died at the hands of Geoffrey de St Omer when it was discovered that he had copied a scroll without permission. However, the knight cannot have known the whereabouts of the copy of the Heavenly Jerusalem scroll as it still exists today in the library of Ghent University.

As a result of the early finds, a Count by the name of Fulk of Anjou went to Jerusalem in 1121 to check on progress. He was given a tour of the workings only after he took the same oath as the others, becoming a brother amongst them. Fulk, who later became king of Jerusalem, provided an annuity of thirty Angevin livres and then returned to Anjou.

Bernard of Fontaine (who would become Abbot of Cloirvaux) was activated to build up his reputation as a Church leader, so that he could draw on his status and persuade Pope Calixtus I that a military order should be formally established to support the kingdom of Jerusalem. The real motive of the Rex Deus group was to keep its activities secret, despite all the comings and goings of several VIPs, and it would soon need a suitable cover story for the considerable wealth that was to become evident.

Next to arrive in Jerusalem was, once again, Hugh of Champagne in 1124. On this trip, he too took the oath and became a Templar, so now there were eleven.

As we said earlier, we could not understand to whom this small band was swearing 'obedience', but if it was to Hugues de Payen, then the joining lord had just announced that he was prepared to be subservient to his own vassal, – a very strange occurrence, which either demonstrates the existence of treasure fever or that they were all sworn to obey a council of Rex Deus members.

The team kept on excavating until Christmas 1127 when they were sure that they had located every scrap of treasure and every scroll. A week later, Payen left to travel to the city of Troyes where he received the draft Rule, written by Bernard but presented to them by the Cardinal of Albano. He then set off on a recruiting tour of Europe, fitting in trips to brief the members of Rex Deus *en route*. This is when he called at the home of his wife's family in Scotland, most likely to deposit the precious scrolls for safekeeping. This was the furthest point from Rome to which they had access and, as such, the most secure place for these heretical documents, for in these scrolls they had found accounts of the life of Jesus and James that told the story of Jewish freedom fighters rather than the arrival on earth of the son of God.

They had found the accounts of the New Jerusalem that would arrive to herald the rule of God and were amazed at descriptions of initiation ceremonies for important recruits that involved a living resurrection. The evidence suggests that knowledge of the existence of these documents was restricted to the senior members of the new Templar Order and the St Clair family who were now acting as guardians of this ancient knowledge.

At the end of Hugues de Payen's tour, he returned to Jerusalem with three hundred knights to do his bidding as the first Grand Master of the Templars. He also had the promise of financial support and the gift of various estates which would be a perfect cover story to explain their sudden possession of very valuable treasures.

The Rex Deus families now had their treasure and they controlled Jerusalem and its Temple for the first time in over a thousand years. However, there was another risk and that was the succession to Baldwin II, who had no male heirs. This was solved by the widowed Fulk of Anjou marrying Baldwin's daughter Melisende to ensure the succession for the group.

The Rex Deus theory that we have outlined here has many attractions, but we had nothing but one man's word that the organisation ever existed. Then, something small but interesting turned up. We had been receiving a steady flow of letters from readers of our previous book, many of whom wanted to pass on information that they thought would be of interest to us, and indeed most of them had been very helpful. In yet another case of curious serendipity, we opened a letter that at any other time would have seemed trivial, but at this particular point it was quite riveting.

Russell Barnes related the following brief story that clearly made little sense to him, but seemed somehow significant. He wrote:

Some years ago I was in contact with the author Sinclair Traill because we shared a common interest in jazz and jazz musicians. He died around fifteen years or so ago and was, I guess, aged almost eighty.

He wore a sturdy gold ring – similar to a signet ring. On the face was an unusual motif which at first glance appeared to be a 'column'. He said the ring and its motif were associated historically with his Sinclair [St Clair] forebears, a name preserved by use as his Christian name. The motif was connected with an ancient building in Scotland.

My memory of this conversation grows dim but the design was similar to either of the pillars reproduced in your book. I wish I could recall what he related with more clarity.

Born in the town of Blandford, his family once owned and resided in a large house (now demolished for modern development) with land surrounding it. Some five hundred yards away from this building is the derelict St Leonard's Chapel, once a hospice run by a religious order. This chapel, erected in the early 13th century, has clear roots reaching back to Fontevrault Abbey, France. The Abbey was favoured by the Counts of Anjou (related to the early kings of England) and is where Richard I (Coeur de Lion) is buried. As a hospice it may have had connections with the Knights Templar of Templecombe, Somerset – some twenty miles away just over the Dorset county border.

Some twelve years ago – by chance – I was in casual conversation with a man (here in Dorset) when I noticed he was wearing an identical ring. He refused to discuss it with me saying that I was

mistaken and could not have seen one before. He terminated our
conversation there and then.

The obvious question sprang into our minds: was this a Rex Deus ring? Staying within our current working hypothesis, it would not seem unlikely that there would have been two branches of the Rex Deus group – those with a genealogy that traced back down the royal line of David and the other that went back along the priestly line. The first set of families would represent the Mishpat pillar of Boaz and the second set the Tsedeq pillar of Jachin. If this reasoning is correct, there would have to be two rings in existence that would remind the wearer of his heritage as one half of the holy gateway of Yahweh.

Chris rang the author of the letter to see if any more light could be shed on the situation.

Russell Barnes answered the telephone and in his soft Dorset accent he explained that he was an ex-policeman and probation officer who now spent his time on his twin loves of jazz and opera. He had read our previous book when it was recommended by a friend, and the episode of Sinclair Traill's ring had come back into his mind. He said that he had seen the second man with the identical ring when he had been in court one day; the wearer he recalled was a lawyer who seemed most alarmed that someone should notice the emblem he wore on his finger.

Russell recalled how both designs had been the same, a square at the base and what looked, at a quick glance, like a chimney rising above it, but on closer inspection it could be seen to be a decorative pillar. He had asked Sinclair Traill if it was a Masonic ring and he received the reply: 'No, it isn't quite Masonic,' the implication being that it was somehow indirectly connected to Freemasonry.

This suggested that there were two possible explanations for these rings that would not require the existence of a secret organisation such as the proposed Rex Deus. Firstly, they could both simply be editions of a ring designed with the image of the so-called 'Apprentice Pillar' of Rosslyn on it, or it could possibly be a device used by the modern Knights Templar in Scotland, are a Masonic-style order who claim direct lineage with the original order from which they take their name. Both of these possibilities could be easily checked out by a telephone call to Robert Brydon, the Templar archivist for Scotland and a man who probably knows more about the history of Rosslyn than anybody alive today.

His answer was short and clear. To his knowledge no such ring had ever been used by the modern order of Knights Templar, nor produced in connection with Rosslyn Chapel. The story of the rings remains to be explained.

Having run through the whole Rex Deus hypothesis in this way, we came to believe that it is unreasonable to deny that there was some greater plan in operation and that the Templars were not lone treasure-hunters, digging in the hope of finding something valuable. Too much time, energy and money was committed by too many important people for it all to be a simple, opportunistic looting of an historical site. Whilst conspiracy theories are not fashionable to promote, it does not mean that major conspiracies do not happen. Where large amounts of money or power are accessible, people will do unusual things to get what they believe is available.

The Templar Order took on a life of its own, after completing its original purpose, almost certainly as a result of the documentation that it found under the Temple. Within a very few years the rumours of strange rituals were circulating about the Order and fabulous stories were told of the Templars' exploits. The scrolls of the Nasoreans, which they had had translated for them, told a greatly different story of Jesus and the Jerusalem Church from the one that they had been brought up to believe. They read that Jesus was a kingly leader and not a god, and the resurrection had been a misunderstanding by Paul. The rituals conducted by Jesus and his followers were ancient, even to them, and they involved initiating candidates into their group by putting them through a living resurrection, where they underwent a figurative death and were wrapped in a white burial shroud. They were then raised from their tomb by a sacred ritual and the 'resurrected' individual became a brother amongst them as one of the new 'soldiers of the Temple', following in the footsteps of those who had died defending the Holy City in AD 70.

The Knights Templar have always attracted a lot of attention and many recent writers have made much of the Order's reputation for possessing human heads and worshipping something called 'Baphomet'. As Freemasons, we are not at all surprised that the Templars had human heads because a skull and crossed thigh bones are still used in the Masonic living resurrection ceremony that has Templar origins.

If any Freemason today was asked if he belonged to a cult that worshipped human heads he would think the questioner quite mad, and yet a quick calculation leads us to believe that Freemasonry around the world probably possesses a total of some fifty thousand skulls! The Templars performed the same ritual as that used as the 3rd Degree in Freemasonry, and they must have had a supply of skulls and of long white burial shrouds in which to wrap their candidates.

The worship of Baphomet has been explained by Hugh Schonfield, who detected that a first-century Jewish code called the Atbash cipher was used to conceal the names of individuals.[14] This code appears in the Dead Sea Scrolls, and in modern Freemasonry, and when applied to the Templar word 'Baphomet' it reveals the word 'Sophia' – the Greek for wisdom.

Whilst the Templars went their own way after 1128, whoever was behind their establishment stayed involved and participated with them in a great period of European architecture. Over the following seventeen years, more than ninety monasteries were established by Bernard of Clairvaux, and the Templars went on to be involved in the design and building of churches and preceptories across Europe as well as eighty great cathedrals, the most famous of which is the beautiful Cathedral of Notre Dame at Chartres.

THE TAROT AND THE TEMPLARS

At this point we were feeling really excited. We had identified the people involved in the establishment of the Knights Templar and discovered exactly how they knew what was concealed below the ruins of Herod's Temple. We now needed to try and work out what beliefs they actually adopted that eventually caused them to be destroyed as a secret heretical cult. Such information as there is on the Templars has been discussed by many people over many years so, as we cast our net wide to search out all possible sources of new insights, we came across a suggestion that Tarot cards have a Templar connection. Neither of us had any interest in the Tarot and we almost ignored the idea, but we thought that we ought to be thorough because strange things had already happened.

We were soon glad that we had invested the time to study these fairground fortune-telling cards.

It has been claimed that the Templars adopted an Eastern technique of telling stories with cards that could have several different versions, depending how the cards were shuffled and described. Some people claim that Tarot cards originated in China or India, but these were entirely different in shape and design and were not at all the same as the ones used in Europe.[15] Several

---

[14] H. Schonfield: *The Essene Odyssey*
[15] A. Douglas: *The Tarot*

scholars have argued that the Templars originated the Tarot and, when we started to look into the meaning given to these cards, they could hardly have come from anyone else.[16]

The Templars no doubt got the idea from the Saracens who had used picture cards since the eighth century, but Templar cards were designed to have two separate layers of meaning, making them a safe method to carry training materials around without the danger of discovery by unintended spectators. These carefully painted picture cards originally held the story of the Templars ready for retelling, but they were destined to become the stock in trade for fortune-tellers everywhere.

The Tarot consists of fifty-six cards known as the Minor Arcana and twenty-two pictorial cards called the Major Arcana. It was the Minor Arcana that became the basis for modern playing cards, consisting of suits of wands (clubs), cups (hearts), swords (spades) and pentacles (diamonds). Originally each suit had fourteen cards: four court cards – king, queen, knight and page (the Jack) – plus cards numbered from ace to ten. The four cards that have been lost to make the current fifty-two-card pack are the knights from each suit. These cards suddenly disappeared soon after the Knights Templar were declared heretics and the Church was determined to obliterate all memory of the Order.[17]

The Major Arcana consists of twenty-two numbered pictorial cards. All but one of these cards mysteriously disappeared around the same time as the knights of the Minor Arcana because the Church considered them to be 'the rungs of a ladder leading to hell' and 'the devil's breviary'. From this we deduce that, after the Templars had been arrested as heretics, some had confessed the true purpose of these cards as coded symbols that could communicate secret teachings under the very nose of the Church, without arousing suspicion. The Major Arcana was also called the suit of Trumps or the Greater Secrets, and only the Fool escaped censorship, surviving as today's Joker of the pack. It is said that the Fool represented the novice at the beginning of his journey towards enlightenment.

Christian clergymen saw fit to remove the other twenty-one cards of the 'Greater Secrets' because they were believed to convey a heretical message detested by the Church.[18] The alternative name, Trumps, comes from a

---

[16] M. Goodwin: *The Holy Grail*
[17] Ibid.
[18] B.G. Walker: *The Secrets of the Tarot*

The High Priestess of the Tarot pack

pageant held in the ancient world called in Latin *a triumph* which centred on the story of a sacred king, or other apotheosised hero, and had strong connections with the goddess Ishtar and her dying and resurrected consort Tammuz. Since the suit of Trumps was removed, people using playing cards have had to designate one of the four remaining suits as temporary trumps for many card games.

The card that was most immediately offensive to the Church was the High Priestess, which is also known as the Papess – the female pope.

This sounds like a strange idea, but it is known that there was a belief in the early Christian Church that the first pope was not St Peter but St Mary Magdalene, who received her spiritual authority directly from Jesus.[19] In the Gospel of Philip she is described as the one that Jesus loved above all his followers:

[19] E. Pagels: *The Gnostic Gospels*

> . . . *the companion of the [Saviour is] Mary Magdalene. [But Christ loved] her more than [all] the disciples [and] used to kiss her [often] on her [mouth]. The rest of [the disciples were offended by it. . .]. They said to him, 'Why do you love her more than all of us?' The Saviour answered and said to them, 'Why do I not love you as [I love] her?*

The Gospel of Mary tells us that she was favoured with visions and insight that far surpassed Peter's. Another document, the *Dialogue of the Saviour*, describes her as the apostle who excels all the rest . . . 'a woman who knew the All'. Gospels that refer to the equality of women were rejected by the Roman Church under the catch-all accusation of being Gnostic, but in these versions it is clear that there was a power struggle between Peter and Mary Magdalene. In a document called 'Pistis Sophia', Peter complains that Mary is dominating the conversation with Jesus and displacing the rightful priority of Peter and the other male apostles. Peter asks Jesus to silence her, but he is quickly rebuked. Mary Magdalene later admits to Jesus that she hardly dares speak to Peter because: '*Peter makes me hesitate; I am afraid of him, because he hates the female race.*' Jesus replies that whoever the Spirit inspires is divinely ordained to speak, whether man or woman.[20]

It is easy to see why, a thousand years after the Council of Nicea had established its Roman creed, the last thing that the Church wanted was information that undermined their claim to the most senior apostolic succession through Peter. The Roman Catholic Church was designed around the idea of the domination of women by men, Even now, the growing liberalisation of other Churches that are admitting female priests appears to be causing annoyance in the Vatican.

We knew that those early Christian teachings that had not come via Rome had a very different view of the role of women. The Celtic Church, which had its roots in Alexandrian Christianity and extended over Ireland, Scotland, Wales and northern England, believed that women had an equal right to the priesthood, and it maintained that view until it was absorbed by the Roman Catholic Church in AD 625, at the Synod of Whitby. It is recorded that early Church Fathers recognised the authority of Mary, but later Church historians focused on her reputation as a harlot.

[20] Ibid.

It is known that the absolution used by the Templar order was distinctly unorthodox. One Templar preceptor, Radulphus de Gisisco, stated that absolution was unusually given in French and not Latin:

I pray God that He may pardon our sins, as He pardoned St Mary Magdalene . . .

It seemed as though Mary Magdalene, the harlot who turned high priestess, was of central interest to the Templars.

At this point of our research we came across a further small, but very significant, twist in history regarding the role of Mary Magdalene. The young Bernard of Clairvaux was utterly fascinated by the history of this first pope and he created the cult of the Black Virgin which acknowledges that Mary Magdalene was black and that she was the Bride of Christ. Bernard personally wrote three hundred sermons devoted to the Song of Songs, a small reference in Solomon 1:5 that reads:

I am black, I am comely, O ye daughters of Jerusalem.

This cult established by Bernard created a new view of women in the twelfth century, when they became respected and the courtly rules of love were established for the first time.

Two hundred years after Bernard, at the very time that the Church was removing this Papess card, stories began to circulate that there had been a female pope in recent times known as Pope Joan. Apparently, Joan was born of English parents and fell in love with a Benedictine monk, with whom she fled to Athens, disguised as a man. After the death of her lover, she again pretended to be a man and entered the priesthood, rising to the status of cardinal, and then being elected Pope John VIII. Embarrassingly for all concerned, she died in childbirth during a papal procession.

Although there is no evidence that can prove the story to be true, it was given full credence by the Church itself, as well as the general public.[21] She still appears in a row of papal busts in Siena Cathedral labelled '*Johannes VIII, femina ex Anglia*' (Pope John VIII, an Englishwoman).[22]

The Vatican must have been quite disturbed by this story because it intro-

---

[21] Microsoft: *Encarta 96 Encyclopaedia*
[22] E.R. Chamberlin: *The Bad Popes*

duced measures to ensure that such a scandal could never occur again. All cardinals who became papal candidates were required to sit naked beneath their gown, on a specially constructed seat that was elevated and open like a toilet seat, where their genitalia could be inspected by their peers from below. A formal verdict had to be declared: *Testiculos habet, et bene pendentes* – He has testicles, and they hang well![23]

The Papess card was sometimes called 'Joan', but the existence of this card before the stories of Joan were in circulation indicated to us that the Templars may have come across ancient documentation that identified Mary Magdalene as the first true pope. In some versions of the Tarot pack, she is shown seated with a scroll in her hand and two pillars either side of her; the left-hand one is black and marked with a letter 'B' and the right-hand one with a 'J'. This clearly identifies the High Priestess, or Papess, as being directly connected with the two pillars of Boaz and Jachin that stood at the entrance to Yahweh's inner Temple in Jerusalem, and that now adorn every Masonic temple.

The mechanism that underpins the Major Arcana is a Möbius strip: a simple structure that curiously is a two-dimensional surface that has only one side. A Möbius strip can be formed by taking a long strip of paper, twisting one end through one hundred and eighty degrees and then joining the ends together, giving a single surface. Because the surface has no end, this figure-of-eight structure has long been used as the symbol of death and resurrection, and in modern usage it signifies infinity.

The story that these cards tell, when laid out in this form, is deeply opposed to the tenets of orthodox Christianity. The Tarot teaches the Jewish and Templar belief that the Fool (who represents the novice) can achieve salvation through his own actions, independently of Christ or his Church, whereas the Church teaches that people can only receive the grace of God through faith in Jesus Christ alone.

The first circle is the solar sphere of daylight and has the cards from the Fool (number 0) to the Hermit (number 9) that move in a clockwise direction on the outside of the ring, signifying the normal world seen by everybody. The tenth card, the Wheel of Fortune, crosses over into the second circle or lunar sphere where the cards are laid inwards, representing the inner path of hidden teachings, and run from Justice through to Judgement. The final card of the World (number 21) links back into the first circle,

[23] G.L. Simons: *Sex and Superstition*

illustrating how the hidden teachings have to relate back into normal life.

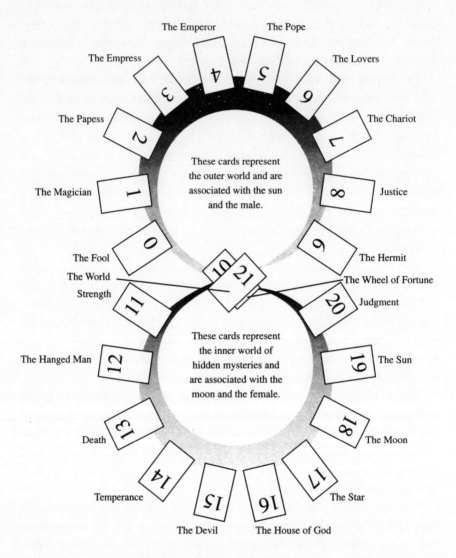

The Emperor

The Pope

The Empress

The Lovers

The Papess

The Chariot

The Magician

These cards represent the outer world and are associated with the sun and the male.

Justice

The Fool

The World

Strength

The Hermit

The Wheel of Fortune

Judgment

The Hanged Man

These cards represent the inner world of hidden mysteries and are associated with the moon and the female.

The Sun

Death

The Moon

Temperance

The Star

The Devil

The House of God

The Eternal Loop of the Tarot pack

We found the fourth and twelfth cards of the Tarot pack to be particularly noteworthy because both show men with one leg crossed over the other. Although this may not sound remarkable, we were very interested to discover that the posture of one leg crossed over a straight leg is described by experts as 'crucial' to Tarot symbolism.[24] This form of leg arrangement appears on the Emperor card and the Hanged Man – a figure suspended from a cross by his right foot, with his left leg bent behind his right leg. This pose was also crucial to Templars as every one of their knights was laid in his tomb with his legs crossed in precisely this manner. The crossed legs form an 'x' shape, which is one form of the Tau, the last letter of the Hebrew alphabet, which signifies death. The more elaborate tombstones of leading Knights Templar were engraved with an image showing this pose, or with a fully sculptured effigy showing the deceased in this unusual position.

The Hanged Man of the Tarot pack   *A Templar grave showing crossed legs*

When the novice (the Fool) is given instruction, he is told that each card within the worldly circle has a direct correspondence with a card in the secret circle. These relationships are recognised by the fact that all paired cards add up to twenty so that the card known as the Hierophant or the Pope (number 5) is associated with the Devil (number 15). Whilst this connection was almost certainly not intended to insult the papacy, it is little wonder that the

---

[24] B.G. Walker: *The Secrets of the Tarot*

Church wanted to destroy these cards when they discovered these types of relationship concealed in the Tarot.

Like the Papess card, the Pope or Hierophant card shows a regal figure sitting between two pillars that are not supporting anything. Barbara Walker, who is a serious and respected Tarot researcher, said of the figure shown on this card:

> *He was surely not intended to suggest Christian orthodoxy. Those few scholars who equated him with the Roman pope did so with many reservations.*[25]

Another interesting point is that, according to Barbara Walker, an alternative name for this figure is 'The Grand Master', which strongly suggested to us that this card could represent the Templar Grand Master. This seems even more likely when we remember that today the Grand Master of Freemasonry still sits on a throne-like chair between two pillars that support nothing. These Masonic pillars are said to represent those that stood in the porchway of the inner sanctum of the Jerusalem Temple – the building that was the home of the Knights Templar. We knew from our previous researches that Freemasonry had inherited its structure and principal ritual from the Knights Templar in Scotland, and we would expect that an official depiction of the Templar Grand Master would show him seated between two pillars.

As we thought around this idea of the Hierophant card, another important connection sprang to mind. James, the brother of Jesus, became the high priest of the Jerusalem Church (the Nasorean movement) after the crucifixion – a position that Christian scholars have recognised by calling him the first 'Mebakker' or Bishop of Jerusalem.[26] It is known that James wore a bishop's mitre which was derived from the crown of Amon-ra, the creator god of Thebes, the city that had provided ancient Judaism with the central tenets of its theology.[27] The ancient Egyptian hieroglyph for the god Amonra shows how the regalia of Christian bishops came from Thebes via Jerusalem.

The name 'Hierophant' is defined by *Chambers English Dictionary* as meaning 'one who reveals sacred things' – exactly what the Templar Master

[25] B. G. Walker: *The Secrets of the Tarot*
[26] R. Eisenman & M. Wise: *The Dead Sea Scrolls Uncovered*
[27] C. Knight & R. Lomas: *The Hiram Key*

The Egyptian hieroglyph for the creator god Amon Ra

would have been doing as he initiated new members.

The only conclusion that we could come to is that the Knights Templar saw themselves as the high priests of Jerusalem 'resurrected' and returned to continue the fight to build a world fit for the True and Living God Most High to rule over. Here, in the most unlikely of places, was evidence that they reconstructed the ancient Davinic cult of the Holy Temple and they probably considered Rabbinical Judaism of the synagogue and Christianity to be significant but corrupted forms of Yahweh worship.

As the new High Priests of Yahweh, the Templar Grand Masters sat upon a throne with the two ancient Jewish pillars of Mishpat (Boaz) and Tsedeq (Jachin) representing the union of sacerdotal and secular power on Earth under the heavenly rule of Yahweh. Upon their heads they wore the crown of the Mebakker, just as James had done eleven hundred years earlier. The 'kings of God' had returned to take the role of the joint messiah that had first been united in one person by Jesus.[28] The Hierophant or Grand Master card of the Tarot must be an accurate depiction of the office of the Templar Grand Master!

As the Templars had rebuilt their own ancient religion they answered to the pope in name only, secretly rejecting his authority and denying the divinity of their hereditary forebear, Jesus Christ, but probably accepting him as a martyred prophet.

The Templars were eventually accused of being non-Christian, were

[28]. Ibid.

destroyed as an order in 1307, and their teaching cards slowly became available to the general world. Anyone looking at the Grand Master card would see the mitre and wrongly assume that it must represent the pope. The Roman Catholic Church almost certainly knows of these secret meanings within the Tarot and it has, understandably, long tried to ban the faithful from having anything to do with them. Interestingly, they were outlawed just nine years after the first public exhibition of the Turin Shroud, first in Florence, then in Germany, Marseilles, Paris and the rest of Europe soon after.[29]

Having made what we consider to be a huge step forward in confirming the real purpose of the Knights Templar, we returned to the rest of the Tarot pack to see what other information could be locked up in these historic cards that have now become playthings. We found that the original suits – Swords, Wands, Cups and Pentacles – had become associated with Grail legends, representing Sword, Spear, Grail and Dish.

Now, it occurred to us that these designations could be connected to the artefacts that the Templars would have found below the ruins of Herod's Temple. Swords and spears would have certainly been taken underground by the Jewish defenders when the battle was being lost, and we have already recounted Josephus' description of how Simon bar Giora and his men had hidden in the secret passages. We also knew that sacrificial cups and dishes had been hidden below the Temple because they are fully listed in the Copper Scroll found at Qumran.

At first we were doubtful that there would be a hard connection between the Grail legends of King Arthur and the Knights Templar but we quickly changed our minds. A very interesting connection between the Grail and the Tarot emerged in what are described as the 'four courts of the Grail'. It is said by Arthurian experts that this shows a web of lineage and bloodline:

North Court Court of the Disc and the House of Benwick
West Court Court of the Grail and the House of Pellinor
East Court Court of the Sword and the House of Pendragon
South Court Court of the Spear and the House of Lothian and Orkney

It was the Southern Court that immediately stood out for us because the House of Lothian and Orkney could only refer to the St Clair family (today Sinclair) who were the last princes of Orkney and whose Roslin Castle is in

---

[29] S.R. Kaplan: *The Encyclopaedia of Tarot*

TAROT	PLAYING CARD	GRAIL
Swords	Spades	Sword
Wands	Clubs	Spear
Cups	Hearts	Grail
Pentacles	Diamonds	Dish

Lothian. Henri St Clair had been involved in the First Crusade right along-side Hugues de Payen, and his niece Catherine married Payen, receiving the lands of Blancradock30 near Edinburgh, now known as Temple, as a dowry.31 The family was certainly instrumental in establishing the Knights Templar and became guardians of the scrolls excavated from the Temple at Jerusalem, which they later re-interred below Rosslyn 'Chapel' – the replica of the ruins of Herod's Temple.32

CONCLUSION

The Dark Ages had arrived with the invention of the Roman Church and human advancement had gone into reverse gear. Jerusalem had been taken by the Turks, a thousand years after the destruction of the city and its Temple, and the First Crusade had been mounted to liberate it from the hea-then hordes. From studying the circumstances of this crusade and the establishment of the Templars we identified a group of people acting in the background who were involved in a plan to excavate the ruins of the Temple. We were told of a group of families, known collectively as 'Rex Deus', who claim to be descended from surviving priests of the Jerusalem Temple, and this made sense of the strange events of the early twelfth century that we had already uncovered.

The Templars excavated under the Temple for nine years and removed treasures and at least twenty-four scrolls. In these scrolls they discovered the details of the Jerusalem Church. They established themselves as the new cult of the Temple with their Grand Master as the joint messiah of Israel, uniting the pillars of Mishpat (Boaz) and Tsedeq (Jachin) just as their forebears, Jesus and James, had done. The secret rituals of living resurrection described

---

[30] Anonymous: *Secret Societies of the Middle Ages*
[31] Baron St Clair Bonde: private communication
[32] C. Knight & R. Lomas: *The Hiram Key*

in the scrolls were adopted as the means of initiation into this resurrected cult of the 'priesthood of the Temple', following in the footsteps of those who had served Yahweh and died defending the holy city in AD 70.

The Templar cult secretly denied the authority of the pope and his Church, believing Jesus to be a martyred prophet but not a god.

The Tarot pack of cards had been created by the Templars as a means of instructing novices without raising the suspicions of the Church and was outlawed by the Church after the fall of the Order. We then found that the Tarot and the Templars seemed to have some connection with the Grail stories of King Arthur and that the St Clairs of Roslin were likely to be involved.

Chapter 5

THE HOLY GRAIL OF THE TEMPLARS

THE ORIGINS OF KING ARTHUR

Although we had doubted at times that it would be possible to find the answer to the third question of our quest, we now knew who was behind the development of the Knights Templar. We had been able to name the main players, and the information we received about the Rex Deus families was a major breakthrough that gave us a probable answer to the fourth question: why did the Templars decide to excavate below the temple? Their mission had been to recover the treasures and scrolls that they knew their ancestors had left for them.

Tarot cards had proved to be a remarkable source of information concerning the Templars when viewed in the context of our other findings. Although we consider Tarot cards completely useless as a means of peering into the future, they have been a remarkably helpful mechanism when it comes to illuminating the past. People today often bare their inner thoughts to the world in many ways, from autobiographical books to documentary films, and students of recent history can readily build up a comprehensive picture of the attitudes and aspirations of any group or individual they care to examine. Anyone studying the medieval period has a much harder time because there are precious few documents that express human feelings regarding non-standard ideas and beliefs.

From the mid-twelfth century to the beginning of the fourteenth century, the Knights Templar were a fabulously wealthy and influential order who reported directly to the pope, and it would have been suicidal for them to allow anyone to know that they had 'alternative' thoughts. They could not overtly write down their real opinions, but they did record them covertly; and that is why the Tarot pack must be considered such a valuable historical 'document'.

The Templar use of Tarot cards seemed to be connected with the legend of the Holy Grail and we now needed to investigate these stories to see what strength of linkage existed. Perhaps the Grail stories were a further covert means of recording secret Templar ideas and beliefs. There was good reason to be hopeful because we had seen the St Clair family being brought into the picture as the Southern Court of the Spear, and Pendragon, found in the Eastern Court of the Sword, was the name of King Arthur's father.

In recent years, many people have claimed to have identified some obscure artefact as being the 'true' Holy Grail, usually said to be the cup used by Jesus at the Last Supper. However, after considering the available evidence, it seems to us that there is no such thing as the 'true' Holy Grail, as it has several definitions. This Grail idea has become a metaphor for an impossible task, almost as futile as seeking the pot of gold at the end of a rainbow, and it has been identified as many different things by those who have written about it over the last eight hundred years.

According to the best known tradition, the Grail was the sacred cup used by Jesus at the Last Supper that had been retained by Joseph of Arimathea after he collected the blood from the body of the crucified Christ in it. This legend tells us that he subsequently brought the sacred artefact to Britain, where it was transmitted from generation to generation of his descendants. Exposure to the Grail can do good or bad, depending on the merits of the onlooker. Those without sin are furnished with food, but the impure of heart are struck blind, and the irreverent lose the power of speech.

This version of the story is interesting because it raises the suggestion that there is an alternative apostolic succession through Joseph of Arimathea and his family. Moreover, this line is claimed to have secret knowledge, unknown to the established Church.[1] This sounds highly fanciful, but it would fit very well with the Rex Deus theory, as the line of Joseph of Arimathea could easily have been one of the group that came to Europe with its secret knowledge.

---

[1] G. Phillips: *The Search for the Grail*

Other definitions of the Holy Grail include 'the stone upon which kings are made', and, very interestingly, a book that contains the secret teachings of Jesus.[2]

It seems that the Holy Grail can be almost anything you want it to be. Therefore, we really had to find the origins of each interpretation so that we could establish a chronology and gain some understanding of the purpose of these stories. The first references to the Holy Grail appear in Arthurian legend which is known in outline to many people, thanks to films such as *Excalibur*, *First Knight*, or *King Arthur and the Knights of the Round Table*. Most people probably believe that these stories stem from folk tales that go back to times when England and Wales still consisted of a series of small kingdoms, which would mean that they predate the Templars by many centuries.

According to the most common version of the legend, Arthur was the illegitimate son of Igerna, wife of the Duke of Cornwall, who was raped by Uther Pendragon whilst under the enchantment of a magician called Merlin. As a very young man Arthur proved that he was the rightful king of Britain by pulling the otherwise immovable sword, Excalibur, from the stone where it had been placed by an earlier king.

Once king, he married Guinevere and established his Round Table, a group of courageous knights who helped him make the kingdom stable and law-abiding. Relationships are always complex in the story and those of Arthur were no exception when he unknowingly fathered an illegitimate son, Mordred, when magically enchanted and seduced by his half-sister, Morwenna. When the boy grew to manhood he appeared at Arthur's Court, at Camelot, and challenged him for the kingdom. In the meantime, Lancelot, one of the knights, had an affair with Guinevere which estranged him from Arthur for many years. The Round Table fell into decline and disrepute, with Arthur himself becoming sick, and the kingdom becoming a waste land. It was said that the land could only be saved by finding the Holy Grail and so the sick Arthur sent all his remaining knights out to search for it.

Sir Lancelot succeeded in finding the Grail and returned to Arthur just in time to heal him and support him in the last mighty battle with his son Mordred. Both Lancelot and Mordred died in the ensuing combat. Arthur was mortally wounded, although legend has it that he did not die but sailed away westwards to the land of Avalon, there to be healed of his wounds, ready to return to save his country at some future time of need. His sword

[2] G. Phillips: *The Search for the Grail*

Excalibur was thrown into a lake where it was caught by the arm of the Lady of the Lake who took it into her care until it should be needed again.

The important questions for us were how old is this story, and does it have any connection with the Knights Templar? At face value, it seems to be far older than the Templars, but we soon found that this is not so.

Certainly, the earliest known references to an Arthur-like character came from a fifth-century monk called Gildas who recorded a last unsuccessful battle, against the encroaching Anglo-Saxons, by a warlord known as Aurelius Ambrosianus in the West of Britain. Four hundred years later, another monk, by the name of Nennius of Bangor, wrote a history of Britain where he named the warlord 'Arthur' and stated that the final lost battle had been fought at a place called Mons Badonicus in AD 500.[3]

However, this early reference to an historical warlord called Arthur describes a very different character from the one of modern legend. The first reference to a King Arthur that we would recognise appeared, out of the blue, in 1136 – just eight years after the formation of the Order of the Knights Templar and the year in which Hugues de Payen died!

The story was entitled *The Matter of Britain* and it was written in the city of Oxford by a secular canon called Geoffrey of Monmouth.[4] Here, for the first time, Arthur is depicted as something of a messianic saviour of his people who comes from a magical mating of Igerna with Uther Pendragon. Geoffrey identifies Arthur's reign as being in a place he calls Caerleon, beginning in the year AD 505 and ending when the king is carried westwards to the sacred isle of Avalon, where he is to rest until such time as he will be resurrected and return triumphant. His magical sword is here called *Caliburn*, which echoes the named sword, *Caladcholg*, which was one of the Hallows of Ireland in Irish legend.

Unlike later Arthurian tales, Geoffrey of Monmouth's early version makes no reference to a Holy Grail, to Lancelot or the Round Table. Geoffrey's Latin narrative became extremely popular and was soon translated into the Welsh by an unknown scribe, into French by Wace of Jersey and into Anglo-Saxon by Layamon. The story spread across all of Europe and for centuries people considered it to be historical fact.[5]

[3] N. Chadwick: *The Celts*
[4] A.O.H. Jarman: 'Geoffrey of Monmouth and *The Matter of Britain*', *Wales Through the Ages*, vol. I
[5] T.W. Rolleson: *Myths of the Celtic Race*

We now knew that the timing was spot on for there to be a direct connection to the founding Templars, but we wondered why Geoffrey of Monmouth had been motivated to write about this obscure early British warrior king at this particular period of history. The date of writing, and the fact that the legend of Arthur spread across Christendom at precisely the time that stories of Templar secret practices were rife, could be entirely coincidental. Was there anything to link Geoffrey to the Templars, and what could it mean if there was?

History records that Geoffrey was a Welshman, born in 1100 in Gwent, his family having come over from Brittany a generation earlier at the time of the Norman Conquest. He was a secular canon in Oxford for many years before becoming archdeacon of Monmouth and, finally, Bishop of St Asaph (in North Wales) in 1152.[6]

At no time did Geoffrey claim to have invented the story of Arthur, preferring to build dramatic effect by informing his admirers that he had translated it from an 'ancient document' given him by his uncle. Most books on the subject record that this uncle of Geoffrey's was Walter Map, the Archdeacon of Oxford,[7] but the only Walter Map that we could find was not born until the year after Geoffrey first published his account of King Arthur, and became Archdeacon of Oxford more than forty years after Geoffrey had died.[8] Maybe there were two Walter Maps, but in any event, most scholars seem disinclined to believe in the existence of this unknown document. If it did exist why did Geoffrey never produce it?

This whole situation struck us as very odd.

Geoffrey's book was a major success, so why did he not simply take the credit for a great work of fiction based upon some obscure myths? Instead, he insisted that it was based on facts that had been drawn from an unidentified ancient document that he could not produce, and he failed to provide a satisfactory explanation of how he, a Welshman of Breton stock, living in Oxford, had gained access to this document.

We felt that something was wrong here and looked more closely at the story that Geoffrey had written.

---

[6] A.O.H. Jarman: 'Geoffrey of Monmouth and *The Matter of Britain*', *Wales Through the Ages*, vol. I
[7] *The Wordsworth Dictionary of Phrase and Fable*
[8] *Chambers Biographical Dictionary*

THE HIDDEN MEANING

A particularly interesting part of Geoffrey's story was the ending where Arthur was mortally wounded, but, instead of dying, he was carried away to the land of Avalon, a perfect land across the sea to the west. Here he waited for a time in the future when he would rise again and become the saviour of his people.

We had come across a belief in *a perfect land that lay over the great sea to the west* before, in two interlinked ways.

Josephus records that the Essenes (and therefore the Jerusalem Church) believed that good souls reside beyond the ocean to the west, in a region that is not oppressed with storms of rain, snow or intense heat, but has refreshing gentle breezes.

This was also the description given by a people called the Mandaeans who have lived in Southern Iraq since they left Jerusalem shortly after the crucifixion of Jesus, in order to escape the purges of Paul. These Jews left Jerusalem in the first century AD and, according to their traditional history, John the Baptist was the first leader of the Nasoreans and Jesus was a subsequent leader who betrayed special secrets that had been entrusted to him.[9] The Mandaeans still conduct baptism in the river, have special handshakes and practise rituals said to resemble those of modern Freemasonry.[10] For them this wonderful land across the sea has only the purest spirits, so perfect that mortal eyes cannot see them. This wonderful place is marked by a star called Merica, that sits in the sky above it.

We believe that this star and the mythical land below it were known to the Knights Templar from the scrolls that they discovered, and that they sailed in search of *la Merica* or, as we now know it, America, immediately after their Order had been outlawed.[11] (Our explanation about the origin of the name of America has been received with open arms by a wide range of scholars who were all very unhappy with the previous and erroneous explanation relating to Amerigo Vespucci.)

Interestingly, the tree is an important religious symbol of divine life in Mandaean belief, and the souls of their people are often represented as taking refuge in vines or trees.[12] This imagery of the tree of life and the powers

---

[9] E.S. Drower: *The Mandaeans of Iraq and Iran*
[10] A. Daraul: *Secret Societies*
[11] C. Knight & R. Lomas: *The Hiram Key*
[12] Drower, op.cit.

of dense vegetation is also common to Celtic legend and the stories of Arthur.

As we reflected on the mythical warrior king that Geoffrey of Monmouth had described, we could see a story that we had heard elsewhere.

Stripped back to its basics, the Arthurian legend says that although Arthur's mother was married she had become pregnant to another man, without any disgrace falling upon her because she had accepted copulation under the influence of a magician. Arthur grows to be the champion and true king of his people. He then gathers around him twelve knights as his key followers and leads his people into war against invading enemies, but he is eventually mortally wounded. However, he is not dead in the usual sense, but goes to a perfect land in the west until such time as he will come again to be the saviour of his people. After he departs the land falls into decay and ruin.

This legend could be seen as the Rex Deus story of the Nasorean priesthood, replanted into Celtic history. The story of the conception of Arthur even had a strong resonance with the Rex Deus account of how virgins like Mary became ritually pregnant to a high priest before being married off to another man. His rise to power with his twelve knights could represent the twelve tribes of Israel. The final terrible battle where almost everyone including Arthur dies is the telling of the fall of Jerusalem in AD 70. Like Arthur's kingdom, the land of Israel had spiralled into corruption and decay which was followed by a fight to the death when all was lost. However, whilst the Nasorean priesthood of the Jerusalem Temple had been almost wiped out, some had escaped and sailed westwards to Greece, where they spread out across Europe and waited for the day that would come when they could return and restore their kingdom to its former glory.

That moment of glory had just occurred with the return of the knights to Jerusalem. After a thousand years they had gone back in a great crusade against Gog and Magog.

We looked closely at what was happening to the Knights Templar in the years that Geoffrey must have been writing his book in Oxford – and we found our connection!

Payen de Montdidier, one of the original nine knights who had excavated under the Jerusalem Temple and then formed the Knights Templar, became Grand Master of England in 1128. He was charged with the duty of establishing a number of preceptories, one of the most important of which was at Oxford, built on lands given by Princess Matilda, the daughter of King Henry I and granddaughter of William the Conqueror.

Oxford was an important but small city in the twelfth century and the building of a Templar preceptory would have been a major event. As a high-profile secular canon in his early thirties, it would be surprising if Geoffrey did not meet Payen de Montdidier on many occasions, and Geoffrey's obviously inquisitive and imaginative mind must have been fuelled by the stories that this senior Templar had to relate.

Payen de Montdidier was probably not so indiscreet as to talk to anyone outside the Order about the existence of the scrolls and the treasures that he and his colleagues had discovered, but it seems likely that he was only too happy to discuss everything else, including some of the ancient events that had been learned from the scrolls. It does not seem an overly ambitious leap of logic to deduce that Geoffrey's new-found inspiration had come, not from his unborn uncle Walter but from the lips of Payen de Montdidier, a founding Templar who made references to certain 'ancient documents'.

To follow our lead further, we had to find out more about the visionary devices that suddenly became so popular in the first half of the twelfth century.

THE RISE OF THE HOLY GRAIL

Geoffrey of Monmouth made no reference in his story to the Holy Grail, so we were very interested to know who had introduced it and why.

We found that the earliest reference to the Grail was, without doubt, from the pen of William of Malmesbury, a monk and historian from Malmesbury Abbey. He composed his saga towards the end of his life in around 1140, some four years after Geoffrey of Monmouth had published his book *The Matter of Britain*. It was William who first claimed that Joseph of Arimathea had come to Glastonbury in AD 73, bringing both the Holy Grail and a Holy Thorn tree which he planted there.[13]

Malmesbury Abbey lies between Oxford and Bristol, and is no more than twenty-five miles from one of Payen de Montdidier's early preceptories known as Temple Guiting, near Cheltenham. It appears that William of Malmesbury was a leading historian of his day and was well known for works such as *Gesta Regum Anglorum*, a chronicle of the kings of England from the Saxon invasion up to 1126; *Historia Novella*, which covers the kings up to 1143; and *Gesta Pontificum Anglorum*, a history of bishops and chief monasteries of England.

We had been surprised when we discovered that William had been

---

[13] P. Berresford Ellis: *Celtic Inheritance*

publicly critical of Geoffrey's work and he does not make any reference to King Arthur, or any other part of the legend created by Geoffrey of Monmouth, in his first account of the Grail. The two stories were only brought together at a later date.

History does not record such details as a meeting between William and Payen de Montdidier, but as a librarian, preceptor and chronicler of the Church right through to his own time, William would have been extremely interested in the Templar's preceptory and church building programme. It seems very reasonable to assume that he would have sought out Payen de Montdidier, at times only twenty-five miles away, and listened to his stories.

Not surprisingly, very few people look closely at the politics of the men involved in the creation of the modern legend of King Arthur and the Holy Grail, but when we looked a very interesting picture emerged.

A verbal battle broke out around these new romantic tales, with accusations and counter-accusations concerning the validity of sources. Here we saw a situation where Geoffrey of Monmouth had written a harmless story about an unheard-of ancient British king, yet within three years he was attacked, in a most aggressive manner, by three other authors who all denied that he had authoritative information. William of Malmesbury, Caradoc of Llancarfan and Henry of Huntingdon all wrote new stories of Arthur, and each was counter-accused by Geoffrey of false work because only he had had access to the 'ancient document' that recorded the true history.

We were surprised to find that all three of these second-wave authors were under the direct patronage of a man called Robert of Gloucester,[14] who just happened to be the illegitimate son of Henry I and half-brother to Matilda, who had provided the land for the Templar preceptory at Oxford. Could it be that Payen de Montdidier had been very indiscreet in providing an 'outsider' with details of the Rex Deus/Templar story, and there was a careful plan to bring control of their stories back into the fold?

A pattern was appearing out of what should have been unconnected events. Too many people seemed to be involved in the creation of the stories of King Arthur and the Holy Grail, and we decided to look into the web of influences and the family powerbases.

The first thing that surprised us was how unbelievably inaccurate some of the most popular books covering this topic are, with completely false relationships identified. Our second surprise was just how involved the real

[14] G. Ashe: *The Quest for Arthur's Britain*

relationships were, and how significant Princess Matilda was to a series of events in Jerusalem, Germany, England and Scotland.

Henry I came to the throne of England in 1100, the same year as Baldwin I had become the first king of Jerusalem. Henry was the third son of the Norman invader of England, William the Conqueror, and he was married to Edith, the daughter of Malcolm III of Scotland (the man who slew Macbeth in revenge for the murder of his father as recorded in the Shakespearian play) and Queen Margaret (later St Margaret of Scotland). Edith's mother was a member of the Anglo-Saxon royal family in exile and her father was the Scottish king who founded the Canmore dynasty, so when she gave birth to her daughter Matilda, the child was a product of Norman English, Anglo-Saxon English and Scots royal bloodlines.

In the year that Hugues de Payen and his fellow knights started digging under Herod's Temple, the sixteen-year-old Matilda married Henry V, king of Germany and head of the Holy Roman Empire, a man twice her own age. Matilda's new husband had a reputation for being rather weak, but shortly after the marriage Henry created his own pope in place of the officially appointed Galasius II. This antipope, known as Gregory III, held office for three years up until 1121.

In 1125, Henry V of Germany died and two years later Matilda decided to return to her family in England. The following year, 1128, was particularly significant, with all the following events occurring:

1. Bernard of Clairvaux gained a papal rule for the Templars, making them a holy Order.
2. Matilda married Geoffrey IV of Anjou, the grandson of King Baldwin II of Jerusalem (the original sponsor of the Templars), and the son of Count Fulk V of Anjou, the man who had financially supported the Templars for the previous seven years and who was destined to be the next king of Jerusalem in 1131.
3. The Templar Grand Master, Hugues de Payen, visited England and Scotland.
4. Payen de Montdidier was made Templar Grand Master of England.
5. Matilda gave the land for the Oxford preceptory to Payen de Montdidier.

This was the year that everything came together for the group that had been laying careful plans for over thirty years, and there can be little doubt that the 26-year-old Matilda was fully involved at this stage.

In December 1135, Henry I died and Matilda was about to be proclaimed queen of England when a number of influential barons, who opposed her and her bellicose husband Geoffrey, elected her cousin Stephen of Blois as king, despite his earlier vow of loyalty to Matilda.

For three years, King Stephen established himself by continually supporting his barons and building strong relations with the Church, but in 1138, civil war broke out when Matilda and her half-brother, the powerful Robert, Earl of Gloucester, moved to seize the throne. The feud continued and, although Matilda was never queen, she eventually became known as 'Lady of the English'. It was precisely at this time that William of Malmesbury, Caradoc of Llancarfan and Henry of Huntingdon all wrote their new versions of the Arthurian legend and accused Geoffrey of Monmouth of false work. Because Matilda, her husband Geoffrey of Anjou and her half-brother Robert of Gloucester had been ousted by Stephen, this was their first opportunity to combat the unofficial version of the story that they wanted to control.

If it was Rex Deus that planned the capture of Jerusalem and set up the Knights Templar as excavators of the Temple treasure, then we can be certain that their bloodline was carried into the English Royal Family in the form of Henry II, the first king of the Plantagenet dynasty that would last for over three hundred years to the reign of Richard III. The son of Matilda and Geoffrey IV Count of Anjou, Henry took the name 'Plantagenet' from his father's nickname which was derived from the Latin *planta* (sprig) and *genista* (broom plant), in reference to a sprig that Geoffrey had habitually worn in his cap.

His mother's line gave Henry II an impeccable pedigree. Through two separate lines he was great-grandson of William the Conqueror and of St Margaret of Scotland (daughter of King Edgar Ironside and an Anglo-Saxon princess), as well as second cousin to the reigning king of Scotland, Malcolm IV. It was his father's line, however, that connected him with the new kings of Jerusalem and the founders of the Templars. When Henry was crowned king of England, his uncle was Baldwin III, the reigning king of Jerusalem.

It was Henry's son – Richard the Lionheart – who became the most famous Crusader of them all when he led the Third Crusade in response to Saladin's conquest of Jerusalem in 1187.

Now that we had reconstructed the circumstances of the twenty-five years from 1118 onwards, we could see that the stories of Arthur and of the Holy Grail had not occurred at random, but were a very controlled product of the powerful families of Europe, particularly those directly connected with the Templars and the ruins of Herod's Temple in Jerusalem.

These stories all build on the idea of an ancient lineage connecting Jesus with medieval Europe. Grail researcher Graham Phillips observed:

> In each romance the Grail or Grails are kept by the family of Perceval, the direct descendants of Joseph of Arimathea. The authors go to considerable lengths to explain this lineage and its significance – Joseph is appointed as Grail guardian by Christ himself. Here lies the Grail's importance – it is a visible, tangible symbol of an alternative apostolic succession.[15]

We contacted Graham Phillips and heard of his good-quality work first hand. He had no knowledge of a group such as Rex Deus, no particular interest in the Templars and no personal theory to project, and yet he had clearly detected an important aspect to the whole thrust of the Grail legends. He went on to say:

> In the Grail romances, however, we read that it is not Peter, but Joseph of Arimathea who is given the cup Christ used to perform the Last Supper – the very first Mass. To the Church authorities of the Middle Ages, such a notion would be pure heresy. Surely if the cup had been given to anyone it would have been given to St Peter, and would still be in the hands of the popes. We are left in little doubt that this is the primary theme of the romances, as in the Didcot and Vulgate versions of the story Christ instructs Joseph in the 'secret words of Jesus' . . . What the Grail romances are clearly implying is that there supposedly existed an alternative apostolic line of succession through Joseph of Arimathea and his family. Moreover, this line is claimed to have secret knowledge, unknown to the established Church.[16]

Perhaps, we thought, among the six hundred and nineteen vessels made of silver or of gold that the Copper Scroll tells us were hidden beneath the Temple, one had been particularly impressive and the Templars took it to be

---

[15] G. Phillips: *The Search for the Grail*
[16] Ibid.

of special significance. Whilst the others were distributed to the families that had facilitated the recovery and some were melted down for financial return, at least one had been identified as being particularly important. This artefact, combined with the story of the descendants of Joseph of Arimathea, had created a notion of a Holy Grail: a single artefact that was the embodiment of the Jewish Christian need for a link with God.

As we already knew, the Holy Grail cannot be tied down to a single artefact and the confusion probably stems from the complexity of the message that was established right from the very start. A work of unknown origin, called *The Lancelot Grail*, tells of a vision of Christ appearing and saying to a hermit:

> *This is the book of thy descent, Here begins the Book of the Holy Grail, Here begin the terrors, Here begin the marvels.*

This multiple role of the Grail has been evident to most people who have researched the subject:

> *Although by the fourteenth century the Grail had become solely the cup of the Last Supper, we can clearly see that the word did not apply exclusively to that particular relic when the first Grail Romances were composed.*[17]

Perhaps the best known of all the early Grail storytellers was Chrétien de Troyes, but modern observers realise that he did not have a definitive picture. One question which has occupied the passions of Grail scholars more than any other is just where Chrétien found the original material for his inspiration because, while later authors owed obvious debts to the French poet, many of the obvious variations suggest that there was a common original narrative shared by them all, which for some unknown reason became lost. The authors who followed Chrétien were often at pains to reassure the reader of the lofty credentials of their sources, usually by alluding to mysterious and secret documents which were variously claimed to be direct transcriptions from Christ himself.[18]

Chrétien de Troyes wrote *Perceval, ou Le Conte du Graal* in 1180,

---

[17] G. Phillips: *The Search for the Grail*
[18] M. Goodwin: *The Holy Grail*

dedicating it to Phillipe d'Alsace, Count of Flanders, from whom he said he had first heard the story. We could not help but remember that one of the few things that is known about Payen de Montdidier is that he was related to the Counts of Flanders. On further digging, we found that Phillipe d'Alsace's father was a cousin of this founding Templar who we believe had inspired Geoffrey of Monmouth.

If Payen de Montdidier had told stories to his cousin, the Count of Flanders, who had in turn embellished and repeated them to his son Phillipe, then Chrétien could well have been quite truthful when he said that he first heard the stories from Phillipe d'Alsace. Chrétien had previously been closely associated with the Court of Champagne, and Maria, Countess of Champagne, had been his patron to whom he dedicated many of his earlier romances.

The other great writer of a Grail romance was Wolfram von Eschenbach who created his epic *Parzival* in about 1210, after visiting Jerusalem and spending time with the Templars of his day. Whilst the story would appear to be a development of Chrétien de Troyes' work, most scholars argue that they are unconnected. In *Parzival*, Wolfram has the hero split between spontaneous nature and the rigid Christian belief in God, separate and superior to nature. He also describes the interwoven nature of good and evil . . . black and white.

What is certain is that the original stories of Arthur and the Holy Grail were completely at odds with the teachings of the Church, and it was only a matter of time before the unwanted material was dealt with.

The Church has always had methods of dealing with unwanted ideas with the power to grip the imaginations of its subjects: it attacks the ideas as heresy (in modern times, since burning at the stake is no longer an allowed response, this is often done by ridicule), or it adopts the alien idea, sanitises it and integrates it within its own teachings. One of the earliest examples was how the Catholic Church adopted the hermits of the Celtic Church as full-blown saints. People like St Columba, St Brendan, St Asaph, St Rhwydrws and St Patrick would probably be horrified if they knew that their memories had been absorbed into the alien faith of Rome.

The solution for the Church was the creation of *The Vulgate Cycle*, which is a Christianised form of the story put together by a group of Cistercian monks.[19] They took the suspect strands of the Grail legend and turned it into

---

[19] G. Phillips & M. Keatman: *King Arthur, The True Story*

a respectable Christian story, making all the early Celtic knights into good Roman Catholics, despite the fact that if they had really existed they would have been Celtic Christians. In this way, the story and the lineage of the Roman Church absorbed a potentially dangerous story.

In due course this *Vulgate Cycle* was drawn on by later writers, such as Thomas Malory in his Arthurian romances, *Le Morte d'Arthur*, written in about 1469. By now, the myth was well established and it settled into its present form with, for example, the writing of Tennyson, the paintings of the Pre-Raphaelites and the Arts and Crafts movement of William Morris in Victorian times.

However, the real problem for the Church was to come in the mid-fourteenth century when its power decreased to an all-time low and the stories of the Grail would become attached to the memory of the Templars, who were said to have been guardians of the Holy Grail.

As we shall see, the Church was about to fight for its survival.

CONCLUSION

The legends of King Arthur and of the Holy Grail both sprang from different authors who can be linked to the Templars and the kings of Jerusalem. Payen de Montdidier, one of the original nine knights who had excavated under the Jerusalem Temple, became Grand Master of England and provided Geoffrey of Monmouth with information that he should not have divulged. Within three years, his story had spread across Europe and a bitter argument erupted between Geoffrey of Monmouth and three other authors sponsored by Robert of Gloucester, with each camp claiming to have sole access to the genuine source of the legend.

The story of Arthur appears to be a description of the history of Rex Deus, and the Holy Grail represents a separate line of apostolic succession from Joseph of Arimathea that has precedence over the lineage claimed by the Vatican through St Peter.

Chapter 6

THE BIRTH OF 'THE SECOND MESSIAH'

THE LAST CRUSADES

We had found that the Order of the Knights Templar was founded through the joint efforts of a range of Rex Deus members who infiltrated key positions to ensure that their grand plan to recover artefacts from beneath the ruins of Herod's Temple could not be blocked. They succeeded in establishing the Templars and the Order rapidly grew to achieve fame and fortune. By the time that the first Grand Master – Hugues de Payen – died, the Templars were already building their preceptories and round churches across Europe and, as their reputation spread, they were soon said to be the guardians of the Holy Grail.

Having found the principles of their beliefs in the Tarot, and having detected strong connections between them and the authors of the Arthurian legends, we needed to study the period of their demise more closely.

The First Crusade in 1096 had led to the capture of the Holy Land by Christians and the establishment of the Latin Kingdom of Jerusalem. However, the Muslim armies did not just sit back, and when they retook the region of Edessa, a Second Crusade was launched in 1147, under Louis VII of France and Emperor Conrad II. This venture failed to repeat the glories of the First Crusade, its only success being the capture of Lisbon in Portugal, by English and Frisian Crusaders on their way to the Holy Land by ship. A Third Crusade was led by the well-known crusading kings, Richard I (the Lionheart) of England, Frederick I (Barbarossa) of Germany and Philip II (Augustus) of France – but they too failed to produce any meaningful result. Frederick was drowned *en route* in Cilicia and from that point onwards the mission started to disintegrate as Richard and Philip tried to go their own ways, rather than work together. Eventually, the ports of Acre and Jaffa were secured, but the Christian army managed to achieve little else.

During the Fourth Crusade of 1202–4, the Christian city of Zara in Dalmatia was attacked, and Constantinople was taken and looted of its treasures and relics before Baldwin, Count of Flanders, was installed as the new Latin emperor of Constantinople. The Fifth Crusade saw Frederick II crowned King of Jerusalem in 1229 only to be deposed by the Tartars fourteen years later.

Following the loss of Jerusalem to the Muslims in 1244, a major expedition to the Middle East was planned and financed by King Louis IX of France who took four years preparing an ambitious plan. At the end of August 1248, he sailed with his army to Cyprus, where they spent the winter making final arrangements for the seizure of the Holy Land. Following the same strategy as the Fifth Crusade, Louis landed in Egypt and the following day he captured Damietta without difficulty. His next attack was on Cairo, in the following spring, but this turned out to be a total disaster. The Crusaders failed to guard their flanks, and the Egyptians opened the sluice gates of the water reservoirs along the Nile, creating floods that trapped the entire crusading army and leaving Louis with little option but to surrender. After paying a huge ransom of £167,000[1] and surrendering Damietta, the king sailed to Palestine, where he spent four more years building fortifications before returning with his army to France in the spring of 1254.

Stephen of Otricourt, the commander of the Templar force that had accompanied Louis and had suffered tremendous losses attempting to salvage the ill-conceived venture, had to be pressurised to lend the ransom.[2] A feeling was beginning to grow among the nobles of Europe that Crusades had outlived their usefulness and Louis' disaster confirmed this. His crusading failure, however, left him with more time to devote to sorting out the problems of his own kingdom. At last he could tackle the long-standing

[1] E.M. Hallam: *Capetian France 987–1328*
[2] M. Barbour: *The New Knighthood*

problem of the relationship between France and the English who held large parts of the French kingdom.

To establish good relations with Henry III, of England, Louis invited him to visit Paris in 1254,[3] when the English king and his company were accommodated at the Paris Temple, by the Knights Templar, as it was the only place near to Paris that was large and grand enough.[4] The outcome of this convivial meeting was the Treaty of Paris, 1259, which restored the English king's right to hold Gascony, under the rule of the French king.

Having secured his borders, Louis announced his intention of leading another Crusade, despite strong opposition from his nobles. During this period of extraordinary military demands on France, the pope granted Louis the right to levy taxes on the French Church, a concession that his grandson would take as a right.

Embarkation of the new Christian battle force was delayed because of an illness that struck the king low. Although he improved enough to set sail, he soon suffered a major relapse and died in Tunis, before his army had carried out any useful military action. His entrails were buried in Monreale and his bones were carried back to St Denis, where they were buried in 1271. There, his relics became the focus of a growing cult which unofficially recognised the dead king as 'St Louis', although it was some years before his actual canonisation.

It seems to have been a common phenomenon in France at that time for cults to arise around holy relics. In an age that knew very little science, almost everyone was driven by superstition and the body parts of famous people, and relics connected with them, were often deemed holy and were believed to be capable of causing miraculous cures. The centres of heterodoxical belief that sprang up from time to time around the mystical relics of once powerful individuals often posed a problem for the Church because the populace could suddenly turn its allegiance towards icons and ideas that were outside Church control.

The Church has always responded to the new beliefs that it finds in new lands, or that spring up in its own territory, in a three-tiered process:

1. **Ridicule.** First the Church derides and criticises unwanted ideas. If this is unworkable, or it simply fails to get results, it moves to the next stage.

[3] E. M. Hallam: *Capetian France 987–1328*
[4] M. Barbour: *The New Knighthood*

2. **Absorption.** It simply takes existing beliefs and Christianises them. This has happened in cultures all over the world. Today, Roman Catholic priests in parts of Africa are not only allowed to marry, they are allowed to have several wives because their old tribal customs have become part of the 'new' Christian way to God. If this absorption process fails, the Church used to move to a final stage.

3. **Destruction.** The Church tortured, maimed and killed the people who would not surrender their minds to the Vatican.

In the early thirteenth century the Church had shown how it dealt with those who would not surrender to papal dogma during the so-called Albigensian Crusade, which devastated much of France in a process of theological cleansing. At first, it had attempted to reconvert the Albigenses heretics through peaceful means, but when this failed, Pope Innocent III ordered an armed Crusade which, within twenty years, wiped out hundreds of thousands of people and left only a few small surviving bands of Albigenses hiding out in isolated areas. These unfortunate people were still being hunted down by the Inquisition as late as the fourteenth century. Simon de Montfort's massacre of the inhabitants of Beziers during this unholy Crusade demonstrated the cruelty which accused heretics received from the Roman Church as a matter of course. It was on this occasion, when asked how the soldiers could tell a heretic from a Christian, that de Montfort gave his infamous reply: 'Slay them all. God knows his own.'[5]

This domestic Crusade caused huge bloodshed amongst the Albigenses and innocent Christians alike, yet for all of its ferocity the Church failed to bring the Albigenses under its control.

In times of great hardship, such as long-term famine or terrible plagues, people turn to the Church for help, and if it continues to fail them, it is human nature that they seek for new ideas to try and find a solution. Philologist and observer of the psychology of religion, John Allegro, comments that:

religion serves the necessary function of exorcising the devils of accumulated stress, the seemingly inevitable accompaniment of everyday living.[6]

[5] W.L. Wakefield: *Heresy, Crusade, and Inquisition in Southern France, 1100–1250*
[6] J. Allegro: *Lost Gods*

He also says that as the inadequacy of the traditional authorities becomes increasingly obvious, so there will be a natural tendency to seek out new sources of power. Relics capable of performing magical intervention on behalf of their devotees were just such new sources of power.[7] So, when the cult of the relics of Louis IX became too strong, a source of strength for the kings of France,[8] in an attempt to defuse its power, Pope Boniface VIII absorbed the new threat by accepting a petition from the faithful of St Denis and immediately made Louis IX a saint of the Roman Catholic Church.

Louis' son, Philip III, did not seem to have realised that the days of effective Crusades had gone for ever when he took part in an abortive Aragonese crusade which cost him his own life and his country the sum of £1,229,000, a truly enormous amount in those days.[9] Philip III's wild adventures finally tipped the French economy beyond the limits of what it could normally recoup from the usual sources of royal income. The annual income of the French crown then was £656,000, and the normal running expenses of the state were some £652,000.[10] The cost of Philip's abortive crusade left a crippling debt that would have considerable repercussions for both State and Church. It was the final demonstration to his son, Philip the Fair, that the days of the Crusade, and the Christian military orders it had created, were over.

THE TROUBLES OF PHILIP IV

Philip IV, known as 'the Fair', was only three years old when Louis IX died, so whilst he never really knew his sainted grandfather, he grew up in the shadow of his pious achievements. He remembered with bitterness the reluctance of the Templars to pay his grandfather's ransom after the failed Crusade, and would eventually quote that incident during his attack on the Order.[11] With young Philip's crown came the tradition of a saintly grandfather to live up to and a virtually bankrupt nation to lead. He became devoted to the cult of St Louis because, for him, it represented French monarchy at the height of its powers, combining the roles of king and priest in one individual.

[7] J. Allegro: *Lost Gods*
[8] R. Fawtier: *The Capetian Kings of France* (trans. by Butler & Adams)
[9] E.M. Hallam: *Capetian France 987–1328*
[10] Ibid.
[11] M. Barbour: *The New Knighthood*

Philip was educated by Giles de Colonna, later to become Archbishop of Burgues, who was a forceful personality with strong opinions about the duties and responsibilities of kingship. By the time Philip became king at the age of seventeen, he had developed a powerful sense of self-importance from a belief in his mentor's words that told him:

Jesus Christ has not given any temporal dominion to his church, and the king of France has his authority from God alone.

King Philip the Fair

Being the grandson of a saint was of great importance to Philip and the instruction he received from Giles de Colonna created a monarch who would bow to no man and would not be subservient to the will of the Church.

Philip IV inherited three things from his father: a debt-ridden kingdom, an arranged marriage and a love of hunting. When he became king in 1285, the 17-year-old Philip calculated that paying off the debts incurred by his father would take over three hundred years – even if he used all of his disposable income, even without interest payments – and he was not about to accept a lifetime of penury.

By the age of twenty-six, Philip was at war with Edward I of England, which meant that he had extraordinary expenses to meet, along with his inherited debts. He urgently needed other sources of income and had to use all the means of revenue-raising at his disposal. When these did not yield enough income, he needed to look for other sources of funds to stay solvent. His father had come up with the idea of levying extraordinary taxes on the Jews in 1284, and Philip continued this family tradition in 1292 and in 1303. Then, as there had been little political backlash, he hit on the idea of a one hundred per cent tax on Jewish possessions. In 1306, Philip the Fair ordered the seizure of all Jewish property and the deportation of the entire Jewish community. Also, following his father's inspired example, he instigated a harsh tax on the Lombard and Florentine bankers (in 1295 this tax yielded £65,000), but these ruthless and extraordinary measures still did not provide sufficient funds.

Philip's expenses were running at about £4,000 a day at this time, and so, to have sufficient currency to meet his debts, he was forced to devalue the coinage. His father and grandfather had used the financial services of the Knights Templar in Paris to carry out the monetary obligations of the state, but Philip decided to move his treasury from the moderating influence of John of Tours, the Templar Treasurer in Paris, and to install his own treasury staff at the Louvre.

He recalled all coinage, had it melted down, and then coins with the same face value were reminted, but with a much lower precious metal content. This action was one of the first recorded instances of currency devaluation. Inflation was not a common problem in the medieval period, but by 1303 the buying power of the French mark had almost halved, compared to its value in 1290. By systematically debasing the coinage, the crown raised £1,200,000 between 1298 and 1299, and £185,000 in 1301.[12]

Some historians believe that Philip was obsessed with emulating the crusading activities of his grandfather, Louis IX, and that the decline of the two major crusading orders, the Templars and the Hospitallers, gave him the opportunity to try to combine them under a new leader, a role he saw for

[12] E.M. Hallam: *Capetian France 987–1328*

himself. It has even been suggested that Philip may have considered giving up the throne of France to become a new king of Jerusalem at the head of a combined order.[13] We view this as unlikely because his actions did not show that this idea was very important to him: not once during his twenty-nine-year reign did he attempt to take part in a Crusade. However, Philip's actions relating to the Paris treasury of the Templar Order seem to confirm a financial motive.

To pull the French currency back on to a firm basis he was going to need a new source of precious metals suitable for coining. The Templar treasury was just such a source.

John de Tours was the second consecutive treasurer of that name of the Paris Temple. He was appointed in 1302 and fragments of the surviving records show he used an early, but quite sophisticated, type of double-entry accounting. The Templar treasurers had developed methods of administration to finance Crusades. These techniques involved secure storage of deeds and wills, the safe keeping of valuables and the accounting of payments for the management of estates. They provided the means for a government to maximise its taxation revenue. The kings of Europe had quickly realised that the Templars had the financial infrastructure they lacked and the Templars, confident of their temporal independence, were happy to co-operate in providing the world's first banking facilities.

Their wealth and financial network was to prove a fatal attraction to Philip, but he had a problem in that the Templars were responsible not to him but only to the pope.

THE BATTLE OF THE CHURCH'S FINANCES

The pope had granted Philip's grandfather the right to levy extraordinary taxation on the Church and the lay community during times of war, to meet the needs of the state and the defence of the kingdom. Philip revived the tradition and taxed the Church as another convenient and regular source of revenue, to try to reduce his debts. To stop Philip doing this to pay for his military expeditions, Pope Boniface VIII issued a bull, in 1302, forbidding the clergy to give any financial subsidy to lay powers without the permission of Rome. Philip's rapid response was blunt and forthright. He issued an order prohibiting the export of gold, silver or merchandise from France, thereby preventing funds crossing from his country to the Vatican, and

[13] N. Cohn: *Europe's Inner Demons*

cutting off a large source of papal revenue at a stroke.

This hit the Vatican in its purse, but did little to help the highly inflated French economy, and it could not avert the major currency crisis that occurred in 1303 when there were widespread calls for a return to the coinage values of St Louis' day.

As a result of Philip's attack on papal revenues, Boniface issued a decree stating that all princes were subject to his rulings, in matters temporal as well as spiritual. Philip had a very different view and he refused to be bound by secular edicts of the pope, sending a reply to Boniface which left little doubt as to his feelings on the matter:

> Philip, by grace of God, king of France, to Boniface, acting as
> supreme pontiff, little or no health. Let your extreme folly know,
> that in temporals we are not subject to any one.

To ensure that his rejection of the pope's authority was perfectly clear to everyone, Philip publicly burned the papal bull to the accompaniment of a mighty fanfare of trumpets.[14] It was politically impossible for Boniface to overlook this blatant act of rebellion against his authority and he summoned the French clergy to Rome to discuss how he could preserve the traditional freedoms of the Church against the stubbornness of this upstart young king. Philip, in turn, called a national assembly in Paris of both clergy and deputies of the third estate, where he so moved the assembly that they passed a resolution to stand by their monarch, in defence of his rights. Such was the force of Philip's personality that even the clergy present denied the temporal jurisdiction of the pontiff. Philip did not want either Boniface, or his minions, to misunderstand the extent of his determination to assert his temporal rights, so he ordered the seizure and confiscation of the lands and properties of all the churchmen who had obeyed the pope's edict to go to Rome.

Philip's escalation outraged Boniface who responded by publishing the bull *Unam Sanctam*. This asserted that not only was every human being subject to the rule of the pope but also they had to appear in Rome if so ordered. The battle of the egos was really getting into its stride now.

To assist him in ruling France, Philip had as his chief officer of state William de Nogaret, a man with no cause to love the Roman Church as his

[14] Anon: *Secret Societies of the Middle Ages*

parents had both been burnt at the stake as heretics, during the Albigensian Crusade. De Nogaret, Philip's main adviser from 1303 to 1313, described the king as:

> full of grace, charity, piety and mercy, always following truth and justice, never a detraction in mouth, fervent in the faith, religious in his life, building basilicas and engaging in works of piety.[15]

Boniface VIII, in his earlier incarnation as Cardinal Benedict Gaetani, had a colourful history of sexual adventures, and Nogaret was aware of this background when he accused him, among other things, of gross sexual misconduct.

The pope was bisexual, and certainly catholic in his sexual tastes, having kept a married woman and her daughter as his bedfellows, as well as attempting to seduce a number of handsome young men, apparently with a good measure of success. He was quoted as saying that the sex act was 'no more a sin than to rub your hands together'.[16] Boniface certainly practised adultery and sodomy, but it seems very unlikely that he went as far as Nogaret suggested – when the chancellor convened the States General, he accused the pope of practising simony, sorcery and specifically of keeping a small tame demon in his ring, who would appear at night and conduct unspeakable depravities with the pontiff in the papal bed.

Undeterred by this imaginative attack, Boniface sent commissaries to France to insist that the French clergy conformed to his instructions, and it seems that some vigorous argument occurred before the king, his wife and his son publicly pledged themselves to stand by all churchmen who supported the independence of France against papal usurpation. By now the proceedings were becoming farcical, as the king intercepted the papal bull that should have excommunicated him, but didn't, because its publication was prevented. At this point in the discussions, Boniface's self-control seemed to break down completely and, relying on the Donation of Constantine, which he claimed gave him the power to make or break kings, he offered the throne of France to Albert, emperor of Austria.

This quarrel was now extremely serious and neither side would back down, but Philip had a masterstroke to use against the 84-year-old pontiff.

---

[15] E.M. Hallam: *Capetian France 987–1328*
[16] N. Cawthorne: *Sex Lives of the Popes*

Working on the premise that any enemy of his enemy must be an ally, Philip had given asylum to members of the Colonna family, who were personal enemies of Boniface. Nogaret set off for Italy with Scairra Colonna and a force of three hundred horsemen, and on the morning of 7 September 1303 enough 'French patriots' were hired to hold an impromptu riot outside the gates of the pope's palace at Anagni.

An adequately bribed papal retainer opened the gates and allowed the 'patriots' inside, where they rushed to and fro shouting, *'Live the king of France, die Boniface.'* Under cover of this diversion, Colonna and his Italians forced their way into the presence of Boniface who, dressed in his pontifical vestments, was on his knees before the altar, expecting to die. The awe of the Italians was too strong to allow them to kill the pope, but they did keep him a prisoner for three days, during which they subjected him to considerable physical abuse. He was finally freed by the people of Anagni, who eventually drove out the French forces.

Despite the fact he had not managed to capture the pope, Philip still called a meeting of the States General, in Paris, to try Boniface *in absentia*. The charges included heresy, not believing in life after death, and murdering his predecessor Pope Celestine V, as well as restating the previous charges. Unfortunately, Boniface died of a seizure, probably brought on by the stress of his incarceration, within a few weeks of returning to Rome and so the charges were never tested in a court.[17]

A FRENCH POPE

When Pope Boniface died, the Church was in a spiritual and political mess of huge proportions. The Roman Catholic Church had always considered that it had the right to rule the temporal affairs of the world, since its hierarchy represented the kingly rule of Christ on earth. It argued that bishops and priests should exercise the sovereignty of Christ in the affairs of all nations, and that the pope was the supreme ruler of the world, pontifical supremacy being the fundamental article of Roman Catholic religion.

The surfeit of ecclesiastical rule, and a growing awareness of the corruption associated with it, started to lead to a greater questioning of the Church's role which, in turn, was increasingly making the Church nervous of 'heresies' – meaning any views that had not emanated from the Vatican. There was growing doctrinal dissension within the Church and a strangely

[17] *Sismondi Republicques Italiennes*

large number of natural disasters seemed to be plaguing the world, which started to build a view amongst the general population that God was no longer on the side of the Church.

At times like this, cults of relics and a nostalgia for golden times past become a great source of comfort to ordinary people who have lost confidence in those they would usually look to for support and guidance. The Church's Crusades had reduced many kingdoms to poverty, without reclaiming the Holy Land, and by the beginning of the fourteenth century, the first outbreaks of the Black Death were bubbling forth as if from Hell itself. If the responsibility for God's ill-will was not to be pointed at the Church, then other scapegoats would have to be found. The Jews, as we have mentioned, had already been persecuted, but soon other victims would be needed.

Boniface's replacement, Pope Benedict XI, initially met with Philip's approval when he quickly removed the sentence of excommunication that Boniface had issued against the French king. However, as Benedict settled into the papacy, he felt forced to act to restore the authority of the holy see, which Boniface had failed to uphold. Philip had no intention of re-opening the battle for temporal supremacy that he felt Boniface had already lost, and so he short-circuited an unnecessary and unwanted debate by arranging to have Benedict poisoned. This left the papacy vacant, but there was considerable difficulty in selecting a new pope.

The suggestions of the French cardinals counterbalanced those of the Italian cardinals and a stalemate ensued within the conclave for ten months. To break this impasse, Philip's agents suggested that one side should select three candidates from which the other side should choose a pope. Bertrand de Gotte, Archbishop of Bordeaux, a man who had many reasons to dislike both Philip and his brother, Charles of Valois, was selected as the compromise candidate of both sides. The Cardinal of Prato advised Philip that Bertrand was an ambitious and malleable character who could serve the king's purposes and, if the king spoke to him, would see where his own best interests lay.

Philip immediately set up a private meeting with Bertrand at the abbey of St Jean d'Angely in Gascony where he told the ambitious prelate that it was within his power to make him pope, and he would do so – if six preconditions could be agreed. The favours that Philip required in return for the throne of Peter were:

1. A perfect reconciliation between himself and the Church.
2. Admission to the communion for himself and his nominees.
3. The tithes of the clergy of France for five years to pay for the war in Flanders.
4. The persecution and destruction of the memory of Pope Boniface VIII.
5. James and Peter Colonna to be made cardinals.

The sixth condition Philip declined to name, saying:

The sixth favour is great and secret and I reserve the asking of it for a suitable time and place.[18]

What could this final 'great and secret' favour have been that could not be named by this usually brazen king? Philip had not shown himself to be shy in stating what he wanted, yet there was something in his mind that he dared not speak until the time was right. We believe that this last commitment that he would require of the pope would have been impossible to disclose because absolute secrecy was the key to his devious plan, which was still two years away from being sprung.

Philip's later actions reveal that this secret favour can only have been that the pope must support his right to arrest the Knights Templar on grounds of heresy and allow him to seize their funds for the French treasury. As the Templars answered only to the pope, Philip knew that he may well not get away with his intended piracy if he was not seen to be acting with papal blessing.

The king and the archbishop did not like or trust each other, but Bertrand was an ambitious man and he agreed to Philip's terms, which included the condition that Bertrand must stay within France. The seat of the papacy had to be relocated and Bertrand was crowned Pope Clement V at Lyons on 17 December 1305. In acceding to Philip's conditions, the new pontiff compromised the authority of the papacy for the next fifty years, the 'Avignon Period', and since likened by the Roman Church to the Babylonian Captivity of the Jews.

The new pope's very first act was to create twelve of Philip's followers cardinals, including the Colonna brothers, and he quickly set about meeting his pledges to Philip – apart from the destruction of the memory of Pope Boniface

---

[18] Anon: *Secret Societies of the Middle Ages*

which the Cardinal of Prato persuaded Philip to withdraw. In return, and to show his support for Philip in his financial difficulties, Clement actually gave the king papal approval for the banishment of the Jews from his kingdom and the seizure of their property for his failing treasury.

At this time there was a widespread acceptance amongst the nobility of Europe that they were not going to be able to dominate the Muslims of the

Pope Clement V

East by sheer force of arms, and many started to question the need for military orders if they could not hold the Holy Land. Back in 1274, in the aftermath of the Sixth Crusade, the second council of Lyons had discussed combining the Knights Hospitaller and the Knights Templar into a single military order. The leaders of both Orders had strongly rejected the idea of giving up their individual wealth and status and they used their considerable influence to ensure that such a merger did not happen. However, the suggestion never quite went away, as many people were jealous of the privileges that the Templars and Hospitallers enjoyed, including their exemption from most tithes and taxes.

By the spring of 1291, the port of Acre fell to the Muslims and the Grand Master died alongside a large number of his knights. The Christian world had lost its last foothold in the Holy Land and, as the Templars withdrew to

Cyprus, they had to consider their future most carefully because they knew that the calls for re-organisation and rethinking would soon become much more forceful.

The public position of the Templars was now very difficult. For many years, they had luxuriated in the growing legends of their almost supernatural fighting abilities; they had basked in the reflected importance of their legendary linking with the mythical guardians of the Grail, and had been happy to be seen as the latter-day knights of the Round Table. Indeed, between 1190 and 1212, they had promoted a version of the Grail legend, known as *Perlesvaus*, which was written by one of their own members and clearly describes the Templars as the guardians of the Grail and the successors to Arthur.[19] Now, however, the party seemed to be ending.

Thrown out of the Holy Land by the Muslims, they were now living as rather unwelcome guests in the kingdom of Henry of Cyprus, and they would soon have to rethink themselves entirely or face the possibility of growing calls for amalgamation with the Hospitallers. These hard times demanded a forceful and visionary Grand Master, a worthy successor to the leadership traditions of Hugues de Payen, to revitalise and rethink the Order in its time of need. Following the death of the Grand Master, William de Beaujeu, at Acre, Theobald Gaudin was elected to take his place, but he died after only a few months. Then, everyone expected the man who had come second, Hugh of Pairaud, to be elected to lead the Order, but, instead, a knight from a village near Besançon in Eastern France became the last Grand Master of the Knights Templar – a man who would become feared by the Church, after his death, as the Second Messiah.

THE LAST GRAND MASTER OF THE TEMPLARS

Jacques de Molay had been born into a family of minor nobles in 1244 and was initiated into the Order of the Temple, at the age of twenty-one, in the town of Beaune in the Côte-d'Or. His initiation ritual was conducted by Humbert of Pairaud, the English Master of the Temple, with the assistance of Aimery of La Roche, Master of the Temple in France.[20] The young Templar went on to serve in the East under the Grand Master, William of Beaujeu, and most likely arrived in Outremer (as the Eastern lands were called) after the Council of Lyons in 1275, when he would have been about

---

[19] R. Barber: *Knight and Chivalry*
[20] G. Lizerand: *La Dossier de l'Affaire des Templiers*

thirty years of age.[21] He visited England and some historians believe that he became Master of the Temple in England, before he became Grand Master of the entire Order.[22]

The historian, Malcolm Barbour, an authority on the Templars, fixes the possible dates of Jacques de Molay's election to the Grand Mastership between April 1292 and 8 December 1293. Barbour comments that Molay is reported to have gained the Mastership by subterfuge, in competition

Jacques de Molay

against Hugh de Pairaud. The only evidence of underhand dealings was given in testimony by Templar Hugh Le Fleur, during the trial, when the story could have been part of the anti-Templar propaganda, intended to discredit Molay's Grand Mastership.[22] However, this story of subterfuge is also

[21] M.L. Barbour: 'James of Molay The Last Grand Master of the Temple', *Studia Monastica*, 1972, vol. 14 pp 91–124
[22] T.W. Parker: *The Knights Templar in England*
[23] Barbour, op. cit.

reported at some length in a book published anonymously in English in the eighteenth century, entitled *Secret Societies of the Middle Ages*:

> *When the order had established its head-quarters in the isle of*
> *Cyprus, James de Molay, a native of Besancon, in the Franche*
> *Comte, was elected Master. The character of Molay appears to have*
> *been at all times noble and estimable; but if we are to credit the*
> *statement of a knight named Hugh de Travaux, he attained his*
> *dignity by an artifice not unlike that said to have been employed by*
> *Sixtus V. for arriving at the papacy. The chapter, according to De*
> *Travaux, could not agree, one part being for Molay, the other, and*
> *the stronger, for Hugh de Peyraud. Molay, seeing that he had little*
> *chance of success, assured some of the principal knights that he did*
> *not covet the office, and would himself vote for his competitor.*
> *Believing him, they joyfully made him great-prior. His tone now*
> *altered. 'The mantle is done, now put the hood on it. You have*
> *made me great-prior, and whether you will or not I will be great-*
> *master also.' The astounded knights instantly chose him.*[24]

The truth of this story is difficult to judge, but Molay proved to be neither a sound military strategist nor a particularly astute politician, so the story may be a case of sour grapes and the benefit of hindsight about his failure to cope with the problems of the Templars in the early fourteenth century.

Soon after his election, Molay visited the newly installed Pope Boniface VIII in Rome. The Templars had sustained tremendous losses at the fall of Acre and the Master was obviously concerned about gaining the pope's support to strengthen the Order's weakened position. The future of the Order was discussed and the pope brought up the question of the possibility of combining the Templars with the Hospitallers. When Philip the Fair later raised the same matter, Molay asserted that Boniface had totally rejected the idea.[25] After this visit, Boniface issued a papal bull granting the Templars the same rights in Cyprus as they had enjoyed in the Holy Land, which appears to confirm Molay's statement. After his visit to the pope, Molay travelled on to both England and France, desperately seeking support for a Crusade to retake the Holy Land which would re-establish his Order's legitimacy.

[24] Anon: *Secret Societies of the Middle Ages*
[25] G. Disgard: *Les Registres de Boniface VIII*

On his way to London for a meeting with Edward I of England, Molay stayed in the Paris Temple,[26] where he was obviously on quite good terms with the French king, as he acted as godfather for Robert, Philip's son. Molay kept in touch with European monarchs he met on this tour, as he is known to have received a letter written by Edward I from Stirling and dated 13 May 1304, recommending the Master of the Temple in England to Molay's favour, and indicating that at some unspecified future date Edward would, possibly, undertake a Crusade to free the Holy Land. Unfortunately, Edward was never able to tear himself away from attacking Wales and Scotland long enough to carry out this pious wish.[27]

Molay stayed on Cyprus until 1306, but even this island was increasingly difficult to secure; with Saracen pirates raiding Limassol almost at will, the Grand Master's only response was to ransom the captives they took. Molay made himself and the Order very unpopular when he supported an unsuccessful coup against Henry, king of Cyprus, by his younger brother Amaury.[28]

Molay had to believe in the recovery of the Holy Land because that was the only way he could see of securing any future for the Templars, but the politics of France were moving remorselessly against him and he was no match for the Capetian monarchy.

By the year 1306, the Hospitallers were renewing their attacks on the isle of Rhodes which finally resulted in the expulsion of the Turks, and when the Teutonic knights transferred their main focus of attention to Russia, it left the Knights Templar as the only inactive order. Molay and his men were still suffering attacks in their base in Cyprus, and the Grand Master is said to have been considering a complete retreat to France. However, because the king of France was in conflict with the papacy, such an action could have been considered to be threatening to Philip, as the Templars still represented a serious military force which was loyal to the pope.

We believe that Philip told his puppet pope of his secret final requirement just six months after Clement's coronation because, on 6 June 1306, the pope wrote to William de Villaret, the Master of the Hospital, and Jacques de Molay, requiring them to meet him in France to discuss the combining of the two orders. He instructed that they *travel as secretly as possible and with*

[26] *Acta Aragonensia,* 1, 26
[27] Reported by M. Barbour from *Calender of the Close Rolls 1302–7*
[28] C. Kohler: *Documents Chypriotes du Début de XIV's Siècle*

a very small train as you will find plenty of your knights on this side of the sea'.[29]

Villaret replied that he could not attend, pointing out that he was in the middle of a major attack on the island of Rhodes, and we cannot help but conclude that Pope Clement and King Philip knew full well that the Hospitaller would not be able to break off from his offensive campaign. Molay, on the other hand, was doing little more than fending off routine Muslim attacks in Limassol and he did not have a suitable excuse not to attend. The Templar Grand Master was probably glad to be away from the continual skirmishing and he set out for the French port of La Rochelle with a fleet of eighteen ships.

One ship should have been quite sufficient and there must have been some purpose behind such an exodus. Molay's idea of 'a small train' seems just as odd, consisting of sixty of his most distinguished knights, 150,000 gold florins and twelve packhorses laden down with unminted silver.[30] The inescapable conclusion is that Molay knew that Pope Clement danced to Philip's tune and, should the discussions go badly, he hoped to buy the king's favour and thereby avoid the threatened amalgamation of his order.

The fleet anchored in La Rochelle and Molay and his entourage made their way to the Paris Temple. When the convoy arrived in Paris, the king greeted the Grand Master, receiving him and his treasure with a great show of pomp and ceremony. Molay deposited the Order's portable store of treasure within the Temple precincts, watched by the debt-ridden and financially beleaguered king.

We have found that Philip was personally already deeply in debt to the Templars, as this passage from Curzon's *La Maison du Temple de Paris* shows:

> *Philip le Bel more than any other man profited from this handy means of getting hold of money [borrowing from the Paris Templar Treasury] for himself but showed himself less scrupulous when paying it back. 29 May 1297 sees him borrowing £2500 for which he agreed to be accountable to the Templars. Later on he obtained from the treasury of the Temple the sum of 200 thousand florins, this additional loan had been made unknown to the grand master*

[29] Anon: *Secret Societies of the Middle Ages*
[30] F.W. Bussell: *Religious Thought and Heresy in the Middle Ages*

Jacques de Molay and the treasurer was dismissed from the Order,
even the insistence of the king couldn't gain him a pardon again.[31]

Molay probably felt that he had Philip the Fair where he wanted him, caught out as a debtor, and if calling in the debt failed, he could always gain the king's co-operation with a generous application of more money in the form of a loan. As an opening gambit in his last great battle, Molay produced a Memorandum, to Pope Clement, which listed the reasons why the Templars were opposed to combining with the Order of the Hospital. The six reasons he cited were:

1. That what is new is not always best; that the Orders, as they were, had done good service in Palestine, and, in short, he used the old argument of anti-reformists, It Works Well.
2. That as the Orders were spiritual as well as temporal, and many a one had entered them for the weal of his soul, it might not be a matter of indifference to such to leave the one which he had selected and enter another.
3. There might be discord, as each Order would want its own wealth and influence, and seek to gain the mastery for its own rules and discipline.
4. The Templars were generous of their goods, while the Hospitallers were only anxious to accumulate – a difference which might produce dissension.
5. As the Templars received more gifts and support from the laity than the Hospitallers, they would be the losers, or at least be envied by their associates.
6. There would probably be some disputing between the superiors about the appointment to the dignities of the new order.[32]

Molay could not give the real reason why the Templars could not join with the Hospitallers – that they were the secretly restored priesthood of the Jerusalem Temple. After some further discussion, about a possible new Crusade in the East, which he thought would be pointless without a simultaneous effort by all the Christian powers, Molay took his leave of the pope and returned to Paris.

By spring of the following year, Molay was beginning to become

---

[31] H. de Curzon (trans. A.R. Thorne): *La Maison du Temple de Paris*
[32] Anon: *Secret Societies of the Middle Ages*

concerned about vague rumours of serious impropriety, on the part of the Templars, which were circulating in France and he decided to pay Clement a further visit. In the company of the Preceptors of Aquitaine, France and Outremer, the Grand Master went to Poitiers to meet the pope. Clement told the Templars that serious charges of various crimes had been made against the Order, which had been reported to him by his chamberlain, Cardinal Cantilupo. The pope appeared to be satisfied with the denials of the senior Templars, and the Master with his officers returned to Paris, believing that they had allayed the suspicions about their loyalty and good intent.

The people of France were suffering under Philip's increased taxes and debased coinage, and many were close to rebellion. On one occasion, two men incited a large crowd to riot in Paris, to the point that the life of King Philip was under threat. He was only saved from the mob when the Templars gave him refuge within the fortified keep of the Paris Temple where he had to remain for three days until the disturbance was fully quelled.[33]

The two ringleaders, Squin Flexian and his accomplice Noffo Dei, had been captured and they confessed, as they were thrown into prison, that they were former Templars. When the king heard that these criminals were once members of the Knights Templar, he instructed his chancellor to find out more about their backgrounds. Chancellor Nogaret reported that Squin Flexian was a native of Beziers, and had been a Templar and Prior of Mantfauçon, before being expelled from the Order. Noffo Dei, a Florentine, was an unpleasant fellow described by a contemporary writer as 'a man full of all iniquity'.

Whether the king suggested a deal, or whether the two prisoners initiated it, we cannot be sure, but suddenly Philip had two ex-Templars who were willing to accuse the Order of heresy and debauchery in order to gain their own freedom. The pair were immediately removed to Paris and brought before the king, to whom they outlined a series of crimes perpetrated by the Order of the Knights Templar:

1. Each Templar, on his admission, is sworn never to quit the Order; and to further its interests, by right or by wrong.
2. The heads of the Order are in secret alliance with the Saracens; and have more Mahommedan infidelity than Christian faith; in proof of which, they make every novice spit and trample on the cross of Christ, and

---

[33] J.J. Robinson: *Born in Blood*

blaspheme his faith in various ways.

3. The heads of the Order are heretical, cruel and sacrilegious men. Whenever any novice, on discovering the iniquity of the Order, attempts to quit it, they put him to death, and bury him privately by night. They teach the women who are pregnant by them how to procure abortion, and secretly murder the new-born babes.

4. The Templars are infected with all the errors of the Fraticelli; they despise the pope and the authority of the Church; they have contempt for the sacraments, especially those of penance and confession. They feign compliance with the rites of the Church merely to escape detection.

5. Their superiors are addicted to the most infamous excesses of debauchery; to which, if anyone expresses his repugnance, he is punished by perpetual captivity.

6. The temple-houses are the receptacles of every crime and abomination that can be committed.

7. The Order labours to put the Holy Land into the hands of the Saracens, and favours them more than the Christians.

8. The installation of the Master takes place in secret, and few of the younger brethren are present. Hence, there is a strong suspicion that he denies the Christian faith or promises, or does something contrary to right.

9. Many statutes of the Order are unlawful, profane and contrary to the Christian religion; the members are, therefore, forbidden, under pain of perpetual confinement, to reveal them to anyone.

10. No vice or crime committed for the honour or benefit of the Order is held to be a sin.

The scene was set. Philip the Fair had the pope's blessing to seize the treasury of the Knights Templar, which was the richest prize in Christendom.

As chance would have it, in investigating the arrest of the Templars, we were about to solve one of the great mysteries of the past: the origin of the Shroud of Turin.

CONCLUSION

The romantic view of brave deeds and knights with almost magical qualities started to decline through the thirteenth century and, by the beginning of the fourteenth, Christendom was in near chaos. Despite a huge expenditure in terms of both lives and money, the armies of Europe had been defeated by the Muslims, and the papacy had become captive to a bankrupt French king. In France, times were hard, money was short, disease was rife and the Church was failing to lead or inspire the masses.

With the Holy Land lost forever, the Knights Templar had become an order with no purpose. They still had their secret rituals and great wealth, but their last Grand Master was now fighting a battle for survival against a weak pope and an avaricious king.

Chapter 7

THE LINEN ENIGMA

FAITH IS BLIND

Despite living in an age built on rationalism, every man and women who has found a route to God through the suffering of Jesus Christ fully understands that their unquestioning belief in the reality of his physical resurrection is the very essence of their relationship with their maker. To have absolute proof that the son of God had died for them would make belief too easy, too much like the rest of life: hard edged and matter-of-fact.

All spirituality requires a strong element of mystery and ambiguity, for if it were not so, logic would sterilise the human soul and certainties would render hope impossible. Yet, in our daily lives, most of us have learned to trust the evidence of our eyes, and religious belief causes us to live with the difficult contradiction between the rules of the seen world and those of the unseen world.

Put simply: miracles deny science and science denies miracles.

Very occasionally, however, something happens that seems as though it might break the deadlock, when 'science' – religion's old arch-enemy – appears that it might support the rationality of Christian belief. One of the greatest examples of this rare occurrence was provided by a small piece of discoloured linen, currently housed in a side chapel of the fifteenth-century Cathedral of San Giovanni Battista in the Italian city of Turin.

What makes this particular sheet of cloth so special is the faint image that is inexplicably present on the surface of the fibres. It shows the full-length front and back view of a man who appears to have been brutally beaten and crucified. The wounds correspond exactly with the biblical accounts of the crucifixion of Jesus Christ, right down to the scourge marks, nail wounds, head wounds and a single stab wound in his side.

This is the famous Shroud of Turin. An artefact that many believed could conclusively prove the historical truth of the resurrection of Jesus Christ.

Our previous researches had led us to speculate that this famous Shroud could have originated from the demise of the Knights Templar, but we were about to find hard evidence that would fully explain the image.

Having established that the French king Philip IV had well-laid plans to steal the Templars' wealth, we also found that he had come across the confessions of two ex-Templars which provided him with the perfect excuse to move against them. Before we went on to investigate the details of the arrest of the Templars we felt we needed to consider a question that we had not originally set out to answer: is the image on the Shroud of Turin that of Jacques de Molay, the last Grand Master of the Knights Templar?

THE HISTORY OF THE SHROUD

Despite the protestations of various Christian researchers, there is absolutely no evidence that the Shroud existed before it was put on public display in a small church in the French town of Lirey in 1357. The cloth with its apparent image of the crucified Christ was lent to the local church by Jeanne de Vergy, the widow of Geoffrey de Charney, a minor nobleman who had died in the previous September. The people of Lirey were not slow to realise the importance of this great relic and the occasion was honoured by the striking of a special medal bearing the arms of both Geoffrey and Jeanne.[1]

No explanation was given then, or proffered since, as to how the Charney family came to possess such an apparently miraculous artefact.

The Shroud proved to be an immediate success, attracting large numbers of pilgrims, and the previously obscure church soon became famous across all of France. For many months things went well, but then the public displays came to an abrupt end when Henry of Poitiers, who was the Bishop of Troyes, stepped in and ordered that the Shroud must be destroyed. Somehow, Jeanne managed to avoid complying with this order and the Shroud was hidden away for over thirty years, until another member of the Charney family, again called Geoffrey, restarted the displays in 1389.

[1] A. Forgeais: *Collection des plombs histories trouves dans la Seine*

This Geoffrey de Charney died in 1398 and the Shroud passed to the keeping of his daughter Margaret and her husband Humbert, the Count de la Roche, who took the relic into safe keeping at the castle of Montfort. Fifty-five years later the aged Margaret sold the Shroud to Duke Louis of Savoy (the son of Pope Felix V) in return for two castles. The Savoy family later provided all of the kings of Italy and have controlled the Shroud ever since 1453. It is still the property of the Savoy family and they have kept it in its present home of the Chapel of the Holy Shroud, in the Cathedral of St John the Baptist in Turin, for over three hundred years.

In 1898, the young state of Italy decided to celebrate the fiftieth anniversary of the Statuto, the constitution of Sardinia on which the laws of the land were based. We found it interesting to note that the Savoy family had become kings of Sardinia in 1720 and were central to the establishment of the Italian constitution. In typical Italian fashion, every city across the country was competing to outdo all others by staging the most colourful and impressive events to mark the occasion. As the major city of the ancient Piedmont region, Turin was planning a range of events, including an exposition of the city's most holy relic: the burial shroud of Jesus Christ.

Baron Antonio Manno was appointed chairman of the Committee for Sacred Art which was to co-ordinate exhibitions and displays, including the premier sacred marvel, the linen cloth which the faithful believed had wrapped the body of Christ in his tomb. It occurred to those concerned that this could be a great occasion to photograph the Shroud and, despite much controversy, an amateur photographer by the name of Secondo Pia was allowed to take some photographs on 28 May 1898.

Pia was amazed when he saw the developed plates because they showed an image far clearer and more lifelike than it had ever looked before. Describing the experience he later wrote:

Shut up in my darkroom all intent on my work, I experienced a very strong emotion when, during the development, I saw for the first time the Holy Face appear on the plate, with such clarity that I was dumbfounded by it. It was a great glory and I was seized by trepidation at what I had seen.[2]

The two plates produced by Pia were negatives which reversed the tones

[2] Giuseppe Pia: 'The First Photograph of the Holy Shroud', *Sindon*, April 1960

141

to produce a 'natural' picture with raised areas of the body being lighter and recessed areas, such as the eye sockets, being darker. This new way of seeing the Shroud image captured the imagination of the entire world and the debate about its authenticity as the image of Jesus Christ has raged ever since.

WHAT IS THE SHROUD?

The physical characteristics of the Shroud are easy to define, but the cause of the image has never been understood.

The cloth type is a relatively sophisticated herringbone pattern with a 3:1 twill weave that came into use in Europe around the beginning of the fourteenth century. This late dating has caused some problems for those who believe it is a Christian relic. It is not absolutely impossible that such a cloth could have been woven in the first century, but it is extremely unlikely. Even some writers who claim that the Shroud is the image of Jesus admit that this type of weave is a weakness to their case.[3]

Another source of information about the origin and history of the Shroud has been the traces of plant pollen caught on the fibrils of the cloth. It occurred to Dr Max Frei-Sulzer, a Swiss forensic investigator, that it should be possible to track which areas of the world the Shroud had visited by examining the cloth for pollen deposits. Dr Frei-Sulzer's analysis showed that the Shroud did indeed have plenty of pollen present, but none came from olive trees, which totally precludes an origin in the Holy Land, because Israel has always had large numbers of these plants.[4] This result was later confirmed by Israeli scientists.

For many years, the most important test of all was denied to those involved in the debate because it involved the destruction of part of the Shroud. The technique known as radiocarbon dating had been rejected because the amount of sample required was too great. However, as methodologies improved, the potential damage to the Shroud reduced to the point where it was felt to be acceptable. In October 1986, an article appeared in *Nature*, arguably the world's most prestigious general science journal, announcing that the famous piece of linen was finally to be scientifically dated:

[3] H. Kersten & E.R. Gruber: *The Jesus Conspiracy*
[4] M. Frei-Sulzer: 'Nine years of palynological studies on the Shroud', *Shroud Spectrum International* 1 (3), 3–7 June 1982

The Roman Catholic Church is about to see one of its most famous relics submitted to the obvious test: pieces of the Shroud of Turin are to be taken to seven laboratories around the world for radiocarbon dating. Given the sensitivity of current techniques, less than 5 milligrams of cloth can yield a date with an accuracy of ± 60 years or so. By grouping all the laboratory results together, the statistics should be considerably better . . .[5]

The dating method relies on the fact that living materials absorb carbon dioxide, a gas which contains one atom of carbon and two atoms of oxygen. Most carbon atoms have a nucleus of thirteen protons and this common form is known as carbon 13, but there are other forms of this element. In the higher levels of the Earth's atmosphere, elements are struck by cosmic rays, which are highly energetic neutrons, thus creating a radioactive form of carbon with fourteen protons in its nucleus. This carbon 14 is an unstable radioactive isotope which, over time, loses its extra protons to become normal carbon. The rate at which this happens has been studied since 1950, when Willard Libby first proposed using this material as a means of dating substances which had once been alive.

All green plants create food by absorbing sunlight in a process called photosynthesis, and as part of this process they take in carbon dioxide and convert it into sugar and oxygen. In the carbon dioxide that they take in are very small amounts of this high-energy carbon 14, and as long as a plant remains alive the amount of carbon 14 remains constant. When the plant dies, the accumulated carbon 14 starts to decline at a precise rate that is known.

It is therefore possible to calculate the date at which a plant stopped living. The same calculation can also be applied to animals because they take in carbon 14 through eating the green plants. The actual dating is established when scientists measure the remaining carbon 14 in the subject and then compare that result against standard graphs, known as calibration curves. This gives the date at which the object ceased to be alive, but, due to possible small errors in the measuring process, the scientists allow a 'time window' of a number of years either side of the identified date.[6]

Once the decision was taken to apply this testing method to the Shroud,

[5] Philip Campbell: 'Shroud to be dated', *Nature* 323, p 482 (Oct. 1986)
[6] S. Bowman: *Interpreting the Past, Radiocarbon Dating*

the British Museum was asked to help oversee the certification of the samples and to produce the statistical analysis of the results. Three laboratories in Oxford, Zurich and Arizona were finally chosen and, following a meeting at the British Museum in January 1988, an experimental method was proposed to the Archbishop of Turin, who then approved it.

There was widespread distrust of the Vatican's motives by members of the Shroud investigation industry and this dissent even went as far as a letter to *Nature* on behalf of the US Committee for the Scientific Investigation of Claims of the Paranormal, raising the question:

> *How are independent observers to know whether any of the samples which the testing laboratories receive are in fact actual linen from the Shroud? Are we simply to take the Vatican's word for it?*[7]

The reply from Dr Tite of the British Museum was published in *Nature* the following month, and assured anyone who was concerned that the British Museum's role was to ensure that the chain of evidence remained unbroken. He was quite unequivocal about his role as an impartial observer of the experiment:

> *. . . I can reassure Dutton that should the proposed procedures be amended to introduce the possibility of tampering with the samples, the British Museum would decline to act as a certifying institution.*[8]

He went further in April of the following year by publishing in full the procedures which would be used in carrying out the experiment, and also announced that a full scientific paper would be published in *Nature* in due course, reporting the whole of the experiment.[9] This satisfied most of the scientific community, although a letter was published by *Nature* which speculated that if the Shroud had indeed wrapped Christ, then it may have been irradiated by neutrons during the holy process of resurrection, with the implied suggestion that this could invalidate the carbon 14 ratios.[10] Quite how the author knew that the assumed otherworldly process of resurrection

---

[7] D. Dutton: 'Still shrouded in mystery', *Nature* 327, p. 10 (1987)

[8] M.S. Tite: 'Turin shroud', *Nature* 327, p 456 (1987)

[9] M.S. Tite: 'Turin shroud', *Nature* 332, p 482 (1988)

[10] T.J. Phillips: 'Shroud irradiated with neutrons?' *Nature* 337, p 594 (1989)

involved the very worldly emission of a neutron flux was not explained in this letter.

Samples were removed from the Shroud on 21 April 1988 in the presence of a number of reputable witnesses. Then they were given, along with three control samples, to three different laboratories at Arizona, Oxford and Zurich. The control samples were not identified to the testing laboratories, so that the accuracy of their results could be gauged against linen of known ages. Two of the control samples were pieces of cloth and the third consisted of threads. The samples used were:

Sample One: a piece taken from the Shroud of Turin.

Sample Two: a piece of linen from a Christian tomb at Qasr Obrim, in Egypt, dated to the eleventh or twelfth century.

Sample Three: a piece of linen from a tomb in Thebes that had been dated to about AD 75.

Sample Four: thread removed from the cope of St Louis d'Anjou from the Basilica of St Maximin, which was known to date from the mid-thirteenth century.

The three laboratories agreed not to compare results until they had confirmed their findings to the British Museum. The Shroud had been exposed to a wide range of different contaminants over its lifetime and so the laboratories used different mechanical and chemical cleaning procedures to eliminate contamination bias as much as possible. When all the measurements were completed, the results of the fifty individual experiments spread over the three test sites were provided to the British Museum, which then undertook a statistical analysis of the evidence.

The details of the calculations and of the age calibration curve used were published in full in an article in *Nature*, so that any doubters could check the methodology and the accuracy of the calculations. The result was quite conclusive and showed that, with 95 per cent confidence, the flax plants which had been used to make the linen of the Shroud had ceased to be living entities between AD 1260 and 1390.

This dating is, of course, spot on for the period of the demise of the Knights Templar and the arrest of Jacques Molay.

The results for the samples taken from the cope of St Louis, when subjected to the same analysis, gave a result at 95 per cent confidence of AD 1263–1283, which was highly accurate as the saint had died in 1270 at the age of fifty-six. The other samples were equally accurate when the radiocarbon results were compared with dates determined by other methods.

The result gave no room for doubt about the age of the linen of the Shroud. As the measurement team said in their conclusions:

These results therefore provide conclusive evidence that the linen of the Shroud of Turin is medieval.[11]

This firm scientific evidence of medieval origins for the Shroud caused a major problem for most sindonologists (as the people who study the Shroud's origins call themselves). Most of the work on the origins had attempted to prove its authenticity as the shroud of Jesus, and a lot of ingenious reasoning had been used to try to extrapolate the known history backwards to show other artefacts which could have been the Shroud. All this work is now discredited by the radiocarbon results and no previous Shroud theory is left that fits the known facts.

The radiocarbon dating should have put an end to the debate, but those who desperately wanted the image on the Shroud to be that of their Saviour were not prepared to let mere science get in their way.

Various people have attacked the dating, such as Holger Kersten and Elmar Gruber who wrote a book which suggested that the three radiocarbon laboratories, the British Museum and the Roman Catholic Church had conspired to mislead the public deliberately by substituting samples of St Louis' cope for the samples taken from the Shroud.[12] They quote scurrilous pamphlets from radical Catholic sources making unwarranted and unsupported accusations of fraud against Dr Michael Tite of the British Museum. Their reasoning seems to be that the Church wanted to preserve the secret of the origin of the Shroud because it could only have been created by a living body. This they see as evidence that Jesus was alive after the crucifixion, a fact that the Roman Church would not want to be known. However, this line of reasoning caused even them great difficulties when they tried to explain why three academic laboratories, with worldwide reputations, would have risked those reputations by behaving in such an unprofessional manner.

---

[11] P.E. Damon et al.: 'Radiocarbon dating of the Shroud of Turin', *Nature* 337, pp 611–615 (1989)
[12] H. Kersten & E.R. Gruber: *The Jesus Conspiracy*

SOME ORIGIN THEORIES

Writers have come forward with theories which, though they are scientifically possible, are not in the least likely to have happened. Dr Nicholas Allen of the University of Durban-Westville in South Africa has published a detailed theoretical analysis of how the image on the Shroud could have been produced by a form of primitive photography using either silver nitrate or silver sulphate.[13] His detailed chemical analysis is certainly accurate, and his practical experiments with a camera obscura yielded excellent results. However, the process was complicated and very slow, requiring many hours of exposure using sunlight and, although the science was impeccable, Dr Allen made no attempt to put forward any motive or opportunity to explain how the image was made. He also failed to link up his chemistry with the known surface condition of the Shroud. He summed up his work as follows:

> It would seem therefore . . . that the hypothetical photographic technique . . . is the only plausible explanation for the image formation on the Shroud . . . and indicates that people in the late thirteenth and early fourteenth century were indeed privy to a photographic technology which was previously thought to be unknown.[14]

What a quantum leap of logic!

Taking advantage of the scientific plausibility of Dr Allen's photographic argument, a British couple, Lynn Picket and Clive Prince, published a book which 'proved' by experiment that it would have been possible for Leonardo da Vinci to have produced the Shroud by a photographic technique, using only materials available in the fifteenth century.[15] This presents extra difficulties as an origin theory because the Shroud was first displayed almost a hundred years before Leonardo was born. Just because a technique can be carried out today, using more ancient materials, does not imply that an historic personage was either inclined or able to carry it out. No plausible

---

[13] N.P.L. Allen: 'Is the Shroud of Turin the first recorded photograph?' *South African Journal of Art History*, 11 November, pp 23–32 (1993)

[14] N.P.L. Allen: 'Verification of the Nature and Causes of the Photo-negative Images on the Shroud of Lirey-Chambery-Turin', http://unisa.ac.za/dept/press/dearte/51/dearturn.html

[15] L. Picket & C. Prince: *Turin Shroud*

motive was put forward to explain why Leonardo da Vinci would want to create such an image and then go to the trouble of exchanging the real Shroud for his copy. The exchange itself would be a fairly difficult exercise because the Shroud was sold to the Savoy family when Leonardo was only one year old, and its history is fully documented.

Quite apart from the improbability of Leonardo switching the real Shroud for his self-portrait snap-shot, it is quite simple to demonstrate that the Shroud is not a photograph.

Picket and Prince focused their attention on the head of the Shroud image because it had long hair and a beard . . . just like Leonardo. If they had spent more time studying the body position, they would have found that there was no foreshortening such as would occur with a photograph, as we will show shortly.

The other main theory of the Shroud's origin is that it is a painting created by a highly skilled medieval artist. This is something of a non-starter theory for three fundamental reasons:

1. No medieval artists painted in such a lifelike style, devoid of influences of the conventions of art. There are distortions to the Shroud image, but they are not due to artistic interpretation.
2. Medieval painters would not have painted a negative image, which was not thought about prior to the invention of photography.
3. All known medieval paintings show Jesus Christ being crucified with nails driven through the palms of the hands, not through the wrists as on the Shroud.

Artist and physicist Isabel Piczek has produced a detailed analysis of the image in which she states that:

> the Shroud cannot possibly be a painting because while the Shroud shows a continuous uninterrupted visible image it does not show a continuous undamaged visible medium film.[16]

Piczek argues that particles of pigment found on the cloth are the result of copying over the years, pointing out that fifty-two copy paintings are known to have been made. She demonstrated the reasonableness of this sug-

---

[16] I. Piczek: 'Is the Shroud of Turin a Painting?', http://www.shroud.com/piczek.htm

gestion by experiment and went on to analyse the perspective of the Shroud image, concluding:

> *the exact position of the body on it [the Shroud] can only be seen on a life model from above at a distance of circa 15 feet.*

She observes that the image is of a body which is bent in the middle, describing in detail how she deduced this from life studies. She expresses no view as to how the Shroud came to be created, but states very clearly that it is not possible for it to have been a painting. Her article is well argued, and illustrated with detailed photographs and life drawings which support her case, but whilst saying clearly what it is not, she sheds no light on how it came to be created and why.

The reality is that there is no published theory which includes the physical/chemical creation of the image on the Shroud that fits the known evidence. The radiocarbon dating has proved that the Shroud is not much older than its recorded history starting in 1357. Any theory of its creation must take this into account if it is to be credible.

THE STRANGENESS OF THE IMAGE

The image of the man of the Shroud presents a number of odd features which any theory of its creation must explain.

The figure is naked, bearded with shoulder-length hair and he appears to be either dead or in a state of deep unmoving unconsciousness at the time of the image-making. The injuries that the victim received are wholly consistent with the type of physical damage that would be inflicted by a highly professional torturer.

For centuries the image has been widely accepted to be that of Jesus Christ and the features of the face have been copied by artists everywhere when representing the Christian messiah in their work.

We decided that the only way to really understand the Shroud was to try and reproduce it.

First we placed a white linen sheet on the floor. Then, we completely covered a naked subject with black water-based paint and laid him on to it, bringing the top section over to cover him head to foot. This gave us a very crude image that immediately revealed interesting inconsistencies with the original Shroud:

1. There was virtually no image of the legs between the buttocks and calves on our reconstructed back view.
2. The small of the back produced no image.
3. The right hand of the subject appeared to be some six inches further up the body than the image on the Shroud.
4. There was no image of the soles of the feet, except for the point of the heels.
5. Unlike on the Shroud, both shoulders appeared to be at the same height.

The result was particularly interesting as regards the dorsal image, which demonstrated that the body only touches the cloth at five main points: the head, shoulders, buttocks, calves and heels. In between these points no image is made, despite the fact that the subject was dripping with paint. The fluid ran down the body to the points of contact where it puddled.

Although a convection transfer method of image formation could explain the front image, no convection process can work in the formation of the back image which has to be formed by contact. Despite every effort by the subject to lie completely flat and still, a complete rear image was not produced.

This result caused us some initial problems in understanding and explaining what had happened, but as we thought about it, there seemed to be only one possible conclusion. The man who was wrapped in the Shroud was not lying on a hard, flat surface at all . . . he had to have been placed on a soft mattress that supported all of his body.

Dead bodies are not laid out on soft absorbent beds, so it seems extremely likely that the image is not that of a corpse but of a living subject who had been horribly tortured.

Because the victim was wrapped in a death shroud, most investigators have taken for granted that the subject was dead and therefore he had been laid out on a slab. Many claim to have conducted experiments, yet people such as Kersten and Gruber show diagrams of the Shroud being placed around a figure on a completely flat surface save for a small supporting item under the head. Yet it is quite impossible to reproduce anything like the limb relationships seen in the Shroud image when the subject is placed in this position.

As we looked at our crude results and studied the Shroud image with a more informed eye, we spotted a very important point that we had previously totally missed. Whilst the frontal image of the figure on the Shroud is delicate and precise with a very life-like effect, the back view is relatively crude and has no gradated tones. It almost seemed that two different processes had created the two halves of the Shroud!

We soon realised that the 'soft bed' theory would also explain the apparently impossible length of the arms, which rest too far down the body for a figure lying down flat. NASA investigators had noted that the angle of projection of this distortion of the lower left arm appears to be sixteen degrees. A simple trigonometrical calculation reveals that to cause this angle with an arm of twenty inches in length the difference in height between the lower right pelvis and left shoulder would need to be about five and a half inches. This is exactly what would happen if the victim had been placed in a bed with pillows behind the head and shoulders, raising the top of the torso relative to the hips and pushing the hands down the body.

On a flat surface the hands cannot extend as far down the body as seen on the shroud

But on a soft surface the hands move into the position shown on the shroud

On a soft surface the hair is supported as shown on the shroud

To test this 'soft bed' hypothesis, we constructed a second experiment with the subject on a mattress with the head raised six inches higher than the pelvis and a cushion beneath the feet. The results were remarkable.

Both of our experiments had produced images that were rather crude and unclear, but there was sufficient evidence to draw a number of important conclusions:

1. A full-length dorsal image is achievable on a soft surface.
2. Raising the height of the shoulders by approximately six inches in relation to the hips does cause the hands to fall into the correct position (as long as the upper arm is also supported by the surrounding cushions).
3. The sole of the foot does leave an imprint if the feet are against a cushion.
4. The angle of the head in relation to the torso is immaterial; because the Shroud follows the contours of the body, the face will always appear to be square on to the viewer. The more that the head is thrown back, the more it simply has the effect of making the neck on the image appear progressively longer.
5. Whilst the hair would be expected to fall away from the face on a flat surface, it seems reasonable to expect it to be able to remain framing the face if the head is resting on a soft pillow.

These experiments have demonstrated that by placing the body on a soft mattress or a series of cushions, all the unusual features of the original Shroud image can be fully explained. The only logical conclusion appears to be that the man whose image is on the Shroud was not dead and was not intended to die. He had been placed on a soft bed with his head and shoulders raised in a position to assist his breathing as soon as he had been taken down from the cross. It seems that he was intended to recover from his ordeal. This raises the question as to why someone would flog and crucify a man, then put him on a bed with a death shroud running vertically under and over his body.

An obvious answer would be that the victim had been terribly tortured in this parody of the crucifixion of Jesus to extract a confession for some crime against Church dogma, but he had to survive in order to stand trial for heresy. No early-fourteenth-century Frenchman would fit this description better than Jacques de Molay.

REPRODUCING THE FACE

The face on the Shroud is very detailed and we attempted to see if a reasonable-quality face image could be produced from a cloth contact print. The subject's face was painted in a base grey paint with extra layers of dark grey painted on to the high points of the face where sweat would accumulate. The paint was allowed to dry and a piece of linen was soaked, wrung out and then placed over the face and lightly pressed in place. The paint transferred to the wet cloth to form an image.

The image looked very crude indeed, but when we scanned it into a com-

Our attempt at producing a face image from contact print shows considerable distortion

puter and turned it into a negative it did have a remarkably photographic effect. However, it was not of the quality of the face on the Shroud. The thickness of the cloth had caused a certain amount of creasing, and gave areas without image, and we noted that the face was distorted in its width.

This diagram shows why we got a width distortion in our face experiment. When an image is made by a contact print the cloth goes around the side of the face, and when removed and viewed in a flat plane there is a marked increase in apparent width. The Shroud exhibits no such distortion and so we could be certain that the image could not have been created by either a contact or a radiation process, as both would produce this extra width effect.

The only explanation for this seemed to be that the image had been formed by a close vertical convection process. Such a transfer would be the only way to produce the image on the Shroud, but we were at a total loss as to what physical process this could have been. There simply was no science that we knew of that could have created the image in this way.

Whilst we had to admit defeat about the chemistry, we did draw one further conclusion from our simple experiments, and it is this conclusion that demonstrates that the Shroud image could not possibly be the result of a photographic process.

An image formed by a photographic process would produce a very fore-

Apparent width of the face - Contact Print

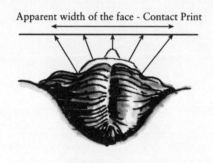

Apparent width of the face - Convection Image

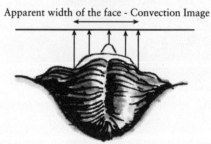

As the cloth wraps around the side of the face it picks up part of the image not visible from a front view and when opened out the face seems strangely wide.

shortened result, with the figure looking squat and having stunted legs and torso. The figure on the Shroud is however slightly distorted in the opposite direction, appearing to have strangely long arms. This is due to the fact that whilst the figure is slightly bent, allowing the hands to move down the thighs, he appears to be lying flat out because his full height is recorded. This could only result from a close contact convection transfer, where the Shroud followed the contours of the subject, and when the Shroud is viewed on a flat plane it would show the subject's full length but record the limb relationships of a bent person. This is a picture-making process that has never been seen before amongst photographers or artists and it produces proportions that are unique.

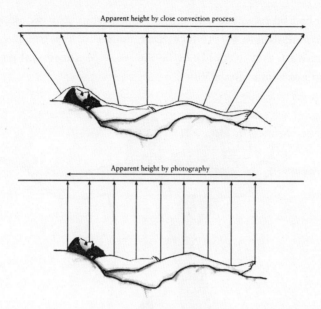

Apparent height by close convection process

Apparent height by photography

As the shroud is lifted from the body and straightened out, the length of the image increases.

Once we understood this simple principle, we could not imagine how something so obvious could have been missed by us and every other Shroud investigator before us.

THE EVIDENCE IN BLOOD

The marks that appear on the Shroud image are consistent with the victim having been scourged, but no previous Shroud researchers, that we are aware of, have looked at these marks with any degree of seriousness. Careful inspection of the marks allowed us to determine that there were discrete clusterings of marks, each of which indicated a different position of the attacker in relation to the victim.

In order to understand how these groups of apparent skin lacerations occurred, we tried to reproduce them using a whip that was designed not to cause pain to our nervous model. We fitted small lead weights to the tips of pieces of string and repeatedly dipped them in black paint to see how we could emulate the distribution pattern found on the Shroud.

We soon found that the marks on the back of the subject had been delivered by a man standing in front of the victim, and not behind as has been generally assumed. There is no doubt at all that the Shroud is the image of a man who had been beaten with a multi-tailed whip, as it would have been completely impossible to produce these marks in any fraudulent way – further evidence that it could not be the work of a medieval painter or a photograph of Leonardo da Vinci!

How the whip marks on the back were delivered from the front.

The victim was completely naked and had had his arms held in an outstretched position approximately at ninety degrees to the torso.

Having understood how the scourging had happened, we turned our attention to the bloodflows of the arms, in the hope that they would tell us something more about the nature of the crucifixion of this person. We were not to be disappointed.

In 1932, a Parisian surgeon by the name of Pierre Barbet used the limbs of corpses to work out what had happened when the victim seen on the Shroud was crucified, and he found clear evidence that there were two distinct flows of blood from the wrists, ten degrees apart.[17]

[17] J. Walsh: *The Shroud*

We could see that the general direction of the flow was along the arm from the wrist to the elbow. We conducted a simple experiment to see what position the arms might have been in, and we were very surprised by what we found. Using transparent paper, we carefully copied the victim's arms, tracing the marks of the bloodflow, and then we turned the paper over so that the blooded areas were facing away as they would have had to do. We then hinged the paper until the direction of the bloodflow was downwards. This process gave us two possible results, neither of which resembled the Roman technique of crucifixion in which the arms were stretched out side-

How the whip marks on the buttocks and legs were delivered from the front.

ways to cause great breathing difficulties to the victim.

In both cases, the maximum distance between the two nails is around thirty-six inches, but only one of them could have been a sustainable crucifixion position. We concluded that the victim on the Shroud was nailed up with his right arm over his head and his left arm out sideways. This suggests that the perpetrators of this physical assault either did not know the correct technique or simply did not care.

This position would also explain why so many observers have concluded that the victim's right arm appears to be dislocated at the shoulder. With an arm nailed vertically, the shoulder joint would have come under great stress and dislocation would have been very likely.

All of our review of what can be known from studying the Shroud and its recorded history indicated to us that our Molay hypothesis could be correct, as the known evidence and our new information were fitting together well. We had lots of answers, but one great problem remained: the chemical processes still eluded us.

At first we had thought that the lactic-acid-rich blood had reacted with calcium carbonate whitening agents to burn the image on to the surface of the fibres of the Shroud, but our experiments had shown that the Shroud was not a contact print.

These experiments had been messy, but had stopped short of driving nails through flesh, and our reconstructions were therefore rather limited imitations of the original process. We had had little difficulty in reproducing something similar to the back view, but the front view of the Shroud had subtleties that were impossible to reproduce.

For many months we were resigned to admitting defeat, but then the answer came out of the ether.

Chris was driving home one evening and he switched on the radio. There was an interview in progress, and the words he heard made his hair stand on end:

It's quite possible the Saracens crucified a Crusader prisoner exactly according to the gospel accounts as a cruel mockery of his faith.

The voice on the radio was saying what we had suspected for some time, but the speaker had come to the similar conclusion from quite different evidence.

The person being interviewed was Dr Alan Mills, an expert on Martian soil who works in the Department of Physics and Astronomy at the University of Leicester, and has a long-standing interest in the process which had created the image on the Shroud of Turin. In 1995, he published the results of his work which put forward a new explanation of the chemistry of the image creation process. In the BBC broadcast, he briefly explained how he had undertaken a very careful review of the literature about the Shroud and had then come up with an explanation of the features seen on it.

We contacted Dr Mills, who explained his work in more detail. He then sent us a copy of his recent paper and very kindly gave us permission to quote from it.[18]

The characteristics of the image which he felt needed to be explained were:

1. The lack of the gross distortions one would expect from a contact print.
2. That image density is an inverse function of the distance of the cloth from the skin, with the process saturating at a distance of 4 centimetres.
3. That there are no brush marks detectable on the image.
4. That the process affects only the surface fibres and does not penetrate to the inverse side of the cloth.
5. That the variations in image density are produced by changes in the density of yellowed fibrils per unit area, not by changes in the degree of yellowing.
6. That the bloodclots had protected the linen from the yellowing reactions.

In our own experiments, we had proved that the formation of the front image could not be made by a contact process and we believed that the fibril yellowing was caused by a lactic acid reaction of some sort.

Dr Mills had noticed two other processes which produce similar sorts of images. Very old botanical specimens that have been kept dry produce faint yellow-brown markings on cellulose that show a remarkable amount of detail in a blue-filtered negative image. He found excellent examples of this effect on the paper mounts of samples stored in the herbarium of Leicester University since 1888. These markings, known as Volckringer patterns, were thought to be caused by a lactic acid reaction. Dr Mills commented:

The 'plant pictures' offer an accessible source of image bearing fibres for preliminary investigations. There are no religious attachments, and no one has felt obliged to explain them as man-made artefacts.[19]

---

[18] Dr A.A. Mills: 'Image formation on the Shroud of Turin', *Interdisciplinary Science Reviews*, 1995, vol. 20 No. 4, pp 319–26
[19] Ibid., p 321

The other related phenomenon he had noticed was one that had caused problems for early manufacturers of photographic plates, when they found that images could be produced in total darkness by the proximity of various materials such as newsprint, resinous woods, aluminium and vegetable oils. Known as the 'Russel Effect', it was generally accepted that the process was connected with the release of hydrogen peroxide. By the 1890s, film manufacturers had discovered how to make emulsions which did not suffer from the effect and interest in this strange image-making process, that needed no light, died away.

Dr Mills found clear evidence that a naked man in still air will produce laminar (non-turbulent) convection air flows for a distance of 80 centimetres, and from this he worked out that any image-forming particle would take about a second to travel the 4 centimetres from the surface of the body to the cloth. He described the key to the process as follows:

Only if the active principle is highly unstable would its smooth vertical transport give rise to a modulated image.

In layman's terms this sentence means something like:

The particles that caused the discolouring of the fibrils of the linen must have been in a chemically unstable condition whilst rising smoothly from the body to the linen if they were to create a recognisable image made up of graduated tones.

Dr Mills is here describing a little-understood process which is known to produce an image with shades of light and dark exactly like a photograph, but using molecular particles of some element instead of light photons. A possible unstable particle which could result in yellowing of linen fibrils is a type of free radical known as a reactive oxygen intermediate. A full description of this image process is given in Appendix 3.

The process, known as auto-oxidation, is a very slow reaction taking a great number of years to reach saturation, after which the image will begin to decline very slowly. Dr Mills' theory predicts that the image on the Shroud will slowly become fainter, which is exactly what has been reported to be the case, and will eventually disappear.

His conclusions were fascinating:

Although images of this nature associated with botanical specimens pressed on paper are not uncommon, that on the Shroud of Turin appears to be unique because of the need for a highly unlikely combination of circumstances that are not individually demanding, namely:

- *a long shroud woven from fine linen*
- *its hurried draping over the recently deceased (unwashed?) body of a tortured man in a sealed, thermally stable place*
- *removal after some 30 hours*
- *storage in a dry, dark place for decades or centuries.*[20]

As we will show in Chapter 8, all of these circumstances fit our hypothesis, but we believe that the subject, Jacques de Molay, was in a coma, not dead. This would assist the process as the body heat would continue for the whole of the period of enshroudment.

In the knowledge that all of the known evidence fits precisely with our theory (see Appendix 3) we now needed to continue our reconstruction of events in October 1307, to see if the motive, opportunity and circumstances would confirm the Molay hypothesis.

CONCLUSION

Carbon dating has conclusively shown that the Shroud of Turin dates from between 1260 and 1380, precisely as we would expect if it were the image of Jacques de Molay. There is no other known theory that fits the scientifically established facts. Through experimentation, we know that the figure on the Shroud was in a soft bed of some kind, which strongly suggests that the victim was not dead and was expected to recover.

The image on the Shroud has been explained in detail by Dr Alan Mills who, quite independently, identified extremely unusual circumstances that we had already described in detail. He even suggested that the victim may have been a Crusader.

[20] Dr A.A. Mills: 'Image formation on the Shroud of Turin', *Interdisciplinary Science Reviews*, 1995, vol. 20 No. 4, p 325

Chapter Eight

THE BLOOD AND THE
FLAMES

THE HOLY INQUISITION

In the autumn of 1307, the near-bankrupt Philip IV of France was about to activate the sixth and final favour that he had extracted from the eventual Pope Clement V, in return for the prelate's elevation to the throne of St Peter. Soon the wealth of the Order of the Knights Templar would solve the king's financial worries.

Jacques de Molay must have believed that he had almost won his battle with Philip and Pope Clement to stave off an amalgamation of the Templars with the Hospitallers. He had made sure that the pauper king had seen the wealth that he had brought with him and deposited in the Paris Temple, giving himself the sense of power that a bank manager feels when confronted by a man he knows is about to ask to extend his overdraft. From the size of the delegation that had accompanied the Grand Master, we believe that it is highly likely that Molay was intending to stay in France to rebuild Templar influence and take control of the unwanted merger debate. Unfortunately for him, however, he had totally failed to understand the utter ruthlessness of his desperate adversary, and he paid a terrible price for his miscalculation.

There is no other image of a human figure that is pictorially or chemically anything like the Shroud, and we knew from Dr Mills' work that the circumstances of its creation must have been very unusual indeed. The avarice of Philip the Fair created those unique circumstances, the members of the Paris Inquisition provided the mechanism, and the unfortunate Jacques de Molay became the model for an image that would intrigue the world for centuries.

The Inquisition was a 'court of justice' founded by the Roman Catholic Church for the express purpose of eradicating all interpretations of scripture that deviated from the official Vatican line; this was normally achieved by maiming and killing anyone suspected of holding such views. In AD 382, the Church had decreed that anyone convicted of heresy was to be executed, but, as Christianity became more firmly established and its outspoken opponents, such as the various Gnostic teachers, were silenced, the persecution of those who did not interpret the scriptures in the approved manner was pursued less vigorously. For a time, the Church was content simply to excommunicate heretics, but this led to intellectuals questioning the Church's supernatural beliefs, so cruel measures were once again needed to put an end to this unsatisfactory state of affairs. To ensure that accused individuals were not too shy about confessing their non-authorised views, the Inquisition was permitted to apply limitless amounts of intense physical pain to anyone they suspected. This practice was formally approved by the inappropriately named Pope Innocent IV in AD 1252.

Shortly before daybreak on the morning of Friday, 13 October 1307, the seneschals of France swooped on fifteen thousand Knights Templar who had gone to bed as highly respected members of a holy order, but were now rudely awoken as accused heretics.

In the capital, Philip IV watched from a safe distance as his officers took possession of the Paris Temple and its contents, along with the preceptors of Aquitaine, the prior of Normandy and the Grand Master – Jacques de Molay himself.[1] There was no resistance from the Templars, even though their building was designed to be fully defensible.[2] Philip considered the Temple, which brooded over the city walls of his capital, so important that he attended in person, once it was secured.[3]

It is remarkable that most of the senior members of the Order received no warning of the trap that was closing in on them. Considering how many junior clerks and officials must have seen the multiple copies of the

---

[1] M. Barbour: *The Trial of the Templars*
[2] M. Barbour: *The New Knighthood*
[3] E. Burman: *Supremely Abominable Crimes*

instructions, they must have been either totally loyal to the king or afraid of reprisals if they talked. The charges of heresy would have helped preserve their silence because actively assisting accused heretics would have attracted the attention not just of Philip's soldiers but of the priests of the French Inquisition who were taking charge of the interrogation of the Order.

Not everything went Philip's way, however.

There must have been a leak in security in La Rochelle because a significant number of the fighting men of the Order, and all of its fleet, had disappeared by the time that the king's seneschals arrived at the harbour. The fleet had slipped away under cover of darkness and was never seen again.

There can be no doubt that most of the fugitives ended up in Scotland under the protection of the already excommunicated king, Robert the Bruce, whilst we believe others sailed due west in search of the land they knew as la Merica.[4]

William Imbert, the Chief Inquisitor of France (also known as William of Paris), was the personal confessor of Philip the Fair and is said to have been '*deeply versed in all inquisitorial arts and practices*'.[5] He was charged by the king with the task of extracting an immediate confession from Jacques de Molay, by whatever means he considered appropriate.

One Templar, by the name of John of Foligny, quickly admitted under the persuasion of the Inquisition, that private Templar ceremonies took place in the oratory of the small chapel of the Paris Temple, which was inside the main tower which housed the treasury. He described this chapel as 'a secret place',[6] and we believe it was a windowless room virtually identical to a modern Masonic temple. We have not been able to find a record of the decoration used in this 'secret room', but almost certainly it will have had a black-and-white chequered floor, walls adorned with non-Christian symbols and a star-studded ceiling with the letter 'G' at its centre.

Within that inner temple, possibly inside a small wooden chest, were four items. A human skull, two thigh bones and a white burial shroud; just as one would expect to find in a Masonic temple today. Like the Jerusalem Church before them, and Freemasonry after them, the Templars kept a linen shroud to wrap the candidates for senior membership, as they underwent ritualised death and resurrection to their new life as full brothers in the community they sought to join.

---

[4] C. Knight & R. Lomas: *The Hiram Key*
[5] Anon: *Secret Societies of the Middle Ages*
[6] *Der Untergang des Templer-Ordens*, II, 35

Of the ten charges brought against the Templars, the most offensive to the Inquisition must surely have been:

they make every novice spit and trample on the cross of Christ.

The cross, as a mystical symbol of the resurrection of the dead Christ, was, and still is, the very essence of Christian belief and any attempt to mock or belittle its importance would have outraged the priests of the Paris Inquisition. When they realised that the Master of a once heroic Christian order had spat upon the cross, their fury would surely have known no bounds. For Imbert, this terrible betrayal of Jesus Christ and his holy Church had to be avenged in the strongest possible way. He was authorised by papal ruling to use torture on all heretics where and when he discovered them with few exceptions, but the Order of the Knights Templar was just such an exception.

Jacques de Molay and his followers answered only to the pope and Imbert knew that, without direct papal instructions, his authority stopped short of putting the Templar Grand Master to 'the Question'. However, Philip had told Imbert that as the king of France he was justified in ordering the torturing of the senior officers of the Templars under the terms of the papal directive which ordered all Christian princes 'to give all possible assistance to the Holy Office of the Inquisition'.[7] Imbert was now happy that he had been legally authorised by the king to make Jacques de Molay, this master heretic, confess by any means he wished.

When subjected to torture by a skilled practitioner, prisoners will, nearly always, confess to whatever the questioner wishes to hear, even when the victims know such a confession will result in their immediate execution. Indeed, in such circumstances, death may become the sole ambition of the unfortunate suspects.

THE INTERROGATION IN THE TEMPLE

As soon as the Paris Temple was secure, Imbert began to question the Grand Master.

The Paris Temple was the financial centre of the city, and as such its cellars did not contain a torture chamber, so the usual instruments of persuasion such as the rack and the pulley were not readily available. Imbert, however, was a resourceful man and had come prepared with the necessary

[7] P.A. Limborch: *The History of the Inquisition*

materials for the task he was planning, including ropes, whips and several generous-sized nails.

We will now describe what we believe happened to Molay at the hands of the Inquisition, and the range of supporting evidence will follow.

Because he was outraged at the Templars' use of a resurrection ceremony, which insulted the 'true' resurrection of Christ, we believe that Imbert had every intention of forcing Molay to endure the same torture that Jesus had suffered. This is most likely to have taken place in the 'secret room' where the Templars had conducted their 'obscene' ceremonies, and where Imbert had found the chest containing the shroud, skull and thigh bones used in the Templar resurrection ceremony. He knew what they were used for because his informants had already told him of a ceremony that involved the candidate taking the role of the victim in the re-enactment of a murder, only to be resurrected from a ritual 'grave'.

Horrified and repulsed, Imbert decided on the form of torture he would use on Molay, who would live to regret his denial of the cross and vile use of these unholy objects.

As a preliminary to any torture by the Inquisition, the victim was stripped naked, as is shown by this contemporary comment:

> The stripping is performed without regard to humanity or honour
> . . . For they cause them to be stripped, even to their very shifts,
> which they afterwards take off, forgive the expression, even to their
> pudenda.[8]

Molay was secured by two ropes attached to his wrists and Imbert proceeded to have his victim beaten with a multi-tailed whip, possibly tipped with fragments of bone.

A crown of sharp objects was thrust with great force on to the Master's head, cutting into his scalp and forehead.

It is recorded that the Inquisition regularly nailed people to posts or other convenient objects as a form of torture and that is precisely what we believe happened in the Paris Temple that day.[9] For the expenditure of just three sturdy nails Molay's inquisitors had a portable and highly effective means of extracting a confession.

---

[8] P.A. Limborch: *The History of the Inquisition*
[9] G.R. Scott: *A History of Torture*

Molay was dragged to the nearest suitable object, perhaps a section of wood panelling or, much more likely, a large wooden door. He was made to stand on something like a footstool and his right arm was pulled, almost vertically, above his head and then nailed in place between the radius and ulna bones of the wrist, carefully avoiding the veins. The violence of the nail's impact on the internal structure of Molay's right arm caused his thumb to swing across the palm so violently that the joint dislocated and his thumb nail imbedded itself into the flesh of his palm.

Then his left arm was pulled out sideways and upwards and nailed to the door at a lower level. Now, the footstool was kicked away and his right foot had a nail driven through between the second and third metatarsal.[10] Once the point was through, Molay's right foot was put over his left, so that both feet could be pinned with a single nail. He was not hung in symmetrical manner, but in a near straight line from the right wrist to the feet, with the left arm stretched outwards. His right shoulder dislocated almost immediately.

Blood loss was minimal and he remained fully conscious, although he must have been in terrible pain.

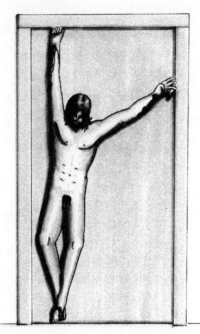

The position of Mohay's crucifixion as indicated by the shroud blood flow

[10] R. Bucklin: 'The Medical Aspects of the Crucifixion of Christ', *Sindon* December 1961

The priests of the Inquisition were highly skilled men and they loved to exercise precise control of their unfortunate victim. The rack was a popular piece of equipment because pain could be applied in considered increments, but the three nails denied them this degree of finesse. However, the choice of a door on which to nail the victim provided an excellent means of instantly increasing their persuasive powers. The simple act of opening the door, swinging it to and fro and occasionally slamming it shut, will have sent horrendous shock waves through the near-demented victim.

This description of events is consistent with the dislocated thumb and right shoulder that have been identified by medical experts who have studied the Shroud. It also explains the directions of the bloodflow seen on the forearms of the Shroud image.

The 63-year-old Templar had known a life of high authority and esteem, and now he found himself degraded and almost destroyed. It would take a strong man indeed not to tell the Inquisition anything they wanted to hear.

The trauma inflicted on Molay's body caused the production of large amounts of lactic acid in his bloodstream, leading to what is called 'metabolic acidosis', a condition often seen in athletes driven to exhaustion.[11] This condition produces severe cramp, and it was further aggravated by the build-up of carbon dioxide that occurred when Molay could not breath out efficiently, leading to 'respiratory acidosis'. As his struggle for survival reached its cruel climax, his body temperature soared and sweat poured out profusely, his muscles became frozen in permanent cramp, his blood pressure plummeted and his heart pounded wildly – but Imbert did not intend him to die. Just as the Master thought he could stand no more, Imbert ordered him to be taken down.

Now was the moment to show Molay that his mocking use of a shroud had not gone unnoticed by the Holy Inquisition. As he was taken down, his torturers laid him face upwards on the cloth and the excess section was lifted over his head to cover the front of his steaming body.

Molay was then placed on the same soft bed from which he had been dragged earlier that morning. His head and shoulders were supported to assist his laboured breathing and the injured man's morbid fluids – sweat and blood with high lactic acid content – ran freely over his entire body.

The shroud made full contact with the back of Molay's supine body so that the blood and sweat left a crude image on the cloth beneath him. The

[11] J.F. Zilva & P.R. Pannall: *Clinical Chemistry in Diagnosis and Treatment*

cloth on the front of his body draped over the high points and the evaporating sweat passed upwards to the shroud. Being on a soft bed with pillows ensured that his head was raised and his waist and knees were bent, bringing his hands down to the top of his thigh.

Imbert was under strict orders not to kill the Grand Master of the Templars, but he had no intention of nursing the confessed heretic back to good health himself. Molay had no family in the area to call in to look after him, but his right-hand man, the Templar Preceptor of Normandy, who was also under interrogation at the Paris Temple at the same time, did. We believe that the family of Geoffrey de Charney's brother, Jean de Charney,[12] was called in and ordered to care for both men, who were destined to die together seven years later, when both were slowly roasted over charcoal for their relapse into 'heresy'.

The Charney family removed the shroud and dressed the wounds. They must have spent many weeks bringing Molay back to something approaching reasonable health, but his scars never healed because two years later he removed his shirt to show the papal representatives the extent of his torture. The shroud was stiff with blood and sweat, but, as a useful piece of cloth, it was washed rather than discarded, and the clean white linen was then folded up and put away in the family home without further thought.

THE CONFESSION OF JACQUES DE MOLAY

Many books on the Templars casually state that Jacques de Molay made a full confession, soon after his arrest, under threat of torture. The impression that most people will have gained from reading commonly available books on the subject is that Molay gave a 'show confession', whereby he betrayed his Order to Philip, in order to win some time for himself. However, we discovered that there are some more detailed accounts of this confession which shed a very different light on the matter.

Once the Grand Master was well enough, he dictated his 'confession' in a letter that was sent to every other Templar Knight, urging them to do likewise, stating that: *'they were deceived by ancient error'*.

However, whilst he admitted the denial of Christ, he steadfastly refused to admit what he referred to as: *'permission for the practice of vice'*.[13]

On the face of it, this was a very odd response for a priest and the leader

---

[12] E. Burman: *Supremely Abominable Crimes*
[13] F.W. Bussell: *Religious Thought and Heresy in the Middle Ages*

of a powerful Christian order. He was prepared to admit heresy, for which he could be burnt to death and damned for eternity in hell, but absolutely denied homosexual acts which, as we know from the comment of Boniface VIII, were considered 'no more a sin than rubbing your hands together'.

One would expect even strong-willed priests to confess under torture to something as trivial as an act of sexual deviance, even when it was untrue, but they would surely die in agony before falsely admitting that they had denied Christ. However, it is entirely consistent with the confession one would expect to hear from a man who knew that Jesus was a Jewish messiah rather than a god. It also ties in with the comments of that English Templar, John de Stoke, who said that Molay had told him to believe in the one omnipotent God, who created heaven and earth, and not in the Crucifixion.[14]

Under torture the Grand Master confessed to the half of the accusations that would ensure his death, and it therefore seems very likely that he told the truth. The Templars did not practise homosexuality, so he denied it, but he admitted that he did not believe that Jesus, or any other man, was a god because there was only one God – and yes, he did reject the cross as a symbol.

Molay is reported to have made his first, verbal confession before the University of Paris on Sunday, 15 October.[15] This was only two days after his arrest and, if this account is accurate, Imbert must have persuaded him to confess very quickly, probably on the day of his arrest, otherwise he would never have recovered sufficiently from his torture to be able to be carried in to speak. It was ten days later that Molay wrote his statement of confession where he admitted denying Christ and the cross, but vehemently denied the other charges of homosexual activities.[16] The next stage of the confession process occurred early the following year when Molay and the grand-priors of Normandy and Aquitaine were taken to the town of Chinon for an audience with Pope Clement, where they once again confessed to denying Christ and the cross. Clement referred to this meeting in a private letter he wrote to Philip, dated 30 December 1308,[17] by which time he was keeping the king fully informed about the papal proceedings against the Templars.

Clement met the obligation of the 'sixth condition' demanded by Philip

[14] M. Baigent & R. Leigh: *The Temple and the Lodge*
[15] Anon: *Secret Societies of the Middle Ages*
[16] F.W. Bussell: *Religious Thought and Heresy in the Middle Ages*
[17] Anon: *Secret Societies of the Middle Ages*

IV, and publicly admitted that the French king had acted within his legal rights, under the terms of the papal directive which ordered all Christian princes 'to give all possible assistance to the Holy Office of the Inquisition'. The attack on the Templars was directly against Clement's interests and demonstrated to the world that Philip did not need the consent of the pope to proceed against an order which was directly under papal protection. No doubt the resourceful king had built in some means of blackmail to persuade the pope to comply with Philip's secret sixth condition.

To confirm his position, Philip held an Assembly of State at Tours in 1308, and obtained from this meeting a declaration of his royal right to punish notorious heretics without needing the consent of the pope.[18] It seems that Clement did try to resist complying with Philip's arrest of the Templars because it is known that he tried to escape to Rome via Bordeaux, but unfortunately his baggage train, his treasures and his holy person were stopped on the king's orders and the pope became a virtual prisoner of Philip from then on.

Clement was required to set up a papal commission to investigate the guilt of the Order and, on Wednesday, 26 November 1309, Molay was brought before this commission at Vienne. Letters were read to him which stated that he had previously made a full confession to all charges put to him. The Grand Master immediately flew into a rage, vehemently denying that he had ever confessed to the charges of homosexual practices. So aggressive was Molay's response that the bishops of the commission ordered him to moderate his tone. He did not deny his confession regarding his rejection of Christ as a god in human form.

The following day, when he had regained his composure, Molay made this statement to the commission:

> *If I, myself, or other knights, have made confessions before the*
> *bishop of Paris, or elsewhere, we have betrayed the truth – we have*
> *yielded to fear, to danger, to violence. We were tortured by our*
> *enemies.*[19]

He removed his shirt to show the assembled bishops the marks that the torture had left on his body.

On 28 March 1310, following a public accusation, hundreds of Templars

[18] P.A. Limborch: *The History of the Inquisition*
[19] Anon: *Secret Societies of the Middle Ages*

in Paris demanded to be brought before the pope, but this audience was denied by Philip.

The pope now drew up an act of accusation against the Templars which claimed that, at the time of their reception, initiates for Templarism were required to deny the virgin birth and assert that Christ was not the true God but a prophet who was crucified for his own crimes and not for the redemption of the world. It was stated that they spat and trampled on the cross, especially on Good Friday.[20]

When he could no longer use the excuse of the collection of evidence for further delay, Clement called a meeting of the general council at Vienne. On 1 October 1311, Pope Clement and one hundred and fourteen of his bishops met to decide the fate of the Templars. The bishops, the majority drawn from outside France, refused to find the Templars guilty, and so Clement closed the council and continued to do nothing. Four months later, Philip went to visit Clement and had a 'private discussion' with him, following which, on 22 March 1313, Clement abolished the Order on his sole authority, without ruling on either its guilt or its innocence. The general council reconvened on 3 April and, in the presence of the king and his royal guards, the pope read his Bull of Abolition. On 2 May, the bull was published and the Order of the Knights Templar officially ceased to exist.

Clement did, however, allow Philip to make a charge for expenses against the Templar estates, to cover the costs of his investigations and imprisonment of the suspects. These 'legitimate costs' soon absorbed the Order's entire assets in France.

THE FINAL DENIAL

Philip the Fair never made any attempt to give the Templars a fair trial. In 1308, the king caused Clement to publish a papal bull on 12 August which gave the results of an examination and confessions of various Templars who were not even interviewed until 17 August! Then in 1310, when Clement called the Order to defend itself and show good cause as to why it should not be suppressed, tIt is recorded that five hundred and thirty-six Templar knights came forward on the promise from Philip that they would be in no danger.

When they appeared before the papal commission in Paris, they told how they had been horribly tortured; one knight by the name of Bernard de Vardo

---

[20] M. Barbour: *The Trial of the Templars*

showed the commissioners a box containing the blackened bones that had dropped out of his feet whilst they had been held over a brazier.

Having got the Templars together, the king broke his promise and had them arrested and prosecuted. Many had previously confessed under torture, and their attempt to defend themselves at the papal commission was held to be a relapse into heresy – the penalty for which was burning at the stake. The Templars were damned by the fact that they claimed innocence. The king had them burnt in batches; on one occasion, when fifty-four knights died in the flames at a burning under the control of Philip de Marigni, the Archbishop of Sens, it is said that the victims screamed in anguish, but none would admit their guilt.

Philip's hatred of the Templars knew no limits, but even he surpassed himself when he ordered that the remains of the former treasurer of the Order, dead for almost a century, who had not wanted to ransom the king's grandfather, should be dug up and burnt.[21]

The final list of accusations against the Templars was rather more specific than the original one.[22] The claims against them now were:

1. The denial of Christ and defiling the cross
2. Adoration of an idol
3. A perverted Sacrament performed
4. Ritual murders
5. The wearing of a cord of heretical significance
6. The ritual kiss
7. Alteration in the ceremony of the Mass and an unorthodox form of absolution
8. Immorality.
9. Treachery to other sections of the Christian forces

According to Templar historian Bothwell Gosse, they were probably guilty of 1,5,6 and 7. He concludes that there may be some part truth in 8, but they were totally innocent of charges 2,4 and 9 (he made no comment about point 3).

The charge that they wore a cord of heretical significance immediately brought to mind the cable tow or noose that every Masonic candidate has to

---

[21] J.S.M. Ward: *Freemasonry and the Ancient Gods*
[22] Ibid.

wear in his initiation. We had found a carving at Rosslyn with a bearded Templar holding just such a cord around the neck of a candidate. The accusation of ritual murders could also be true if the emphasis is placed on the word 'ritual' and we take them as referring to the symbolic murder of every candidate for Templarism/Freemasonry, prior to their resurrection.

Jacques de Molay, the Grand Master, Geoffrey de Charney, Preceptor of Normandy, Hugh de Peyraud and Guy de Auvergne remained in prison before Clement set up a papal commission, under the Bishop of Alba and two other cardinals, not to hear the prisoners but, taking their guilt for granted, to pronounce their sentences. Philip wanted the maximum publicity for this show of sentencing senior Templars and he ordered a public demonstration of Templar guilt. The Archbishop of Sens and the three papal commissioners took their places on a specially erected stage on 18 March 1314, before a huge crowd that had gathered to see the fate of the four Templars. A hush fell over the square as the distinguished prisoners were brought from their dungeons on to the platform. The Bishop of Alba read out their alleged confessions and pronounced a sentence of perpetual imprisonment, but as he was about to go on to explain their total guilt he was interrupted by the Grand Master who insisted on speaking to the assembled crowd. It seems probable that Molay told the bishop that he was prepared to stand up and confess his sin to the crowd personally. He was then allowed to speak:

It is just that, in so terrible a day, and in the last moments of my life, I should discover all the iniquity of falsehood, and make the truth triumph. I declare, then, in the face of heaven and earth, and acknowledge, though to my eternal shame, that I have committed the greatest of crimes but . . .

No doubt Molay paused here for effect as he changed the thrust of his speech to catch out his persecutors.

. . . it has been the acknowledging of those which have been so foully charged on the order. I attest – and truth obliges me to attest – that it is innocent!
I made the contrary declaration only to suspend the excessive pains of torture, and to mollify those who made me endure them.
I know the punishments which have been inflicted on all the knights who had the courage to revoke a similar confession; but the

dreadful spectacle which is presented to me is not able to make me confirm one lie by another.

The life offered me on such infamous terms I abandon without regret.[23]

There were, of course, no journalists in the crowd that day and there certainly was no written script, so we have to accept that the recorded words must be based on the memories of some of the more literate people present on the occasion. Whilst the details may not be fully accurate, it is reasonable to assume that the key words were spoken and the general sentiment is likely to be intact.

Molay appears to have teased his tormentors a little by starting out as though he was accommodating their accusations in return for a life sentence, but he then smartly flips the apparent confession around into a denial of guilt. The most interesting part of his speech, however, is what he did not say!

The Grand Master states that truth obliges him to attest that the Templars are innocent. They were truly a good and godly order but not a Christian one, for nowhere in his one-hundred-and-three-word parting speech did Molay mention Jesus Christ. One would surely expect that the priestly leader of this apparently Christian organisation would take this last opportunity to reaffirm his love of Christ if he were trying to prove that the claims that he had denied his saviour under torture were untrue. Why did he not say something along the lines of: 'The Order is innocent and I hereby express my love for, and devotion to, Jesus Christ the saviour of the world'?

In his capacity as the last High Priest of Yahweh, Molay said that the Order was 'innocent'; which in his view it most certainly was . . . but he did not refer to the principle charge against it and announce that: 'The Order is innocent of denying Christ.'

This Rex Deus Grand Master and his followers made many references to God, but we know of no references whatsoever to Jesus Christ – even in this parting speech of innocence. From the tone of Molay's words, we take it that, once he had openly confessed to the Order's rejection of Jesus as the son of God, he had been forced to say that he accepted that this was iniquitous behaviour and that all Templars were therefore sinners. In front of the crowd

---

[23] Anon: *Secret Societies of the Middle Ages*

at Notre-Dame, he now put the record straight; they were not sinners and they held the greater truth. Jesus Christ as the 'son of God' just did not enter into it.

Molay caused an uproar of support and Geoffrey de Charney stood shoulder to shoulder with him. The commissioners stopped the proceedings to report the horribly changed situation to Philip. His response was immediate; without seeking papal authority Philip unhesitatingly condemned both the outspoken Templars to the flames. On the following day, on a small island in the river Seine called Ile des Javiaux, the two Templars were finally put to death, one after the other. Records tell us that Jacques de Molay and Geoffrey de Charney were slowly roasted over a hot, smokeless fire. The heat was applied with great care, first to their feet and then to their genitals, to ensure that the suffering lasted as long as possible. As his flesh blackened and slowly cooked, Molay cursed both Clement and Philip, summoning them both to appear before the Supreme Judge (God) within a year. When death finally came, it is said that many spectators shed tears at the view of the bravery of the two Templars, and during the night their ashes were secretly gathered up and preserved as relics.[24]

The deaths of Molay and Charney were recorded in a popular verse chronicle by Geoffroi de Paris[25] which says that Molay insisted that his hands were not bound so that he could join them to pray during his final moments. Molay's final comment on his accusers was said to be:

Let evil swiftly befall those who have wrongly condemned us – God will avenge our deaths.[26]

De Charney is reported to have added the following words as Molay's body smoked – words which quickly became well known throughout France:

I shall follow the way of my Master, as a martyr you have killed him. This you have done and know not. God willing, on this day, I shall die in the Order like him.[27]

We have already quoted on several occasions from an intriguing anony-

---

[24] Anony: *Secret Societies of the Middle Ages*
[25] E. Burman: *Supremely Abominable Crimes*
[26] Ibid.
[27] Ibid.

mous book covering certain aspects of the Templars in great detail. Quite why a person should write a book such as *Secret Societies of the Middle Ages* and then remain anonymous is hard to understand. The individual may have been a well-known person, perhaps a politician or even a churchman, but from everything that we have been able to cross-check, he was certainly well informed. Because everything that is checkable has turned out to be very accurate, we are prepared to take other things he said seriously. This unknown author added one last intriguing comment that we could not ignore. Here are his words:

> *We are far from denying that at the time of the suppression of the order of the Temple there was a secret doctrine in existence, and that the overthrow of the papal power, with its idolatry, superstition, and impiety, was the object aimed at by those who held it, and that Freemasonry may possibly be that doctrine under another name.*[28]

Unfortunately, the author (who was clearly not a Freemason) does not elaborate on this point. Our own researches have established a direct lineage between the Templars who fled to Scotland and Freemasonry, and there can be little doubt that the Presbyterian and the later Episcopalian forms of Freemasonry did oppose Catholic power in Britain. Since the unification of English Freemasonry in 1813, the United Grand Lodge of England and all other Grand Lodges have been scrupulous in their avoidance of any religious or political opinion.

CONCLUSION

Jacques de Molay was arrested in the Paris Temple early on 13 October 1307, whilst the king watched from a safe distance. The Templars offered no resistance and the Grand Master was tortured to make a confession. He admitted the Order's denial of Christ, but steadfastly refused to admit that Templars indulged in homosexual practices.

Our theory that Molay was crucified, and that it was his image on the Shroud, has been borne out by the known facts:

1. The date fits the carbon dating of the fabric of the Shroud.

[28] Anon: *Secret Societies of the Middle Ages*

2. We have an explanation of why a shroud was available. (Used for the resurrection rituals. Freemasons still use such shrouds today.)
3. We have two motives for the crucifixion. (The Inquisition had to use a form of torture that needed no large equipment, and Imbert knew that the Templars had denied Christ and 'mocked' his resurrection with their heretical ceremonies, so it was poetic justice.)
4. We know that the victims of the Inquisition were always stripped naked and that the Inquisitors had a reputation for nailing people up to convenient objects.
5. We know from the evidence of the image that the victim was almost certainly still alive because he was placed on a bed not a stone slab.
6. We know that Molay showed off his wounds at a later date.

The case for the Molay hypothesis was looking very strong, but we still needed more evidence before we could be certain.

Jacques de Molay died in the flames after retracting his confession that the Order had sinned, but he conspicuously did not retract his confession that the Templars had denied Christ as the son of God.

Chapter 9

THE CULT OF THE SECOND MESSIAH

A TIME FOR PROPHECY

In the early part of the twelfth century, Judaism as a religion was in a state of almost terminal decline. The driving concept of the religion was the idea of a chosen people and the messiah who would lead them to their destiny.

Jews believed that the coming of the messiah would be announced by the return of the prophet Elijah when the 'Last Days' of the old order had come, and Elijah's spirit would appear in the guise of a Jewish teacher and announce the new king. These teachings encouraged Jewish scholars to look for 'signs of the Times' and to try to predict the 'End of the Days'.[1]

Seven years after the Templars had established their new Order of the Temple, a Jewish child by the name of Moses ben Maimon was born in Cordoba, which was then part of Moorish Spain and one of the few places where Jews were respected and their skills welcomed. His birth came on the anniversary of the death of Jesus: the eve of the Passover in the year 4895, which in the Christian calendar was 30 March 1135.

Although he was born with the name Maimon, he became known as Moses Maimonides. He grew up in a Moorish Islamic civilisation that was at the peak of its achievement and, unlike Christian Europe, intellectualism

---

[1] H. Schonfield: *The Passover Plot*

179

was an encouraged and admired quality. His religious education inspired him to study the full heritage of the Jewish people which is, of course, far more than just a religion, as the Law contains rules for living every part of one's life.

Writing to a fellow rabbi he said:

> *Although from my childhood the Torah was betrothed to me and continues to hold my heart as the wife of my youth, in whose love I find constant delight, strange women whom I first took into my house as her handmaids, have become her rivals and take up much of my time.*[2]

These other rivals for his affection were the sciences in general and the science of medicine in particular, which caused him to become a respected healer – soon rising to become the physician to the court of Saladin. He was a brilliant medical scientist and his books on the subject made him a well-known figure throughout the scholarly world. These books were for general use; they did not contain anything offensive to the religious views of either Muslims or Christians and so were widely read, even being translated into Latin by Christian monks.

The interest in Maimonides' medical works often led informed readers to seek out his thoughts on other matters, and he became one of the most respected and well-known Jewish rabbis in the medieval world. He wrote in several languages and in one Arabic work, called *Guide for the Perplexed*, he harmonised faith and reason by reconciling the tenets of rabbinical Judaism with the rationalism of Aristotelian philosophy. Here he wrestled with such complex issues as the nature of God and creation, free will, and the problem of defining good and evil. His sophisticated and yet clear thinking was to influence leading Christian philosophers, such as St Thomas Aquinas and St Albertus Magnus.

When the Jews of Yemen had a serious religious problem, it was only natural that they would consult Maimonides for guidance. In his reply the rabbi told them that the power of prophecy would return to Israel in AD 1210 – after which the messiah would come. Unsurprisingly, he also told them to keep this information from becoming public.[3]

[2] I. Kobez & H. Friedenwald: *The Jews in Medicine*
[3] G.W. Buchanan: *Jesus – The King and His Kingdom*

1. A carving on the exterior of Rosslyn showing a candidate being initiated into the first degree of Freemasonry whilst kneeling in front of two pillars. The candidate is blindfolded and he has a noose around his neck which is being held by a figure in the tunic of the Knights Templar. His feet are in the precise position that a Masonic candidate still adopts in modern ceremonies, and he is holding a Bible in his left hand. This carving was created circa 1450 AD, almost two hundred and seventy years before the United Grand Lodge of England says that Freemasonry began.

2. Rosslyn Chapel built by Sir William St Clair and begun in 1440. It has clear connections with both modern Freemasonry, the Knights Templar and first-century Jerusalem.

3. The west wall does not have its stonework tied into the main central section and so cannot be the wall of an unfinished structure.

4. The endstones were deliberately worked to appear damaged, like a ruin.

5. A four-inch high tableau hidden away on top of a pillar in Rosslyn shows a figure holding up a cloth which could represent the Shroud of Turin. There is very little damage to the stonework of Rosslyn but this is one of a small group that appear to have had their heads deliberately cut off, presumably to prevent recognition of some individuals as the remaining figures show great character and appear to be portraits of actual people.

6 & 7. Right at the back (plate 6) there is a dismembered head hidden from view which shows a remarkable likeness to the face on the Turin Shroud.

8. The medieval Latin inscription inside Rosslyn that proves that several of the higher degrees of Freemasonry were known to William St Clair in the mid-fifteenth century.

9. The authors standing by the west wall of Rosslyn.

10. The priestly pillar of Jachin at Rosslyn which was for many years disguised by plaster to appear similar to the other pillars.

11. The kingly Boaz Pillar at Rosslyn.

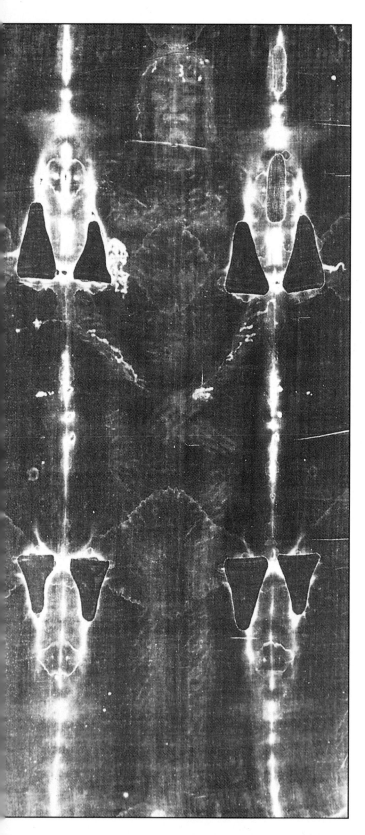

12. The front image of the Shroud of Turin showing the strange perspective, caused by the close convection process.

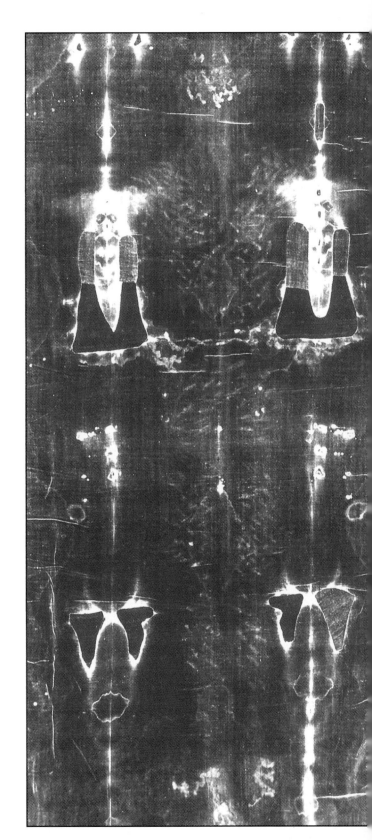

13. The dorsal image of the Shroud of Turin showing the full contact image of the back, caused by the soft underlay.

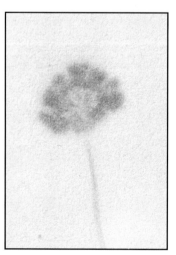

14 & 15. Volckringer patterns of Australian plant specimens. After being collected in Australia in 1868 and mounted on paper, the collection was presented to the Natural History Museum in London in 1921 and has been stored until 1997. During remounting these magnificent images were found on the original paper mounts which clearly show the same three-dimensional, impressionistic quality as the images on the Shroud of Turin.

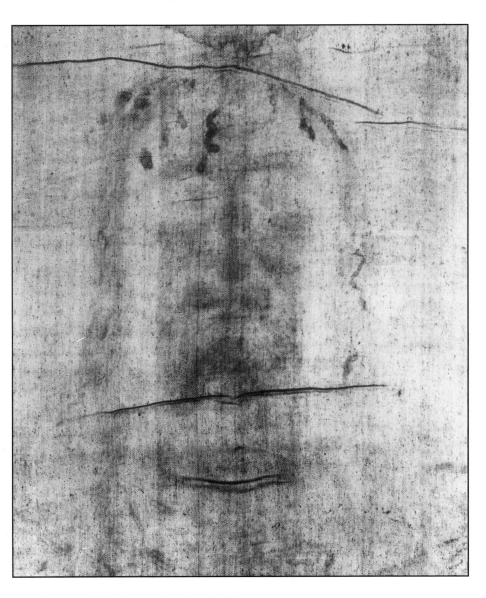

16. The image of the face on the Shroud of Turin.
This Volckringer pattern of the face of Jacques de
Molay was created by the same chemical process as
the images of the Australian plants shown opposite.
The image has the same characteric of no distinct
lines, produces a photographic image when viewed
as a negative and becomes easier to see the further
away it is viewed.

17. The Mount of Olives and the tomb of James in the foreground marked by twin pillars.

18. The site of the Pinnacle of the Temple opposite James's tomb. This is the point from where James was thrown.

19. An open segment of the Copper Scroll held by John Allegro. This was the first segment to come away.

20. The fully opened scroll – the work of Dr H Wright Baker and John Allegro at Manchester College of Technology in 1955.

THE HIEROPHANT

21. The Duke of Sussex: the first Grand Master of the United Grand Lodge of England, seated on the Grand Master's throne between the twin pillars. He was responsible for suppressing the Scottish rituals of Freemasonry.

22. The Hierophant card from the Tarot pack, seated on a throne between two pillars. The similarity to the Grand Master of Freemasonry can easily be seen.

23. Albert Pike of the Supreme Council for the Southern Jurisdiction of the United States who assisted in the mutilation of the original rituals that he considered to be incoherent nonsense and jargon.

24. The Templar Round Church at Cambridge.

25. Our first attempt at reconstructing a shroud image on a flat hard surface, using a model. The front image shows none of the subtlety of a Volckringer image and does not have the perspective distortion so obvious on the shroud.

26. The rear image clearly shows how the model's body touched the shroud at just five points: the head, shoulders, buttocks, calves and heels. Only by using a soft underlay is it possible to create a complete back image by contact.

In 1170, the Shiite Mahdi, ruler of the Yemen, suddenly demanded that all Jews, who had lived there since the Dispersion, become Mohammedans forthwith or face death. At this time, a Jewish messianic revival had begun in Yemen and was spreading to other lands, creating a general belief that the promised arrival of the messiah was at hand. Many pious Jews started to repent of their sins, dispose of their property and give it to the poor. The messianic uproar seemed to be making the situation of the Jews in Yemen even worse, so Jacob al Fayumi wrote to Maimonides, the sage of Fostat, for advice.[4] Maimonides' reply is in the famous letter to the Jews of Yemen known as *Iggert Teman.*

In this letter, which became well known in European centres of learning, he also made comments about the coming of the Jewish messiah, on the basis of his extensive study of Jewish literature which said that the messiah would be in hiding in the Great See of Rome.

This prophecy was stating very clearly that the new messiah would appear to be a member of the Roman Church, but he would secretly be the new messiah of Yahweh!

When writing to the Jews of Yemen, he summarised this folk tradition of the messiah and restated its contemporary meaning:

> *King Messiah will arise and restore the kingdom of David to its former state . . . The Messiah will be a mortal being who will die and will be succeeded by his heirs who will reign after him . . . 'Then the Lord thy God will turn thy captivity and will return and gather thee'.*[5]

We found Maimonides' choice of words to be very interesting. He qualified the title 'messiah' with the word 'king' which indicates that he was aware that there was also a priest messiah. He also went out of his way to ensure that every Jew fully appreciated that this kingly messiah would bring a re-instated royal bloodline of David: a monarchical dynasty rather than a man-god as the Christians believed they had found.

This prophecy, by the greatest Jewish scholar of medieval times, was studied by Christian scholars throughout Europe. It was to prove very important for the Church of Rome, which obviously had a vested interest in

[4] J.S. Minkin: *The Teachings of Maimonides*
[5] B. Cohen: *Moses Maimonides' Letter to Yemen*

not having any sort of second messiah appearing, as such an idea could undermine the authority it derived from its first messiah. Many well-informed people had been made aware that one of the most important Jewish teachers to appear for many years had forecast the imminent coming of a messiah – who would be connected with the Roman Church.

Another man, who like Maimonides was born in 1135, was also instrumental in developing a belief in the arrival of a new messiah. His name was Joachim of Fiore and he became a Calabrian abbot with an apocalyptic vision of the future, based on a strange but highly developed numerical system of biblical analysis. As the Major and Minor Arcana of the Tarot pack had a numerical method of linking cards from the inner world to those of the outer world, so Joachim's calculations connected events of the Old Testament with those of the New Testament.

He calculated that 'The Age of the Son' was coming to a close and that 'The Age of the Spirit' would soon be dawning. He believed that there had been forty-two generations between Adam and Jesus, and for him it followed that the expected new age would start to arrive forty-two generations after Jesus which, he wrote, would start around the year 1260. The abbot warned that this would not be a smooth transition as there would be a protracted battle with the Antichrist to be fought, and won, before the wonderful new age could begin.

After his death, Joachim's ideas became public property and were soon developed by other thinkers in various ways. Some, who founded a group in the crucial year of 1260, called themselves the Apostolic Brethren and began armed resistance against the Church of Rome. They believed that God had withdrawn his authority from the pope and all of his clergy who would soon be destroyed in the coming battle that would lead to the 'Age of the Spirit'. In 1304, the Apostolic Brethren took to hiding out in Alpine valleys to wait for the end of the world – which for them, like the Templars, arrived in 1307 when they were slaughtered by the forces of the Church at Monte Rebello.[6]

For the people of Europe the dawning of the fourteenth century was a worrying time. The Church was failing its people and the expected messiah had still not arrived. The apocalyptic vision of Joachim was soon to become very real as the Black Death began to swathe its deadly way across the entire Christian world.

[6] D. Thompson: *The End of Time*

CHRISTENDOM IN NEED

As Jacques de Molay roasted, he had cursed Philip IV and Pope Clement. Within three months both were dead.

Philip, who had always loved hunting, fell from his horse during a chase and was killed outright. Clement died of a fever, which some said was brought about by poisoning of the communion wine by one of his own priests during a celebration of Mass, but, more likely, he finally succumbed to the cancer of the bowel which had invalided him for the previous two years.

What was even more significant for the superstitious population of fourteenth-century Europe was the frighteningly appropriate fate of Clement's body after his death. His cadaver was lying in state when a thunderstorm developed during the night and lightning struck the church, igniting the building into a ball of flame. Before the fire could be extinguished, the body of Clement had been almost completely incinerated.

For many it seemed that the Supreme Judge had passed His verdict on the truly guilty.

Another Templar at the stake had invited the king's principal henchman, William de Norgaret, to appear with him before the throne of God within eight days. It seems probable that Norgaret may have had a helping hand to make the appointment, for he too was dead within the week.

The story of the deaths of the Grand Master's enemies spread throughout France, quickly building a reputation that the spirit of Molay lived on, and had the power to call down the wrath of God on to his persecutors. The legend grew and, even at the time of the French Revolution, one of the spectators at the beheading of Louis XV is said to have dipped his hand into the king's blood and sprinkled it on the crowd, shouting, 'Jacques de Molay, thou art avenged!'[7]

When it comes to being considered a major cultural hero, the main prerequisite is to be dead. From Jesus Christ himself to more recent and lesser icons such as Che Guevara, James Dean or Buddy Holly, the legend that lives after them surpasses any fame that they might have enjoyed during their lifetime. If the circumstances of their departure are unusually powerful or poignant – all the better. Jacques de Molay died a most terrible and very public death that represented not only the demise of a once great crusading

---

[7] R. F. Gould: *History of Freemasonry*

order, but also the passing of a glorious period of Western pride, where knights had seemed to possess almost magical powers in the battle to establish light over darkness. By the mid-fourteenth century, the Church was at a very low ebb indeed, and circumstances were arising that could have very damaging results for it.

Over the forty-three years after the death of Molay, the memories and legends concerning him had all the necessary qualifications to make him the founding figure of a very threatening cult. An expectation of a second coming was everywhere, thanks to the well-publicised prophecies of Maimonides, and people believed that the plague and other disasters were the beginning of the apocalypse prior to the Messiah's arrival. That Molay's two main enemies had quickly died in strange circumstances had built him up as a great figure and, as we know, his ashes and charred bones were considered to be semi-holy relics.

A generation after Molay's death, Europe suffered a number of disasters. In 1345, Rome was hit by a great flood; two years later there was a revolution; and two years later again a severe earthquake badly damaged all three of the great basilicas. Then the greatest horror of all time struck.

The Black Death, a form of bubonic plague, is caused by the bacterium *Yersina pestis*, and is transmitted to human beings by infected fleas and rats. Victims normally develop a fever, painfully swollen lymph nodes and haemorrhages that turn black: hence the common name of this terrible disease. It is easily transmitted by droplets of saliva when coughing or sneezing.

It is believed that the Black Death began as an epidemic in the Gobi desert in the 1320s and spread to China, where it killed almost one in three people, quickly reducing the population by a staggering thirty-five million. It was then transmitted along trade routes west to India, the Middle East and Europe. By 1349, the plague had killed one-third of the population of the Muslim world. Two years previously, the Kipchaks, nomads from the Euro-Asian steppe, had deliberately infected a European community with the disease by catapulting infected corpses into a besieged Genoese trading post in the Crimea. From the Crimea, the Genoese inadvertently brought the disease to Sicily in a ship carrying infected rats, and in 1347, the Black Death swept through Sicily, North Africa, Italy, France and Spain. By 1349, it had ravaged Hungary, Austria, Switzerland, Britain, Germany, Holland, Belgium and Denmark, and by 1350 it reached Sweden and Norway where it killed more people than it spared.

The Norsemen then carried the disease to faraway Iceland, and on to Greenland, where the plague may have hastened the end of the Viking settlements. According to the Norwegian shipping line owner, Fred Olsen, who is a longstanding confidant of the researcher Thor Heyerdahl, there is reason to believe that the disease was also carried to parts of the Americas by pre-Columbus European traders, where it wiped out the city dwellers of what is now the southern United States and the entire civilisation of the Toltecs, leaving their deserted cities to be occupied by members of the Apache nation who we call the Aztecs.[8]

At least twenty-five million Europeans died in the first wave of the Black Death before it returned again in 1361–3, 1369–71, 1374–5, 1390 and 1400. In total, the Black Death killed a greater proportion of the world's people than any other known disaster, before or since.

The whole social outlook of Christianity was transformed by the disease, which is believed to have killed approximately one-third of the population in the four years between 1347 and 1351. The apocalyptic events led to strange forms of religious practices, including one in which flagellants tried to appease their vengeful God's wrath by bearing crucifixes and ritualistically whipping themselves wherever they went. As ever, some sought out scapegoats and in Strasbourg and Brussels thousands of Jews were slaughtered.

The Church too was held responsible, despite the fact that huge numbers of priests and monks had perished in noble attempts to help the sick. By 1351, the clergy was more than decimated by the disease, the economy of Europe was at rock bottom and the surviving people were in open rebellion against Church and State.

As we will show, just like everybody else, the remnants of the Templars and their many supporters were looking for the second coming. Jacques de Molay was rapidly becoming a super-hero and people wondered whether he might have been the Messiah, killed yet again. Those who knew that the Grand Master had been crucified became convinced and the word must have spread, to the alarm of the Church. After the crucifixion of Jesus, the Holy Land had been smitten and the people of the land largely destroyed. Now it was happening again.

The last thing the Church needed was a miraculous image of a crucified

---

[8] Fred Olsen: private conversation

Jacques de Molay to suddenly appear – but that is exactly what was about to happen!

THE BATTLE OF THE HOLY IMAGE

In June of 1353, King John II, known as 'the Good', granted Geoffrey de Charney permission to set up a collegiate church in the town of Lirey. We believe that this Geoffrey de Charney was the grandson of Jean de Charney, the brother of the Templar Preceptor of Normandy who had died in the flames alongside Jacques de Molay. He was a talented and ambitious knight who managed to get himself close to the king. In 1355, Geoffrey was made the standard bearer to King John and he looked set to go far as a royal courtier.

On 28 May 1356, Henry of Poitiers, the Bishop of Troyes, inaugurated Geoffrey's new church at Lirey and we note that no mention was made of a shroud in the stated assets of the church.

Four months later, on 19 September, Geoffrey was fighting at the Battle of Poitiers alongside King John when things went badly wrong for the French forces. As the English closed in, Geoffrey found himself desperately defending his king, but died in the attempt, and the king was taken hostage by Edward the Black Prince, imprisoned in England and a huge ransom of 3,000,000 crowns was demanded for his release.

With her husband dead, and no king to grant a royal pension, Geoffrey's young widow, Jeanne de Vergy, found herself in difficult financial circumstances and, some weeks after hearing the news, she had to appeal to the acting regent, John's son Charles, to support her. She had an infant son, also called Geoffrey de Charney, and little money, but Charles had financial problems of his own and could not offer much help.

As would be normal in such circumstances, Jeanne set about sorting through Geoffrey's possessions. Amongst those items that were pulled out for inspection was a large linen cloth, neatly folded but stained with age. It was unfolded so that its value could be assessed and, much to Jeanne's surprise, she could see the faint but distinct image of a face within the staining on the cloth. Once it was fully opened out, she could clearly see two full images of a man: one the front view and one the back view. This strange apparition looked, for all the world, like the image of Jesus Christ after he had been crucified.

At first, we were not sure whether or not the family had passed on knowledge of what had happened to Jacques de Molay two generations earlier.

Fifty years is a long time, but all the evidence tells us that Jeanne was a very intelligent woman and, on the balance of probabilities, we think that she probably did work out that the cloth was the one that had wrapped the last Grand Master of the Templars, after he was crucified by the Inquisition. Once we looked more closely at her later actions, we became certain that she knew exactly what she had.

Jeanne de Vergy saw this stained shroud as a way out of her financial difficulties. She persuaded the canons at the new church at Lirey to display it as a holy relic, and such a talented marketeer was she that she even invested some of her meagre funds in having a commemorative medallion struck for visitors to purchase, at a suitable profit.

Vast numbers of pilgrims flocked to the site. The holy relic business was a solid investment for anyone in the fourteenth century, and the Church tended to encourage such things because it strengthened the superstition of the people in a way that benefited the authority of the Church. Bishop Henry of Poitiers soon became aware of this influx of visitors to Lirey and when he saw the Shroud, he made investigations into its origin.

We believe that Henry of Poitiers must have found people who knew of Molay's torture by crucifixion, and he heard that the Charney family had taken the shroud that had wrapped the famous Templar. This would have alarmed the bishop because Molay's death had made him a martyr of huge standing and if it was revealed that he had been crucified on the orders of King Philip, with a crown of thorns upon his head, the imagination of the public would know no bounds.

A new messiah was expected and here was a story that would ignite all of Christendom if it got out. The fact that Molay had miraculously left the image of his suffering on a shroud terrified the bishop, not so much because he feared the power of the dead Grand Master but because he knew that the Church would not survive the tidal wave of emotions that such a new cult would create. The Church may have felt more threatened by this small artefact than it was by all of the Muslim hordes in the Holy Land.

The Templars were already widely believed to be the true guardians of the Grail itself because of their patronage of the Templar *Perlesvaus* version of the Grail legend. Interest in the messianic figure of King Arthur, and the reviving of his knightly values, had continued to grow since the demise of the Order whose members had promoted themselves as the saviour king's successors. In England, at that precise time, King Edward III was even building a new Round Table at Winchester, with a view to establishing a knightly order based on the Templars.[9] Any miracles attributed to Molay, such as his recognisable image appearing in the guise of Christ, could easily tip the balance away from the Church and make surviving supporters of the Templars the disciples of the Second Messiah.

The similarities between the death of Jesus and that of Molay had already been noticed. The contemporary poet Dante had written a poem describing Philip the Fair as the 'Pontius Pilate' of the Templar downfall. If the shroud in the Lirey Church was ever recognised for what it really was, the world would have its Second Messiah.

The Shroud had to be destroyed before it destroyed the Church.

Henry of Poitiers responded quickly by claiming that he had located the man who made it, and ordered that the Shroud be destroyed – instructions that he recorded in the archives of the Diocese of Troyes. He did not, however, identify who this 'man' responsible for its creation was, as one would expect if it were a simple forgery.

The Shroud was duly removed from public display, but Jeanne hid it rather than allow it to be destroyed. She must have realised the magnitude of the situation because the rest of her life appears to have been shaped around getting the Shroud back on public display. It seems likely that Henry was told that the Shroud had been destroyed because he maintained excellent relations with the Charney family for the rest of his life.

Jeanne was still young and she remarried the wealthy nobleman Aymon of Genevainto. He was a member of a family that had great influence within the Church – so much so that by 1378, she was to find herself aunt to the new pope, Clement VII.

For the widow of an obscure knight to engineer herself into such a position of influence seems utterly remarkable, and wildly beyond mere coincidence. A further interesting development in this unfolding drama is the fact that Jeanne's son, Geoffrey, married the niece of Bishop Henry of Poitiers, the man who had ordered the Shroud destroyed.

Jeanne and her son clearly had other plans which once again involved earning money from displaying the Shroud as a holy relic at Lirey. The expositions of the Shroud were restarted in 1389.

The importance of the little church at Lirey grew rapidly as it attracted more and more pilgrims, but this new-found success quickly raised the interest of the current local bishop, a Church lawyer called Pierre d'Arcis. He

[9] G. Phillips and M. Keatman: *King Arthur: The True Story*

heard reports of the growing cult of the Shroud of Lirey and, like Henry of Poitiers thirty-two years earlier, he decided to investigate its provenance for himself. In looking back at Henry's records, he soon discovered the findings of the previous investigation and was alarmed. Henry had wanted to record that the Shroud was not the image of Christ, but it would have been far too dangerous to write down the real terrible secret for any future reader to discover. Instead, he simply recorded that it was a fake and he knew the 'man' responsible. He did not name Imbert, Molay's inquisitor, but from his reluctance to identify this creator of the Shroud, or explain what he knew, we strongly believe that that is who he was referring to.

Alarmed at the renewal of this 'fraud', the bishop sent an instruction to the Dean of Lirey to stop the exposition immediately, but the reply he received was not at all what d'Arcis was entitled to expect. The dean said that he had higher permission, authorising him to exhibit the cloth, and that the relic was under the jurisdiction of the Crown. Furthermore, d'Arcis was informed that the current patron, Geoffrey de Charney, had retaken legal possession of the cloth and gained permission from the king to post a military guard of honour around the relic, in case the bishop should try to seize it by force. Pierre d'Arcis was outraged, outranked and outflanked, so he turned to the last resort of a churchman: diplomacy.

With as much humility as he could muster, d'Arcis petitioned Geoffrey at least to suspend the expositions until a papal ruling could be obtained as to the possible damage that was being done to the souls of simple pilgrims. However, Geoffrey was not prepared to give any ground at all; the lucrative expositions continued just as if no appeal had been made.

Bishop d'Arcis was a trained lawyer and he quickly complained to the king. In the light of d'Arcis' reasonable requests for suspension of the expositions until a papal ruling was obtained, the king had to support him as a matter of law. This he did by ordering that the cloth be surrendered to Bishop d'Arcis and he authorised the bailiff of Troyes to confiscate it – but the bailiff returned from his mission empty-handed, for Geoffrey simply refused to give up the Shroud.

This stalemate lasted until the summer of 1389, after which it was broken in a most unexpected manner. Geoffrey de Charney arranged a meeting with the pope at the papal palace in Avignon and, without consulting with d'Arcis, Pope Clement ruled that the expositions should be allowed to continue, although he did introduce a new condition aimed at placating the ruffled bishop. He ordered that the priests of Lirey must state in a clear and audible voice that the cloth was a 'copy or representation' of the Shroud of Christ, and not announce that it was genuine.

Bishop d'Arcis could not believe that the pope could take such a decision, unless material facts in the matter had been withheld from him. He must have genuinely believed that the Dean of Lirey, in league with Geoffrey de Charney, was acting with 'fraudulent intent and for the purpose of gain'. The souls of his flock were more important to d'Arcis than a papal ban on discussion, and so he decided to compose a detailed report for Clement VII, telling everything that he knew about the origin of the cloth, in order to convince him to reverse the decision made in favour of Geoffrey.

The report Bishop d'Arcis wrote, in Latin, to Pope Clement VII in 1389 has been preserved in the Bibliothèque Nationale in Paris.[10]

When studying this report, the reader cannot doubt the honesty and conviction of d'Arcis. He was a man who saw what he perceived to be a great wrong taking place and, after turning to higher authority for support to stop the exploitation of simple pilgrims for gain, he met with what seemed an entrenched attitude which prevented him from taking the action he saw as right. He believed that the pope did not know the awful truth behind the shroud and he was determined to tell him:

> *Indeed it is a wonder to all who know the facts of the case that the opposition which hampers me in these proceedings comes from the Church, from which quarter I should have looked for vigorous support, nay, rather have expected punishment if I had shown myself slothful or remiss . . .*[11]

Referring to Henry of Poitiers' original investigation, the current bishop said:

> *. . . Eventually, after diligent inquiry and examination, he discovered the fraud and how the said cloth had been artfully made by hand, the truth being attested by the master craftsman who had created it, to wit, that it was a work of human skill and not miraculously wrought or bestowed . . .*

[10] Pierre d'Arcis documents: Bibliothèque Nationale, Paris: Collection de Champagne v154, folio 138
[11] 'The Holy Shroud and the Verdict of History' (trans. H. Thurston), *The Month*, vol. CI, 1903

. . . I am convinced that I cannot fully or sufficiently express in writing the grievous nature of the scandal, the contempt brought upon the Church and ecclesiastical jurisdiction, and the danger to souls.

Clement did not carry out his own investigation, or even consult further with d'Arcis, but instead, on 6 January 1390, he published three documents which ended the quarrel – but in a way which did not satisfy d'Arcis or, indeed, answer any of the allegations he had made in his report.

To Geoffrey de Charney, his step-cousin, the pope sent a letter re-affirming his previous decision and restating the condition that whenever the cloth was displayed it should be announced that it was a 'figure or representation'.

To Bishop Pierre d'Arcis he sent a letter, which totally ignored all the findings of the bishop's Memorandum, and imposed a ban of perpetual silence upon him, warning him that if he ever spoke of the matter again he would be immediately excommunicated.

To the senior clerics of the area of Troyes and Lirey, he sent a letter confirming his ruling and ordered them to ensure that his instructions in the matter were carried out to the letter. With the sending of those three letters, the records concerning the d'Arcis Memorandum come to an abrupt end. Pierre d'Arcis died five years later, without ever mentioning the matter again.

Henry of Poitiers had investigated the shroud and he must have quickly found its links to the Templar's last Grand Master. He did indeed discover the man who had created it: Imbert – the man who had crucified Molay and wrapped him in his shroud. By the time of Henry's investigation Imbert was in his seventies, but when asked he would have been able to supply every detail of the event for the horrified bishop. Unfortunately, the records he did leave, which Pierre d'Arcis mentioned in his report to the pope, disappeared soon afterwards.

We knew that the Shroud had passed from the Charney family to the Savoy family in 1453, when it was bought by Louis, the second duke, and we decided to look a little further into this family, to see if we could find any specific reason why they thought it worth giving two castles to become the keepers of this sheet of linen.

History records that the House of Savoy is one of Europe's oldest dynasties, and ruled over Italy from its establishment as a country in 1861 until it became a republic in 1946. The dynasty is said to have been founded by a Burgundian nobleman with the curious name of 'Humbert the Whitehanded' who died around 1048. Humbert's son Oddone became the second Count of Savoy and he greatly extended his dominions when he married Adelaide, the heiress of Turin in the region of Piedmont. (We recalled at this point that Jacques de Molay was himself a minor Burgundian noble, which may, or may not, be pure coincidence.)

Over the next three centuries, the possessions and influence of the family grew rapidly in France, the Italian peninsular and Switzerland, and, in 1416, Count Amadeus VIII of Savoy was elevated to become the first Duke of Savoy, in return for his support of Holy Roman Emperor Sigismund. We were fascinated to find that at the age of fifty-one, in 1434, Amadeus suddenly decided to pass his title to his son Louis and went off to found a semi-monastic order on the shores of Lake Geneva, where he lived the life of a hermit. Five years later, he was nominated by the Council of Basel to succeed the deposed Pope Eugene IV and was crowned Pope Felix V in 1440. Some European monarchs continued to recognise Eugene as the true pope and in 1449 Amadeus voluntarily resigned his claim to the papacy in favour of Pope Nicholas V, thereafter taking the title of papal vicar-general of the house of Savoy and soon afterwards becoming a cardinal.

Amadeus had an eventful life and when he died in 1451, he left behind him a powerful dynasty that would eventually provide all of the future kings of Italy. It was two years after Amadeus' death that his son Louis bought the shroud from Margaret, the daughter of Geoffrey de Charney.

It had seemed slightly odd to us that Geoffrey de Charney's mother, Jeanne, just happened to remarry into the family of anti-pope Clement VII. Jeanne was not from an especially well-to-do background and she had been penniless after the death in battle of her first husband. She was therefore not exactly the most obvious choice of wife for a wealthy and high-profile nobleman like Aymon of Genevainto.

Could he have married her simply because she possessed the Shroud?

When the Shroud did change hands a century later, it was to the son of another anti-pope – a descendant of a Burgundian family that had established itself in the eleventh century and whose members are likely to have been involved in the First Crusade.

It seems very probable that the Savoy family knew the secret of the Shroud, and the question that sprang to our minds was: are the Savoy family members of Rex Deus?

THE TEMPLARS LIVE ON

When Philip the Fair moved against the Templars on 13 October 1307, the Templar fleet had escaped and many members of the accused order headed for Scotland where Robert the Bruce was already excommunicated and ready to offer them shelter. This substantial Templar remnant was welcomed by the Rex Deus families of Scotland such as the St Clairs, and their beliefs continued to form the basis of what we now know as Freemasonry, Rosslyn Chapel proving the linkage between the two traditions.

However, the Templars were made up of three classes of members: the knights, priests and serving brothers, and it was only the knights who were persecuted. The serving brothers were divided into two classes: men-at-arms and craftsmen – and because the Templars had been major builders of preceptories, churches and wonderful cathedrals, the most common craftsmen amongst them were masons. It is therefore entirely probable that some elements or echoes of Templar ritual might have found their way into the continental guilds of stonemasons, and even into the less formalised masons' associations in England.

Not all of the French Templar knights escaped to Scotland. A great many died at the hands of the Inquisition, but many survived and, according to one important piece of evidence, the whole Templar Order continued in complete secrecy in France, until at least 1804. A document known as the *Charta Transmissionis* appears to contain a list of all Templar Grand Masters after the death of Jacques de Molay.

This document was first drawn up by one Johannes Marcus Larmenius who was the successor to Molay, chosen by the Grand Master as he awaited execution. When Larmenius grew old, he transmitted his power to a man called Theoboldus and he and succeeding Grand Masters thereafter appended their acceptance on the original document, down to the last holder of this exalted position, Bernard Raymond in 1804.

The Charter was written in a ciphered Latin, laid out in two columns on a very large sheet of heavily ornamented parchment with designs of architecture. The cipher works as follows:

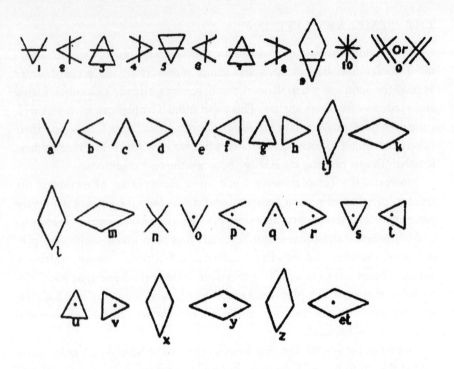

A full transcript of this Charter, which first had to be translated from the cipher into Latin and then into English, can be found in Appendix 2.

It is the unusually reverential way that Larmenius refers to Molay that is particularly interesting. He starts by saying:

> *I, Brother John Mark Larmenius, of Jerusalem, by the Grace of God and by the most secret decree of the venerable and most holy Martyr, the Supreme Master of the Knighthood of the Temple (to whom be honour and glory), confirmed by the Common Council of the Brethren, being decorated with the highest and supreme Mastership over the whole Order of the Temple, to all who shall see these Decretal letters, [wish] health, health, health.*

Further on, Larmenius again makes reference to Molay, interrupting his flow to describe him with these words:

> *. . . the very holy our above said Venerable and most blessed Master, the Martyr, to whom be honour and glory. Amen.*

These words seem to be describing someone far more holy than a past Grand Master: to us it seems more the form of address one would give to a messianic figure.

Another interesting aspect of this document is the hatred that Larmenius has, not only for the Order of the Hospitallers but for Templars who fled to Scotland, deserting their Grand Master to the abuse of Philip the Fair:

> *I, lastly, by the decree of the Supreme Assembly, by Supreme authority committed to me, will, say and order that the Scot-Templars deserters of the Order be blasted by an anathema, and that they and the brethren of St John of Jerusalem, spoilers of the demesnes of the Knighthood (on whom God have mercy), be outside the circle of the Temple, now and in the future.*

If this document is genuine, and informed scholars believe that it is, then there must have been two Templar traditions which were probably reunited by Chevalier Ramsey when he brought the Ancient Scottish Rite to Paris where Bonnie Prince Charlie was in exile.

We were now convinced that the last official Templars were worshippers of Jacques de Molay, and that any cult that arose out of them, like Freemasonry, had to have knowledge of this veneration of the crucified Grand Master. Our task now was to scour every possible source of information about the early rituals of Freemasonry to see if we could connect the story of Rex Deus, the Templars and the martyred Molay.

CONCLUSION

All of the evidence strongly suggests that Jacques de Molay was widely considered by many to be a holy martyr, and by some to be the Second Messiah who had, once again, been murdered by the Roman establishment (the Church this time instead of the army of the empire), and the devastation that swept all of Christendom was God's wrath just as had occurred on the previous occasion. Like the Jerusalem Church, the followers of Molay had been persecuted and the truth had to be carried abroad for safe keeping.

As the Black Death smote down Christendom, the Church feared that the miraculous image of Jacques de Molay that had appeared on the Shroud would let out the terrible secret that they had crucified him too. They had to keep the identity of the Shroud image hidden or they would be swept away by a new cult of Molay, just like the cult of Jesus that created them in the first place. The problem was finally headed off by the Church accepting the public display of the Shroud and encouraging people to believe that it was the image of Christ, even though they had previously denied it.

The secret knowledge went underground.

The indications are that Templarism continued in France and in Scotland and both strands venerated Molay. Larmenius, the French Grand Master who followed Molay, could not have known about the image on the Shroud because it did not go on display until long after his death. However, later Templar descendants could not fail to have realised the significance of the image.

The current owners of the Shroud, the Savoy family, have possessed it since the fifteenth century, and it seems probable that they too have always known its true origin.

Our theory that it was Jacques de Molay's image on the Shroud is further supported by the fact that the artefact was first put on display by a descendant of Geoffrey de Charney, the Templar Preceptor of Normandy, who was arrested with, and died with Jacques de Molay.

Chapter 10

THE GREAT SECRET OF FREEMASONRY

A REX DEUS RELIGION

When the Grand Lodge of London was established in 1717, the members discarded their Scottish origins because they were far too Jacobite for the Hanoverian politics of the day. Almost a century later, the United Grand Lodge of England was formed and the rituals of the 33 degrees of the Ancient Scottish Rite were considered outrageous by the new Grand Master, the Duke of Sussex, who did his best to see them changed and suffocated.

We have learned from our own experience, and from the writings of many previous researchers into Freemasonry before 1717, that it is the policy of the United Grand Lodge of England to discourage investigation into the origins of the organisation. This strongly suggested to us that something was being hidden, even from Freemasons.

Our task now was to try and find pieces of those missing degrees so that we could reassemble the lost secret of Freemasonry, which we definitely felt would connect with the beliefs and history of Rex Deus and the martyrdom of Jacques de Molay. There was no easy starting point, so we set about a trawl of every old book on the rituals of Freemasonry that we could find. Nothing that we came across seemed to deal with the discarded rituals that we needed and we began to fear that the censors had been more thorough than we had hoped.

As we were delving through various Masonic volumes, Tim Wallace-Murphy rang to tell us that his Rex Deus informant had made contact again. During the conversation, Tim had told him about our research and he was most interested and had responded to some of the ideas that we were developing.

Tim had asked the Frenchman if he had ever heard of a building called Rosslyn. He had not, so Tim then enquired if he had ever heard of a medieval reconstruction of Herod's Temple, built in Europe. He replied that such an idea seemed quite probable and he spontaneously said that, if we were to find such a building, we must concentrate our interests on the west wall. When pressed by Tim to explain why the west wall was important, he said that he did not know the reason, but he remembered his father stressing that 'the west wall was key'.

If this was coincidence it was a very strange one, because it is the west wall of Rosslyn that has been confirmed to be a replica of the Herodian ruin in Jerusalem.

Tim then asked his contact if he had ever heard of a Rex Deus ring (such as we had been told about by Russell Barnes). The answer came that he had been told of two rings, one with two pillars on it and one with one pillar on it which has a serpent wrapped around it.

Tim had not told his contact anything about the importance of pillars to our story and for him to have described the rings in this way is of significance. The single pillar with the snake wrapped around it does sound remarkably like the Boaz pillar in Rosslyn, which has a vine spiralling around it. Our earlier assumption that there should be two rings appeared to be correct, but we had been wrong about each having a single but different pillar. We assume that the ring with the single pillar represents the house of David, the kingly line, and the twin pillar ring represents the joint messiah.

The Rex Deus man went on to tell of other very interesting information:

- The colours of the royal house of David are green and gold.
- The Stuart dynasty were members of Rex Deus.
- William I of England (William the Bastard) was from a Rex Deus family, and his son, William II, had been assassinated when he planned to replace Roman Catholicism with Rex Deus beliefs as the official religion of England.

On this last point, Tim enquired what he meant by 'Rex Deus beliefs'. He was told that they amounted to something very similar to Celtic Christianity. This reply fits exactly with what we would expect, as we already knew the Celtic Church was built on Jewish-Christian beliefs, including the rejection of the idea that Jesus was a god. From other research, we have every reason to believe that the founders of this Church in Ireland and Scotland – St Patrick and St Columba – were themselves Jewish.

If William II had considered establishing a Rex-Deus-based religion in England, it would have been quite disastrous for the mission in Jerusalem because the Vatican would hunt down everyone suspected of having contact with the heresy. William was killed on 2 August 1100, while on a hunting trip in the New Forest in Hampshire, and it has often been speculated that he was murdered for reasons unknown. We note that he, Pope Urban II – the initiator of the First Crusade – and Godfrey de Bouillon – the victor of the First Crusade – all died within months of each other. Could there have been a 'hit squad' established to ensure that the mission in Jerusalem was not put in jeopardy?

That the Stuarts were a Rex Deus family did not surprise us because, when James VI of Scotland went to London to become James I of England, he brought Freemasonry with him, which is a form of the Rex Deus 'doctrine' and tells the story of the rebuilding of the Holy Temple. The Anglican Bible is the King James version, which drops the last two books of the Old Testament, the Books of Maccabees, because they are anti-Nasorean.[1] James Stuart was also remarkably candid about his dislike of the Roman Catholic Church, as can be seen from the words he used to introduce his version of the Bible:

> . . . So that if, on the one side, we shall be traduced by Popish
> Persons at home or abroad, who therefore will malign us because we
> are poor instruments to make God's holy Truth to be more and
> more known to the people, whom they desire still to keep in
> ignorance and darkness . . .

The information from Tim's contact certainly seemed to be of very high quality, as the Frenchman's comments fitted well with facts that he could not have known.

---

[1] C. Knight & R. Lomas: *The Hiram Key*

THE MISSING RITUALS

Reading through various papers that could be of possible interest, we came across a strange but fascinating statement given in a lecture entitled 'Freemasonry and Catholicism' in May 1940:

> *Christ betrayed the secret word of Masonry . . . to the people, and*
> *he proclaimed it in Jerusalem, but in saying the Senate word to folk,*
> *he was before his time . . . Let Masons receive Christ back into*
> *Masonry . . . Masonry has been the expression of Christianity for*
> *the last 2000 years.*[2]

Powerful words indeed, and ones that we believed to be correct. As the kingly messiah from the royal line of David, Jesus had been initiated into the highest order of the Nasorean movement which involved a ritual where the candidate underwent a figurative death before being resurrected to a new life in the order. Jesus knew that time was short and so he 'turned the water into wine' (made unclean people into righteous people) by baptising them and we believe he gave his principal followers the secret of the living resurrection which is still used by Freemasons today.

The name of the lecturer meant nothing to us and we tried to find out more about him.

The man who spoke those words was Dimitrije Mitrinovic, a Balkan scholar from Bosnia-Herzegovina, who came to live in London around the time of the First World War. He became a leading figure in the 'Bloomsbury Group' which was a collective of intellectuals who were mainly English. This group took its name from the district near the British Museum in central London where most of the members lived and was made up of prominent thinkers who were individually known for their contributions to the arts or the social sciences. It included people such as Virginia Woolf and her husband, Leonard; the economist John Maynard Keynes and the novelist and essayist E. M. Forster.

It had taken us seven years of wide-ranging research, including specialist Masonic knowledge, to come to our view, so how had Mitrinovic arrived at the same conclusion? We could find nothing more written by Mitrinovic and we were about to give up when we came across a reference to the fact that

[2] D. Mitrinovic: *Freemasonry and Catholicism in the New Order. Lectures 1926–1950*

he had built up a considerable personal library which may have survived him.

We made enquiries at all of the obvious places, but we could find no trace of this missing collection that we felt could contain the information we needed. Phone call after phone call drew a complete blank – but our persistence eventually paid off.

A call to one university, which was well down our list of possible repositories for such a collection, at first gave us the usual answer:

'Sorry,' the lady said in a pleasant manner, 'there is nothing under that name here.'

Just as we were about to thank her for her time, and move to the next one on the list, she suddenly sounded more hopeful:

'Oh, wait just a moment. I want to ask my colleague about a collection that hasn't been catalogued yet. I seem to remember that it had an eastern-European-sounding name.'

There was a small thud as the phone was placed on the desk and then silence for a couple of minutes before she returned.

'You did say the person's name was Mitrinovic, spelt M-I-T-R-I-N-O-V-I-C, didn't you? Well, you're in luck – the collection is here, but it is uncatalogued.'

At last we had tracked down Mitrinovic's personal library, and now we needed to find out if he had collected books that would hold what we were looking for.

We soon managed to gain permission to study the collection and found that Mitrinovic had indeed assembled a number of rare and important Masonic books, including a few that dealt with the older, and unadulterated, rituals of most degrees. As we pored over the many volumes, we were not disappointed. Dimitrije Mitrinovic's superb collection of books by nineteenth- and early twentieth-century Masonic researchers allowed us to build up a revealing picture of the main points of the rituals of these 'lost' higher degrees of Freemasonry.

What we found was simply staggering.

We used several books to reconstruct the key elements of these damaged degrees, the most significant being *Freemasonry and the Ancient Gods*, written by J.S.M. Ward and published in 1921. Unlike most Masonic researchers and writers of his time, Ward has an interesting writing style and an open mind. He was a fellow of several Royal Societies including the Royal Anthropological Society, a prizeman of Trinity Hall, Cambridge, and a highly qualified Freemason. The book that had found its way into our hands was the result of fourteen years' research, prompted by the same feelings of doubt that we had experienced when we looked at the official history of Freemasonry.

Ward was a fair-minded and rigorous scholar who clinically analysed the work of preceding researchers, sometimes pointing out errors in their judgement and sometimes accepting their evidence, although he may have been rejecting their conclusions. We know we would have liked this man and we are grateful that he was encouraged by Freemasons at the time to put his findings into print. He politely demonstrates where such accepted luminaries of Masonic history as Gould made serious errors when trying to follow a rigid line of thinking, assuming that the official dogma was correct and only needed illuminating.

Some of the lost or damaged degrees appear quite ordinary, but others tell a story that made our eyes stand out on stalks because it was one that we recognised very well indeed.

The fourth degree is called 'Secret Master' and is concerned with mourning the death of someone unspecified. The lodge room is hung with black and lit by eighty-one candles, and the jewel of the degree bears the letter 'Z' which is said to refer to Zadok.

During enactment of the ritual, the significance of the treasures of the Temple, such as the Altar of Incense, the Golden Candlestick and the Table of Shewbread, is listed and explained. The candidate is warned not to aspire to anything for which he is unfit, and that he must obey the call of *'duty inexorable as Fate'*. The degree ritual is set at the time when all work on the Temple has been suspended owing to a certain tragedy. The lessons of the degree are to remind the candidate of the importance of *Duty* and *Secrecy*.

This ritual rang several bells for us. We had established that the Knights Templar excavated below the ruins of Herod's Temple, most probably in search of the treasures placed there by their ancestors shortly before the fall of Jerusalem in AD 70. According to Jewish legend, Zadok was the first High Priest of Jerusalem. He made Solomon king and therefore he was a founder of Rex Deus. Amongst the Dead Sea Scrolls, found in Qumran in 1947, is the all-important Copper Scroll that lists where the treasures and holy scrolls were hidden below Herod's Temple and surrounding areas. This scroll also says that a duplicate of itself, with even more information, has been placed under the Temple. Entry 52 says:

*Below the Portico's southern corner in the Tomb of Zadok, under
the platform of the exedra: vessels for tithe sweepings, spoilt tithes,
and inside them, figured coins.*[3]

This Portico is a double arcade running at the eastern extremity of the
Temple, and the southern corner is the pinnacle from where James, the
brother of Jesus, was thrown down. Furthermore, John Allegro, an expert on
the Copper Scroll, believed that this Tomb could not have been that of the
first High Priest, which would have been outside the walls. He says that it
could easily be a reference to the tomb of Jesus's brother, James the Just,
which has a twin-pillared façade before a covered porch or *exedra*.

James was called *the Just* (in Hebrew 'Zadok') or the *Teacher of
Righteousness* (in Hebrew 'Moreh-zedok'). After he was thrown from the
pinnacle, he was stoned and finally dispatched with a blow to his temple
from a fuller's club, on the spot where his tomb now stands. This occurred
in AD 62, shortly before the completion of the Temple, and it is certain that
the Jewish workers would have stopped work as a mark of respect for their
spiritual leader.

The Hebrew word 'Zadok' is exactly the same as 'Tsedeq', which was the
priestly pillar that matched the kingly pillar of 'Mishpat'.

The Dead Sea Scrolls, and another ancient document found early in the
twentieth century, tell us that a group called *The Sons of Zadok* sprang up
and became the community at Qumran that wrote the Dead Sea Scrolls.[4]
This would mean that 'The Sons of Zadok' was the Hebrew/Aramaic title for
the descendants of the priestly line that came to be known as Rex Deus at
some point after the fall of the Temple in AD 70.

The term 'The Sons of Zadok' is repeated throughout the Dead Sea
Scrolls, and other appellations are given to this group, such as ' the Righteous
Seed' and 'the Sons of Dawn'. This brings to mind their hereditary transmis-
sion of holiness and the fact that, since the times of the Ancient Egyptian
kings, resurrection has always occurred at dawn with the rising of the morning star. Freemasons today are ritually 'resurrected' under the light of the
morning star.

The next degree, known as 'Perfect Master', is said to concern the discovery and reburial of the body of Hiram Abif, a character said to have been

[3] J. M. Allegro: *The Treasure of the Copper Scroll*
[4] H.H. Rowley: 'Apocalyptic Literature', *Peake's Commentary on the Bible*

killed by a blow to the head just before the completion of the first Temple at
Jerusalem.

It is important here to mention the technique called 'pesher' which was
extremely significant to the people of Jerusalem in the first century, and is
present throughout the Dead Sea Scrolls. The technique involved looking at
events recorded in long-past Jewish history and going through them and saying, 'The pesher of this is . . .' They would then describe events in their own
time that appeared to be described long before by holy men.

The killing of James the Just could easily have been considered a pesher
of the killing of the man Freemasons now know as Hiram Abif ('the king that
was lost'). Hiram Abif was killed by a blow to his head, rather than betray a
secret that he had been entrusted with. This occurred just before the completion of Solomon's Temple, almost exactly a thousand years before James
the Just was killed by a blow to his head, for refusing to answer a question
that was secret, just before the completion of Herod's Temple. Therefore, the
pesher of the Hiram Abif story is the death of James, the joint messiah of the
Jews.

For this degree, the lodge room is hung in green and is lit by sixteen
candles, four at each cardinal point. The story told is that, at the death of
Hiram Abif, Solomon was anxious to pay a tribute of respect to his friend
and so he ordered Adoniram to build a tomb for the body. Within nine days,
a splendid tomb was built along with an obelisk of black-and-white marble.
Exactly like the tomb of James, the entrance is set between two pillars which
support a square stone with the initial 'J' engraved on it.

The ritual of the sixth to the twelfth degrees of the Ancient Scottish Rite
contain some interesting references, but nothing directly relevant to our
researches. The thirteenth degree is 'The Royal Arch of Enoch' or 'The
Master of the Ninth Arch' and it is set at the time of the building of
Solomon's Temple three thousand years ago. It is very much a 'pesher' of the
Holy Royal Arch Degree, which is the story of the Knights Templar removing a keystone in the ruins of Herod's Temple and lowering themselves down
into a subterranean vault that contains an ancient scroll.[5]

The degree tells how, in times long before Moses and Abraham, the
ancient figure of Enoch foresees that the world will be overwhelmed by an
apocalyptic disaster through flood or fire, and he determines to preserve at
least some of the knowledge then known to man, that it may be passed on to

[5] C. Knight & R. Lomas: *The Hiram Key*

future civilisations of survivors. He therefore engraves in hieroglyphics the great secrets of science and building on to two pillars: one made of brick and the other of stone.

The Masonic legend goes on to tell how these pillars were almost destroyed, but sections survived the Flood and were subsequently discovered – one by the Jews, the other by the Egyptians – so that civilisation could be rebuilt from the secrets that had been engraved on to them. Fragments of one pillar were found by workmen during the excavations for the foundations of King Solomon's Temple. Whilst preparing the site in Jerusalem three thousand years ago the top of a vault or arch was uncovered, and one of the masons was lowered into the vault where he found relics of the great pillar of knowledge.

This has the hallmark of an ancient Jewish legend that one would expect to be passed down the generations of the 'Sons of Zadok' or, to use their current name, the Rex Deus families. We believe that it is an attempt to explain how the Jews believe that they came into the possession of great secrets that were also known to the ancient Egyptians.

The next degree, 'Scotch Knight of Perfection', is set in a room which has at its centre the reassembled fragments of Enoch's pillar, inscribed with hieroglyphics. It is claimed that King Solomon created a 'Lodge of Perfection' to rule over the thirteen lower degrees, and its members held their first secret meeting in the sacred vault of Enoch beneath the partly constructed Temple of Solomon.

This sounds very much like a description of the founding of Rex Deus. The legend claims that Solomon's Temple was built using ancient knowledge that had been passed down to the Jews from a previous civilisation destroyed in the flood. In our last book we detected that the story of the pillars did indeed predate the flood and had passed to ancient Egypt from the land of Sumer, which is the oldest civilisation recorded.[6]

On the pedestal of this degree there are three things: bread, wine and a gold ring for the newly admitted brother! Suddenly, in the degree which seems to refer to the establishment of Rex Deus, we have come across the description of a ring that is worn by all initiates. Could this explain the idea of a Rex Deus ring that we had suspected?

The ritual goes on to recall how other masters become jealous of the hon-

---

[6] C. Knight & R. Lomas: *The Hiram Key*

ours conferred on the members of the Lodge of Perfection and they demand the same honours. King Solomon refuses to let the secrets pass to them and tells them that those whom he had advanced to the Degree of Perfection '*had wrought in the difficult and dangerous work of the ancient ruins, had penetrated into the bowels of the earth and had brought out treasures to adorn the Temple*'. The discontented masters try to enter the Sacred Vault themselves and all are killed, with no trace of them remaining.

The traditional history of this degree tells a story of Solomon's betrayal of Yahweh when, in his later years, the king set up temples in honour of other gods, allegedly to please his many wives. The Perfect Masons were much grieved with this conduct, but, though they kept their faith pure, they were unable to avert the wrath of God, which ultimately led to the destruction of the Temple.

The ritual then takes a particularly interesting turn.

It says that at some later date, descendants of these Perfect Masons accompanied the Christian princes on their Crusades to the Holy Land, from which time onwards these descendants of Solomon's priesthood elected their own Chief. Their valour brought forth the admiration of all the Christian princes of Jerusalem and some of the latter, believing that their mysterious rites inspired them with courage and virtue, asked to be initiated. Their request was granted and eventually their secrets became diffused among the nobility of Europe as Freemasonry.

Here, in the fourteenth degree of the Ancient Scottish Rite of Freemasonry, lies an unarguable confirmation of the acknowledged existence of a group within the forces of the First Crusade who were descended from the Jews who fled Jerusalem after AD 70. The idea that they soon initiated non-members into this Rex Deus order may be a literal truth, or it might be a description of the way that it later developed into a wider organisation and became known as Freemasonry.

Tim Wallace-Murphy's informant had claimed this genealogy, and here was an obscure Scottish Rite ritual confirming such a link! Furthermore, it appears to tell us that as a reward they (the Knights Templar) were allowed, by the new Christian princes of Jerusalem (Baldwin), to elect their own Chief (Grand Master) and that these Christian princes were inspired to join the ranks of the order that would eventually become Freemasonry.

This one degree of Freemasonry has confirmed the whole structure of our hypothesis: there was an ancient hereditary priesthood in Jerusalem that started at the time of King Solomon; these priests did come to Europe and their descendants did return with the Crusader armies to retake their lost city; they did re-establish the ancient rituals and they eventually allowed non-descendants to join; these rituals that were used in Jerusalem for a thousand years, up to the destruction of the Temple in AD 70, did survive as Freemasonry.

The fifteenth degree, 'Knight of the Sword and Knight of the East', is the first part of the Allied Masonic degree of the Knight of the Red Cross of Babylon which we have already discussed in detail in Chapter 2, as it figures in the stonework of Rosslyn in the form of the quotation regarding the strength of truth compared with women, kings and wine. The degree deals with the rebuilding of Zerubbabel's Temple after the Babylonian Captivity of the Jews and the chamber is illuminated by seventy candles in memory of each year of the Captivity. It tells of the return to Jerusalem of the exiled Jews, in great detail that must have been passed down the generations by the Rex Deus families. The colour of the sash worn in this degree is green with a gold fringe: very appropriately, the colours of the house of David.

The next degree is a continuation of the previous Allied Masonic degree of the Knight of the Red Cross of Babylon. The two key individuals are named as the Most Equitable Sovereign Prince Master and the High Priest, and one of the lesser officers is titled Valorous Keeper of the Seals and Archives. This is followed by a degree called the 'Knight of the East and West' which concludes the Allied Masonic degree of the Knight of the Red Cross of Babylon.

Whilst all previous degrees have been focused on the Old Testament, this one leaps forward to deal with the Book of Revelations, mentioning the 'seven seals' and the 'wrath of the lamb'. Everything so far was extremely interesting but then, as we read the next section, our hair stood on end!

The ritual states that the degree was organised by knights engaged in the Crusades in the year 1118, when eleven knights took vows of secrecy, friendship and discretion at the hands of the Patriarch of Jerusalem.

This is an unambiguous reference to the Knights Templar who were founded in 1118!

Unbelievably, many people who style themselves as Masonic historians know nothing of the details of these degrees, and others have wondered why the degree names eleven knights and not the nine who are recorded as founding the Knights Templar. Some have, quite amazingly, tried to use this numerical discrepancy to argue that this must be a reference to some other (otherwise unrecorded) group of knights formed in Jerusalem in 1118.

The reality is far simpler. We have already identified the eleven men who colluded to excavate below Herod's Temple, namely:

1. Hugues de Payen.
2. Geoffrey de St Omer
3. André de Montbard
4. Payen de Montdidier
5. Achambaud de St-Amand
6. Gondemare
7. Rosal
8. Godefroy
9. Geoffroy Bisol

These were the original nine (see page 73). They were then (see pages 83–4) joined by:

10. Fulk of Anjou
11. Hugh of Champagne

The presiding officer is called the 'Most Equitable Sovereign Prince Master', supported by the High Priest. It struck us that the High Priest would have been the Grand Master of the Templar Order, running from Hugues de Payen through to Jacques de Molay, and the more senior person was probably the Rex Deus figure to whom the Templars swore obedience, possibly the kings of Jerusalem from Baldwin II onwards.

The chamber is hung with red, spangled with gold stars. In the east, under a canopy, is a throne elevated on seven steps and supported by the figures of four lions and four eagles between which is an eagle with six wings. On one side of the throne is displayed a burning light, said to represent the sun at high noon, and on the other is a depiction of the moon. In the east there are two vases, one for perfume and one for water. (We know from our previous investigations into the resurrection practices of the Ancient Egyptians that at every king's grave two empty vases have been found and nobody now knows what they once contained.)

On a pedestal in the east is a large Bible from which seven seals are suspended. The floor displays a heptagon within a circle, over the angles of which appear certain letters, and in the centre is the figure of a white-bearded man clothed in white with a golden girdle around his waist. In his extended hand he holds seven stars which are said to represent the qualities that should distinguish a brother: friendship, union, submission, discretion, fidelity, prudence and temperance. The strange apparition is completed with a halo around his head, a two-edged sword issuing from his mouth, and seven candlesticks placed around him.

At this point, we felt that this undeniable Templar link was proof of everything that we had already reconstructed from other evidence, but there was much more to follow.

The twentieth degree known as 'Grand Master' is about the building of the Fourth or spiritual Temple. The historical lecture of the degree tells of the destruction of the Third Temple by the Romans under Titus in AD 70, and how the Brethren who were in Palestine at that terrible epoch were filled with grief at its loss. They left the Holy Land and determined to erect a Fourth Temple that would be a spiritual edifice. We are then told that these people who somehow escaped the mass slaughter in Jerusalem divided themselves into a number of lodges and dispersed throughout Europe.

There could be no clearer retelling of the Rex Deus story than this! Here was the evidence of a degree that is probably medieval, that spells out that the survivors of the battle of Jerusalem in AD 70 did indeed become dispersed throughout Europe, just as the Rex Deus informant had claimed.

The degree goes on to say that one of these groups eventually came to Scotland, establishing a lodge at Kilwinning. The description that one group 'eventually' came to Scotland is very accurate because the St Clairs did not arrive until close to the end of the eleventh century.

We are then told that it was at Kilwinning that these people took the records of their order to be stored in an abbey built in 1140. The Masonic researcher, J.S.M. Ward, states that there seems to be a problem here, observing:

One group came to Scotland and established a Lodge at Kilwinning, and there deposited the records of the Order in an abbey they built there. At this point the first historical difficulty arose, for the abbey was not built till about 1140, and the legend does not state where they were during the period between AD. 70 and AD. 1140.

This fact caused Ward some confusion back in 1921, but it was now plain to us. We know precisely where they were between those dates: the records were hidden beneath the ruins of Herod's Temple, prior to being removed between 1118 and 1128 by the Knights Templar! We also have extremely strong grounds to believe that these ancient documents were taken to be re-interred at Rosslyn in 1140.

The existence of this degree has a monumental impact on everything we have found to date. Described as the 'Grand Master of all Symbolic Lodges' this ritual has a retrospect that tells of the fall of the Nasoreans in AD 70 and how the progenitors of Freemasonry left Jerusalem at that time to spread across Europe; exactly as the Rex Deus informant had claimed! One group, it says, found its way to Scotland to establish a lodge at Kilwinning, an early home of the St Clair family!

The ritual of the twenty-first degree turns the clock back by telling the story of the Tower of Babel and its architect, Peleg. It recalls how Peleg is struck dumb by God for attempting to build a tower to reach up to heaven and he then wanders across Europe, at length settling in the forests of Prussia where he builds a triangular house. Here he laments his former pride and passes his days in prayer to the Almighty who eventually forgives him and restores his power of speech.

The special lesson of the degree is humility. Peleg is said to be a descendant of Noah (the Bible suggests that he was also an ancestor of Jesus Christ), this descent from Noah being via Ham, the grandson of Noah, who the legend says was the first king of Egypt, taking the title 'Osiris' – which is said to have the literal meaning 'Prince who had arisen from the dead'.

In our previous book, we had reconstructed the lost king-making ritual of Ancient Egypt and followed the path of the resurrection rite from Thebes to Jerusalem. We had come to the conclusion that the secret ritual that Jesus 'betrayed' was concerning Osiris and Horus, and that Jesus was himself the 'Prince who had arisen from the dead', by virtue of the living resurrection ceremony.

We found that in the next degree, 'Prince of Libanus', everyone carries a sword and the ritual makes the candidate a member of the Round Table. This ritual states that there are two rooms, and the craftsmen conduc their work in the smaller lower room exactly as we know was the case at Rosslyn in the mid-fifteenth century. Another interesting connection between the Round Table and Rosslyn is the fact that Arthurian-legend knights were buried in their armour, ready to return to defend the realm in time of need, and it is believed that the St Clairs were buried in full armour beneath Rosslyn, to return when a bell is rung to recall them.

The degree called 'Chief of the Tabernacle' comes next, and it explains how the Order of Priesthood was founded by Aaron and his sons Eleazar and Ithamar. The members of the degree are called Levites, after the ancient line of Jewish priests, and they wear white with red edging. The candidate is made a priest and enters an inner chamber which is draped in black and contains an altar and a stool on which are three skulls and a full skeleton. In the chamber is an inscription which reads: '*If you are fearful, go from hence; it is not permitted for men who cannot brave danger without abandoning virtue.*' In this degree there are two High Priests and a principal officer called the Sovereign Grand Sacrificer who wears a golden mitre – this being the head-dress of the creator god of Thebes, Amon-Re, and that of James, the first Bishop of Jerusalem. We are as certain as it is possible to be that the High Priest of Yahweh always wore this head-dress, from the time of Moses onwards, because it is recorded that James, the brother of Jesus, wore the breastplate and mitre of the High Priest when he entered the Temple.

Next, we found a degree that tells how Moses was instructed by God to build the Tabernacle, or sacred tent, for housing the Ark of the Covenant. Called the 'Prince of the Tabernacle' it explains how, by setting up a tabernacle for God, Moses established the royal line of the Jews.

The candidate in this degree is made a High Priest and told that he is now permitted to adore the Most High under the name of Jehovah (an alternative rendering of Yahweh), which is said to be much more expressive than Adonai. He is told that in his progress through the degrees, he has now received the Masonic Science as descended from King Solomon and revived by the Knights Templar.

We could not believe our eyes! Here we have a specific reference to the Knights Templar as the people who reinstated the lost knowledge of the Jews.

Everything that we had deduced from our studies was spelt out here in an obscure and ancient Masonic ritual. The rituals of Freemasonry actually record what we had reconstructed from our own sources, from Tarot cards to Arthurian legend. The Knights Templar had indeed set themselves up as the new priesthood of Yahweh, and to do that they must have been the descendants of the original priesthood. Our anonymous Rex Deus friend was right.

This ritual then goes on to say that the newly made High Priest is told the history of the Royal Art of Masonry which is traced from the Creation through Noah, Abraham, Moses and Solomon, and other important personages, down to Hugues de Payen, the founder of the Templars, and thence to the tragic figure of Jacques de Molay, their last Grand Master. All

Templar Grand Masters were clearly regarded as the High Priest of Yahweh.

Once he has been made a High Priest, the *Grand Word* is revealed to him and he is told that it was discovered by the Knights Templar while in Jerusalem. So far, we have been unable to find this missing Grand Word, as it never seems to have been written down. From the context, it must be another name for God, but the wilful destruction of the old ritual by the Duke of Sussex has denied us whatever insights the knowledge of this word might have conveyed. The legend says that when digging under the spot whereon the Holy of Holies had stood in the heart of Mount Moriah, the Templars discovered three stones, on one of which this word was engraved. When they had to leave Palestine, they carried these relics with them and used them as the foundation stones of their first lodge in Scotland, which event took place on St Andrew's Day. This secret has ever since been transmitted to their successors, who are entitled to be known as the High Priests of Jehovah. Perhaps the Duke of Sussex may yet be thwarted in his attempts to destroy Truth, if this stone proves to be one of the relics buried beneath Rosslyn.

The Masonic historian Arthur Waite observed that there is a Masonic tradition which says that Jesus was schooled in special knowledge, and that he conferred initiation on his apostles and disciples, dividing them into several orders and placing them under the general authority of St John. This doctrine, containing knowledge of the mystic and hierarchic initiations of Egypt, as transmitted by Christ, came into the keeping of Hugues de Payen, the first Master of the New Temple, in 1118, who was then invested with apostolic and patriarchal power, thereby becoming the lawful successor to original Johannite Christianity.

This tradition was a memory even back in the early years of this century, but it seems certain that it was once the central theme of Masonic belief. The idea that the true apostolic succession rested not with the pope but with the Grand Master of the Knights Templar makes it clear why the Hierophant card of the Tarot was mistaken for the image of a pope. It also explains why the early English Freemasons were terrified of the content of these degrees, and the reason for their suppression becomes clear.

For us this degree was a breakthrough – proof positive of our central hypothesis. Hugues de Payen is identified as the reinstated High Priest of Yahweh (Jehovah) and the office is passed down the Templar Grand Masters through to Jacques de Molay – and the Knights Templar are credited with finding the secrets whilst digging under the ruined Temple, and taking them to Scotland!

Everything that we had pieced together in our previous book was being borne out by the content of these obscure and almost-destroyed rituals. We continued to read about the next degree with mounting excitement.

The degree was founded in Palestine, at the time of the Crusades, by a military and monastic order. It alludes to the healing and saving virtues of the 'brazen serpent' among the Israelites, for it was part of the obligation of the knights to nurse sick travellers and protect them from the infidel. The serpent is used in Craft Masonry to join the straps of the apron. This has all kinds of echoes: the serpent entwined around the Rex Deus pillar, and the fact that the Essenes were famous healers and their symbol of a staff with an entwined snake has been adopted as the badge of modern medicine.

The next degree, 'Prince of Mercy', had no great significance for us, but the twenty-seventh degree of the 'Grand Commander of the Temple' was quite amazing. This is said to be a chivalric and military degree where the body which confers the degree is called a 'Court' and its members sit at a round table around the candidate to interrogate him. The ritual tells of the false condemnation of the Knights Templar and the importance of the denial of the cross.

We could find few details about this, but Arthur Waite had noted something that he found distasteful. We thought it completely electrifying. He observed that the cross used in this degree used to be inscribed with two sets of initials: JN and JBM. The shocked Masonic historian stated that he was told that these stood for Jesus Nazareus and Jacques Burgundus Molay.

This was too good to be true. We expected to be able to find material in these ancient degrees that would support our core hypothesis, but we never dreamed that we would find confirmation spelled out so dramatically and decisively. The first and the second crucified messiahs, accommodated on the same cross!

Without doubt, the last Templars and the founders of Freemasonry must have considered Jacques de Molay to be the Second Messiah.

Freemasonry had ceased to be a secret cult when it was converted into a respectable gentlemen's club in early-eighteenth-century London, and we could now understand why the Masons wanted to neuter the ancient tradition, to convert it into something altogether less theologically controversial. Fortunately, like most censors, they were less than a hundred per cent effective and they failed to erase completely all trace of the old knowledge that they so despised.

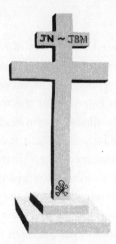

The cross used in Masonic ritual that bears the initials of the first and second messiahs

The degrees of the Ancient Scottish Rite had produced far more than we ever dared to hope. We could expect no more as we read on, but we found even more evidence to support our earlier deductions. The twenty-eighth degree of the 'Knight of the Sun' claims that it is the Key of Masonry. It teaches the doctrines of the natural religion of the 'One True God' which, it says, is the essential part of the ancient mysteries and ceremonies.

This idea of 'One True God' is central to Freemasonry, but is often said to be in collision with the distinctly arrogant belief of most Christians who describe the gods of other religions as false and without standing. Freemasonry is based on the idea that God has always existed and will always exist. He has simply taken many names, as people have perceived Him differently, including Marduk, Amon-Re, Yahweh and Allah.

The degree describes all the Masonic symbols, and the overall purpose is given as the inculcation of truth. A lecture on truth is delivered in sections by nine officers who are called Thrice Perfect Father Adam, Brother Truth, Michael, Gabriel, Raphael, Zaphriel, Camael, Azrael and Uriel. Over the entrance to the chamber where the degree is conferred is written: '*Ye who have not the power to subdue passion, flee from this place of truth*'.

The last seven names used in this degree are those of the major angels. The Frenchman who told the story of the two schools of Jerusalem at the time of Jesus said that the high priests of Yahweh used these names for themselves. Perhaps as the new high priesthood of Yahweh, the Knights Templar also took these names.

The emphasis on 'truth' brought back to mind the sole inscription in Rosslyn that ends: '. . . *truth will conquer all*'.

The twenty-ninth degree has three possible names: the 'Knight of St Andrew', the 'Patriarch of the Crusades' or 'Grand Master of Light'. It is said to have originated when the Knights Templar fled from Palestine, bringing with them the relics of the pillar of Enoch, and used three of its stones to form the foundation of the first lodge of Knight Masons in Scotland. The purpose of the degree was:

> *to pursue the virtues of charity, philanthropy, universal tolerance,*
> *the protection of the innocent, the pursuance of truth, the defence of*
> *justice, reverence and obedience to the Divine, with the expiration of*
> *fanaticism and intolerance.*

We could not help but recall that this ritual dates from a time when the Roman Catholic Church was slaughtering anyone and everyone who dared to have a thought of their own in their heads. Those who practised this degree clearly wanted to defeat such blind ignorance.

We read that the following degree, the 'Knight of the Black and White Eagle', originally gave details of the fate of Jacques de Molay, but unfortunately we have, so far, been unable to find these. The ritual goes on to relate that the knights of the degree have to vow vengeance on those responsible for his death, and take on the duty of continuing the rebuilding of the Spiritual Temple in the tradition of the Templars.

We can't help wondering whether it was the 'Knights of the Black and White Eagle' who despatched King Philip the Fair.

The thirty-first degree, known as 'Grand Inspector Inquisitor Commander', is a purely administrative degree, but the penultimate degree returns to the subject of Jacques de Molay. The degree is conferred in an assembly called a 'Grand Consistory' which is hung in black, and on the hangings are depicted skeletons, tears and emblems of mortality, embroidered in silver. The letters JM in memory of Jacques de Molay are hung above the pedestal of the principal officer called the Thrice Illustrious Commander. The candidate is told of something called 'the Royal Secret of the death of Jacques de Molay'. Unfortunately, this Royal Secret appears never to have been written down.

The use of the word 'royal' strongly suggests that Molay may be considered to be the last of the royal line of King David! Perhaps this degree, in its original form, actually described the crucifixion of this Second Messiah.

As far as we know, the thirty-third degree, of the 'Sovereign Grand Inspector General', is the highest rank that any Freemason can attain.

Facts are sparse, but we know that the lodge is set out with a dais with the name Yahweh in Hebrew in the east, and in the centre is a square pedestal on which are a Bible and a sword. In the north there is another pedestal, displaying a skeleton which holds a poniard in its right hand and the banner of the Order in its left. In the west is a throne raised on three steps, before which is a triangular altar.

All we know for sure of this ultimate degree is that it once told the secret of the founding of the Order and described its ancient origins.

The one clue to the content of this degree came from our friend Robert Temple, a multi-talented Sanskrit scholar who has an encyclopaedic knowledge of advanced physics and anthropology. He is the author of many diverse and fascinating books, including *The Sirius Mystery*, in which he published the first explanation of how the Ancient Egyptians built their edifices on earth, in replication of the layout of certain star groups.

Although he has lived in London for many years, Robert is an American, a direct descendant of one of his country's most famous Freemasons, George Washington, and his family have been Freemasons for well over two hundred years. Shortly after Robert had published *The Sirius Mystery*, he was contacted by an elderly relative who was a 33 degree Freemason. This gentleman told Robert that his book was more correct than he could possibly have imagined and that there was much that he wanted to tell him. Unfortunately, he could not, because Robert would have to be a member of the 33rd degree himself to be told these things, and Robert was not a Freemason at all.

He suggested to Robert that he could join and seek to get an accelerated promotion, so that he could hear these secret things apparently connected with Ancient Egypt and the importance of the stars, but unfortunately, the elderly gentleman died shortly afterwards.

We know that this final degree is concerned with the secret of the ancient founding of the Order and its origins, and this little story of Robert Temple's suggests that the origins do lie in the resurrection and star cult of the Ancient Egyptian kings. Perhaps one day we will find out for ourselves.

THE GREAT SECRET RECONSTRUCTED

Putting all these thirty-three degrees of this ancient Masonic rite together, we have a story that tells how there was a terrible flood at a distant point in time when the secrets of the builders were almost lost. A man called Enoch, from an unknown earlier civilisation, decided to pass on precious knowledge to whatever survivors would remain, to enable them to build new cities and develop new cultures. This was achieved by carving the secrets on to two great pillars designed to withstand the anticipated destruction. The founders of the Egyptian civilisation that sprang into existence in 3200 BC are said to have found one of these pillars, and the first king of Egypt took the name 'Osiris', meaning 'Prince who had arisen from the dead'.

Fragments of the other pillar are said to have been found some time later, by the Jews, on the spot where Solomon's Temple was built three thousand years ago. To us, this sounds like a rationalisation by the early Jewish people to explain how they had come into possession of secret knowledge that predated all known history, but was also known to have been shared by the Egyptians before them. It may well have been a convenient way of avoiding crediting the Egyptians with the creation of the mysterious resurrection cult that had become so important to them. It is known that early Jewish symbolism was very Egyptian in style, and even the name Moses is Egyptian.

Such an explanation would fit the thesis of our previous book which concludes that the theology of first-century Jerusalem was largely evolved from the beliefs and legends of ancient Thebes. There is a strong indication that the Masonic story of the killing of Hiram Abif is a first-century Jewish pesher of the killing of James, 'Zadok', the brother of Jesus. It seems very likely that the line of priests who were the ancestors of the Rex Deus families were known from ancient times as the 'Sons of Zadok'.

The Masonic story then tells us that Solomon did indeed establish a special priestly order that continued until the destruction of the Temple in AD 70, at which time it was dispersed across Europe. Then, much later, the descendants of these people returned to Jerusalem with 'Christian princes' and established a new order in 1118, when eleven knights took vows of secrecy, friendship and discretion. We are then told that these knights were the Knights Templar and that they removed fragments of Enoch's pillar, from under the Temple in Jerusalem, which they took with them, along with written records of their order, to Kilwinning in Scotland where they formed their first 'lodge'.

We are also told of the existence of a Council of the Round Table where each member carries his sword. Recalling that the Templars built round churches and preceptories, it seems highly likely that meeting at a round table became the inspiration for the Arthurian legend of the Knights of the Round Table.

The story in these hidden rituals confirms that the High Priesthood of Yahweh was re-established in Jerusalem by the Knights Templar, and that every Grand Master from Hugues de Payen to Jacques de Molay held this supreme office. They possibly wore a gold mitre when they sat on their throne between two pillars.

Amazingly, Jacques de Molay is included side by side with Jesus the Nasorean on a cross, suggesting that they were viewed as the first and second messiahs. As in the story we have heard about Rex Deus, the names of the great angels are used by leading figures, and all of Freemasonry is said to be about 'truth'. Finally, we are told that there is what is described as a 'royal secret', concerning the death of Jacques de Molay, contained within these ancient Masonic rites. Unfortunately, we have so far failed to find out what it is.

Could it contain the details of Molay's suffering and the story of the Shroud image?

The overriding message contained in these rituals is that Freemasonry has come from a source that was ancient even to the first Jews, and that its message was taught by Jesus and his brother and heir, James. From them it was transmitted to the Knights Templar who eventually passed it on to Freemasonry. At the heart of this teaching is a love of truth and a natural tolerance that embraces all monotheistic religions as being parts of God's own greater truth.

The great and unexpected secret, so carefully concealed at the heart of Freemasonry, is a belief that there was a 'Second Messiah', a High Priest of Yahweh who was crucified and eventually killed, following false accusations. Thirty-five years after the death of Jesus Christ, the land of his birth was being racked by disaster, and a huge proportion of the population was dying a horrible death. Thirty-five years after the death of Jacques de Molay, the entire world was again being racked by disaster, on a scale never seen before or since, and a huge proportion of the population was again dying a horrible death.

The strange reality is that the teachings of the Essenes in general, and Jesus in particular, died away after the first crucifixion, leading to some twelve hundred and seventy-five years of ignorance that we call 'the Dark Ages'. Following the second crucifixion, these teachings spread back out into the world and there was a renaissance of intellectualism, scientific advancement and spiritual tolerance.

It is no coincidence. The arrival of the Roman Church heralded the age of unreason and the arrival of Freemasonry was the driving force that reawakened the world to the rights of the scientist and the social democrat. Freemasons such as Francis Bacon, Sir Robert Moray, Benjamin Franklin and George Washington created a new world order. The goals that they strove for were based on the demands of Freemasonry – truth, justice, knowledge and tolerance.

Neither is it a coincidence that the Essene words that repeatedly run through the Dead Sea Scrolls are truth, righteousness, judgement, knowledge and wisdom.

The words used by Dimitrije Mitrinovic, that *'Masonry has been the expression of Christianity for the last 2000 years'*, have been shown to be entirely accurate.

OUR QUESTIONS ANSWERED

When we started on our quest, we originally set ourselves six questions. We were doubtful what we could achieve, but we have enjoyed more success than we ever imagined possible. Our questions now have answers:

1. *Have some Masonic rituals been deliberately changed or suppressed?*
It is beyond all doubt that the rituals of Freemasonry have undergone deliberate and substantial revision, particularly in England between 1717 and 1820. These changes soon spread to most of the world and attempts were made to remove any evidence of the damaged rituals' previous existence.

2. *Is there a great secret of Freemasonry that has become lost, or has been deliberately hidden?*
Those people who have accused Freemasonry of concealing a great secret from the rest of mankind were right all along – although today's Freemasons are themselves completely innocent of any conspiracy because they too have been excluded from the truth. It was hidden in the eighteenth and early nineteenth centuries by people such as the Duke of Sussex and Albert Pike.

3. *Who was behind the formation of the Knights Templar?*
We have uncovered a network of influential people from a small group of families who were involved in the taking of Jerusalem and the establishment of the Order of the Knights Templar. A man who claims to be a direct descendant of Hugues de Payen has stated that this twelfth-century group were all descended from the hereditary High Priesthood of Yahweh, established by King Solomon, known as Rex Deus – the Kings of God. From our

study of the Templar origins of the Tarot and Arthurian legends, we were able to build up a clearer picture of how these knights re-established the High Priesthood of Yahweh and re-activated the apostolic line that was snuffed out by Rome in AD 70.

The startling evidence of the damaged degrees of Scottish Rite Freemasonry fully confirms this story, and suggests that the original order may have been called 'the Sons of Zadok', which is one of the designations used by the people who wrote the Dead Sea Scrolls.

4. Why did the Templars decide to excavate beneath the ruins of Herod's Temple?

The Templars and their fellow Rex Deus members carefully planned the retaking of Jerusalem, and the subsequent excavation of the ruined Temple of Herod, to recover artefacts that were left there for them by their ancestors in AD 70. These included fragments of Enoch's pillar, huge quantities of coins and gold and silver objects, as well as scrolls which, amongst other things, are said to contain the ancient records of the Order.

5. What were the beliefs which led to the destruction of the Templars as heretics?

The evidence is strong that the Templar Order (the High Priesthood of Yahweh) knew that Jesus was a man not a god, and they asked their members to focus their love upon God rather than the false idolatry of the cross. They also considered themselves to have the true apostolic succession, the Roman pope being a respected but entirely secondary figure.

Any one of these beliefs would have lead to the Templars' destruction by the Catholic Church.

6. Can the deeper rituals of Freemasonry shed further new light on the origins of Christianity?

The solving of the mystery of the Shroud of Turin is nothing compared to the import that our findings will have for open-minded Christians. However, those who feel unable to open their minds will stick with the mythology created by the people of the Roman empire who never knew Jesus and failed to understand the Jewish theology he taught.

The old rituals of Freemasonry are not a threat to Christianity, only to ignorance. It can never serve the truth to stifle knowledge and we suggest that it is time to revisit the origins of Christianity, to see if we can reconstruct a better picture than that crudely assembled by the Roman empire after their destruction of the Jerusalem Church in AD 70. There were many great scholars who became involved in the early centuries of Christianity, but they did not have the evidence that is now available to us.

Perhaps the words of David Sinclair Bouschor, Past Grand Master of Minnesota, sum it up when he said, after reading our earlier work, that what we had found could be:

> ... the beginning of a reformation in Christian thinking and a reconsideration of 'the facts' which we have so blindly accepted and perpetuated for generations.

THE END OF THE SHROUD ENIGMA

Nothing in history can be said to be true beyond any doubt. Despite the way that conventional history and religious legends are represented as 'fact', it can only be prudent to accept the most probable solution as being the case. Until now, there has been no 'probable solution' for the seventh question which imposed itself upon us: *what is the definitive origin of the Shroud of Turin?* There were only a number of hunches, all of which contradicted either common sense or the known facts.

Now, we have an explanation for the Shroud that makes complete sense and fits all of the known facts, including the all-important carbon dating. We have provided a motive and an opportunity, as well as describing a bizarre set of circumstances that meet the essential environmental chemical conditions to produce this unique image, as defined by Dr Mills of Leicester University.

In summary we can be as sure as it is possible to be about any historic event that the Shroud of Turin does bear the image of the last Grand Master of the Templars, for the following reasons:

1. Molay was arrested at the Paris Temple where at least one shroud would have been kept for ritual purposes, just as they are kept in all Masonic temples today.
2. Molay was arrested on a charge of heresy, specifically for denying Christ and the cross. This could have prompted his priestly Inquisitor to see poetic justice in a form of torture that mimicked the treatment meted out to Jesus.

3. The French Inquisition had an established reputation for nailing people up to the nearest object as a rapid and effective torture.

4. The evidence of the bloodflows indicates that the victim was not nailed to a symmetrical cross. One arm appears to have been raised vertically above the victim's head, which would explain the apparent dislocation of the shoulder that has been speculated on for many years.

5. The physiological evidence of the image on the Shroud shows, without doubt, that the victim was placed on a large soft bed, not a stone slab. This indicates that the victim was alive and expected to recover.

6. The victim was in a coma for some twenty-four hours before the Shroud was removed, washed and put away for precisely fifty years. This was an essential requirement for the 'free radical' chemistry recently identified as the cause of the image.

7. The Shroud was first put on display by the Charney family who were descendants of the man who was arrested with Molay and later burned alive alongside him.

8. The arrest and torture of Molay occurred in October 1307, which falls neatly into the range of the date of the Shroud established by carbon 14 dating, which identified that the flax plants used to make the linen of the Shroud had ceased to be living entities some time between 1260 and 1390.

9. We know that the Knights Templar wore their hair and beards in the style of the Nasoreans, just as Jesus had done. This means that Molay would have had shoulder-length hair and a full beard, exactly as the image on the Shroud. Although physical likenesses on their own are poor evidence, we can observe that one of the few drawings of Molay happens to look remarkably like the Shroud image.

10. The Masonic rituals of the Ancient Scottish Rite tell the story of the Templars, and the appearance on the same cross of initials said to represent both Jesus Christ and Jacques de Molay suggests that there was once a wider knowledge that Molay was crucified.

The world now has a cogent and well-substantiated explanation for the strange image that appears on the Shroud of Turin. The consequences of accepting the evidence will be painful for many people because it will ask them to re-examine their preferred beliefs – but we trust, in time, truth will conquer all.

THE TOPOLOGY OF THE PAST

This is our second book concerning our quest to understand the past. We first set out on our researches with a blank piece of paper, to see what we could find out about the origins of Freemasonry. We have travelled further and wider, and continued for longer, than we ever intended, but we have enjoyed the journey, and what we have found has made all the effort more than worthwhile.

Having discovered that the inner secrets of traditional Freemasonry confirmed all of our suspicions, we suddenly felt as though we had just reached the peak of a great mountain, after battling for many years through almost impenetrable jungles and scaling the sheer walls of rock that seemed to block our path. Now we are on this summit, we can see the fantastic landscape stretched out behind us.

The path that we have followed is an ancient one that has been neglected and fallen into near ruin – but we hope others will now broaden and strengthen it. From where we now stand, it is clear to us that this path is not the only one – there are many. We can see that Freemasonry had many influences stemming out of the distant past, that re-met and re-merged centuries later. Christianity, too, has a hugely complex history, with many pathways criss-crossing and sometimes re-merging.

Some of the main pathways that are labelled 'the way of Jesus' appear to come from starting places other than first-century Jerusalem, whilst other less popular routes can be seen to run right back to the Nasoreans.

From what we can see, none of these paths has a more direct line back to the Jerusalem of Jesus and James than Freemasonry.

As we look out from our new vantage point, we can see many other hills; on top of some of them are people huddled together with their eyes squeezed shut. They are all facing inwards and repeating the same words: '*This is the only highground, there can be no other.*' These people stand on ground they call Roman Catholicism, or English Freemasonry, or a thousand other places of institutionalised thinking, and they refuse to open their eyes to take in the gigantic and wonderful landscape of other, and complementary, truths that surround them. They fear knowledge because it might show them that there are other valid places to stand, some of which might be even better than the safe and familiar hilltop they fear to examine in the context of the whole landscape.

Traditional Freemasonry had its eyes wide open when it said:

We must be tolerant of other men's religious views, because all religions have much that is true about them, and we must combat ignorance by education, bigotry by tolerance, and tyranny by teaching true liberty.

Having persevered through the twists and turns of our strange journey, recorded in this book, we hope that you will add your voice to a call for an open-minded revisiting of the past, particularly that concerning the origins of Christianity.

For ourselves, our next care is to find the ancient records of Jerusalem, excavated by the Templars and taken first to Kilwinning in 1140 and, we believe, subsequently re-interred below Rosslyn.

When Rosslyn is excavated the truth will conquer all.

Appendix 1 The Time Line

BC

972	Solomon becomes king of Israel and builds his temple for Yahweh
922	Solomon dies leaving religious and financial chaos across Israel
586	Final destruction of Solomon's temple
539	Start of the building of Zerubbabel's temple
6	Probable date of the birth of Jesus

AD

32	John the Baptist killed; Jesus assumes priestly as well as kingly messiahships
33	Crucifixion of Jesus
37	Mandaeans driven out to Mesopotamia by Saul
62	Killing of James the Just at the Temple
	Simeon, first cousin of Jesus is the new leader of the Jerusalem Church
66	Jewish Revolt begins
68	Destruction of Qumran
70	Destruction of Jerusalem and Herod's Temple by Titus
325	Council of Nicaea established by Emperor Constantine
1070	Hugues de Payen born
1090	Bernard of Clairvaux born
1094	Hugues de Payen succeeds his father as lord of Payen
1095	First Crusade starts
1099	Jerusalem taken by Crusaders; Godfrey de Bouillon elected chief
	Henri de St Clair takes the title Baron of Roslin
	Death of Pope Urban II
1100	Death of Godfrey de Bouillon, first king of Jerusalem
	Death of William II of England
	Baldwin I made king of Jerusalem
1101	Hugues de Payen marries Catherine de St Clair; given Blancradock as dowry
1104	Hugues de Payen travels to Jerusalem with Hugh of Champagne
1113	Bernard and the Fontaine family join the Cistercian Order
1114	Hugues de Payen and Hugh of Champagne again visit Jerusalem
1115	Bernard becomes Abbot of Clairvaux

1118	Nine knights under Hugues de Payen start to excavate the ruined Temple
1120	Fulk of Anjou takes oath to join Templars
1125	Hugh of Champagne takes oath in Jerusalem, making eleven Templars
1128	Council of Troyes grants Rule to Templars
	Hugues de Payen visits Roslin, as part of a tour of Europe
	Payen de Montdidier becomes Templar Grand Master of England and embarks on a major preceptory building programme
1136	Hugues de Payen dies
	Geoffrey of Monmouth writes *Matter of Britain*
1140	Lordship of Payen reverts to Count of Champagne
	Templars take relics from the Temple to Scotland
	William of Malmesbury writes story of Holy Grail and Joseph of Arimathea
1152	Geoffrey of Monmouth becomes Bishop of St Asaph
1153	Bernard of Clairvaux dies.
1174	Bernard of Clairvaux made a saint
1180	Chrétien de Troyes writes *Le Conte du Graal*
1190	An anonymous Templar writes *Perlesvaus*
1210	Wolfram von Eschenbach writes *Parzival*
1244	Birth of Jacques de Molay
1285	Philip IV (the Fair) succeeds his father at the age of seventeen
1292/3	Jacques de Molay elected last Grand Master of the Templars
1294	Boniface VIII made Pope
1296	Boniface issues bull, *Clericis Laicos*, forbidding clergy to pay taxes
1297	Louis IX canonised by Boniface
1299	Philip refuses to support Boniface in Crusade against Aragon
1300	Templars defeated at Tortosa and some carried as prisoners to Egypt
	Molay returns to Cyprus and considers a retreat to Europe
1302	Boniface VIII issues papal bull, *Unam Sanctam*, proclaiming Supreme Papal Power over kings
	William de Nogaret appointed principal adviser to Philip
	Philip IV publicly burns bull and seizes the lands of prelates loyal to the pope

1302 *cont'd* Boniface offers throne of France to Emperor Albert of Austria

1303   Nogaret attacks Boniface at Anagni

Boniface dies of fits brought on by attack

Edward I of England makes peace with Philip

1304   Benedict XI poisoned by Philip's agents after ten months in office

1305   Philip offers an old enemy, Bertrand de Gotte, Archbishop of Bordeaux, the papacy in return for six favours

Bertrand de Gotte crowned Pope Clement V at Lyons

Robert the Bruce excommunicated

1306   Pope calls Masters of Templars and Hospitallers to France to discuss combining both orders

Molay travels to Paris Temple with twelve horses laden with treasure to be greeted by Philip

Molay travels to Poitiers to meet with Clement and submit reasons for not combining orders

Hospitallers take Rhodes

Robert the Bruce crowned king of Scotland

The arrest of all Jews in France

1307   Molay travels again to Poitiers to discuss charges against the Order with Clement

Friday, 13 October, the arrest of the Templars by Philip the Fair

Jacques de Molay crucified, but not killed, and Shroud of Turin created

University meets in Paris Temple and reports on confession of the Master

1308   Pope attempts to escape from Bordeaux, but returned to Poitiers by Philip

Templars brought before Philip and Clement at Poitiers; Philip only hears confessions against Templars

Clement authorises Paris Commission to inquire into the charges against the Templars

1309   Paris Commission calls for Templars to appear before them in November

Molay brought before Paris Commission; reports being tortured to confess

Clement sets up Avignon papacy

1310   536 Templars assemble at Poitiers to defend the Order

1310 *cont'd*	Hearings of witnesses against Order begin in Paris
	Council of Sens condemns 54 Templars to be burnt in Paris
	Archbishop of Reims burns 9 Templars
	Archbishop of Sens burns 4 Templars
	Papal Commission recommences hearings without any defence counsels
1311	Papal Commission completes its hearings
	Pope arrives in Vienne for General Council
	General Council does not rule against the Templars
1313	Philip goes to Vienne
	Clement publishes bull abolishing Templars without ruling on guilt
1314	Molay asserts innocence of Order publicly and again reports having been tortured
	Philip convenes his secular council to condemn Molay to the fire
	19 March, Jacques de Molay and Geoffrey de Charney burnt at stake in Paris
	Philip and Clement both die
	Battle of Bannockburn – won by the intervention of a Templar battle force
1328	England recognises Scotland as an independent nation
	Manuscript of Renaud le Contrefait has first reference to Tarot cards
1329	13 June, pope accepts Robert I and his successors as kings of Scotland
1330	William St Clair dies taking the heart of Robert I to Jerusalem
1348	Black Death enters France via Marseilles
1350	Third of population of France dead from the Black Death
1353	Geoffrey de Charney Jr obtains grant to found church at Lirey
1356	King John II taken prisoner at Poitiers
	Geoffrey de Charney Jr dies
1357	First-known exposition of the Shroud of Turin
	Henry of Poitiers bans expositions of Shroud
1361–72	New outbreak of Black Death
1376	Tarot cards forbidden in Florence
1378	Clement VII, nephew to Jeanne de Charney, made pope
1382–88	New outbreak of Black Death
1389	Geoffrey de Charney II starts to redisplay Shroud

1389 *cont'd*	Memorandum of Pierre d'Arcis
1390	Pierre d'Arcis condemned to silence about Shroud
1440–90	Building of the reconstruction of the ruined Herod's Temple in Roslin
1534	The English split with the Roman Catholic Church
1578	Shroud first taken to Turin Cathedral
1598	First documented minutes of a Masonic lodge
1601	James VI becomes a Mason at the Lodge of Perth and Scoon
1602	Schaw Statutes, St Clair Charter
1603	James VI of Scotland becomes James I of England
1625	Charles I becomes king
1637	New English Prayer Book forced on Scotland
1638	The Covenant signed in Greyfriars' Kirkyard
1641	Sir Robert Moray initiated into Freemasonry in Newcastle
1643	The English Civil War starts
1646	The end of the main phase of the English Civil War at Oxford Elias Ashmole initiated in Warrington Lodge
1649	Charles I executed Charles II offered crown of Scotland only if he signs the Covenant The Commonwealth of England established
1650	Earl of Montrose executed Charles II signs the Covenant
1658	Oliver Cromwell dies
1660	Charles II king of England
1679	Archbishop Sharp of St Andrews killed Covenanters defeated and imprisoned in Greyfriars' Kirkyard
1684	Scottish lodges known to have weapons funds
1685	Charles II dies James VII king
1689	William and Mary sign Declaration of Rights and become joint monarchs
1690	James VII defeated at Battle of Boyne
1702	William of Orange dies Anne becomes queen
1706	Act of Split Succession passed by Scottish Parliament
1707	Parliaments of Scotland and England combined
1714	First recorded minutes of the Grand Lodge of York

1715	First Jacobite campaign to restore the Stuart line
1717	Formation of Grand Lodge of London
1724	Ramsey tutor to sons of Bonnie Prince Charlie
1725	Formation of Irish Grand Lodge
	Lodge of St Thomas founded in Paris
1730	Ramsey visits England
1736	Formation of Scottish Grand Lodge
1745	Second Jacobite campaign to restore the Stuart line
1748	Dermott joins London Freemasons
1752	Grand Lodge of Antients founded by Dermott
1761	Grand Lodge of France issues patent to spread the Scottish Rite in America
1799	The Unlawful Societies Act brought in by William Pitt
1801	The Supreme Council of the Thirty-third degree for the United States of America is formed
1813	Formation of United Grand Lodge of England
1819	Supreme Council for England established
	Duke of Sussex initiated into 33 degree by Admiral Smyth
	Rewriting of Masonic ritual started by Duke of Sussex
1830	All Masonic Craft ritual rewritten
1845	Supreme Council for Scotland established
1855	Albert Pike joins in the rewriting of the rituals of the Scottish Rite
1876	England breaks links with Supreme Council for Scotland
1881	The Encampment of Baldwyn complains that the English Supreme Council is exceeding its powers over ritual
1898	First photography of the Shroud
1947	Discovery of the Nag Hammadi cache of Gnostic gospels and the Dead Sea Scrolls at Qumram
1951	Excavation of Qumran starts
1955	The Copper Scroll opened and deciphered as an inventory of hidden treasures
1988	Carbon dating of the Shroud establishes its earliest possible origin to be 1260
1991	First public access to full collection of the Dead Sea Scrolls

Appendix 2 The Charter of Transmission of J.M. Larmenius

(Deciphered and Translated by J.S.M. Ward)

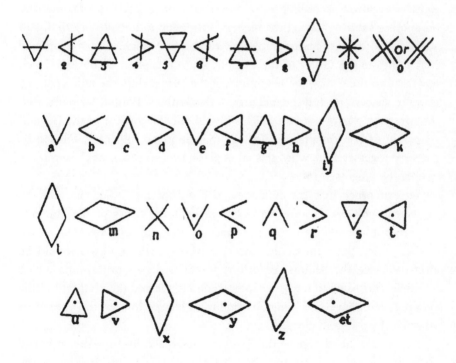

The Key to the Cipher

I, Brother John Mark Larmenius, of Jerusalem, by the Grace of God and by the most secret decree of the venerable and most holy Martyr, the Supreme

Master of the Knighthood of the Temple (to whom be honour and glory), confirmed by the Common Council of the Brethren, being decorated with the highest and supreme Mastership over the whole Order of the Temple, to all who shall see these Decretal letters, [wish] health, health, health.

Be it known to all both present and future, that, my strength failing on account of extreme age, having taken full account of the perplexity of affairs and the weight of government, to the greater glory of God, and the protection and safety of the Order, the brethren and the Statutes, I the humble Master of the Knighthood of the Temple have determined to entrust the Supreme Mastership into stronger hands.

Therefore, with the help of God, and with the *sole consent of the Supreme Assembly of Knights*, I have conferred and by this decree I do confer for life on the eminent Commander and my dearest Brother Theobald of Alexandria the Supreme Mastership of the Order of the Temple, its authority and privileges, with power according to conditions of time and affairs, of conferring on another brother, having the highest distinction in nobility of origin and attainments and in honourable character, the highest and Supreme Mastership of the Order of the Temple, and the highest authority. Which may tend to preserving the perpetuity of the Mastership, the uninterrupted series of successors, and the integrity of the Statutes. I order, however, that the Mastership may not be transferred without the consent of the General Assembly of the Temple, as often as that Supreme Assembly wills to be gathered together, and, when this takes place, let a successor be chosen at the vote of the knights.

But, in order that the functions of the Supreme Office may not be neglected, let there be now and continually four Vicars of the Supreme Master, holding supreme power, eminence, and authority over the whole Order, saving the right of the Supreme Master; which Vicars should be elected among the Seniors, according to the order of profession. Which Statute is according to the vow (commended to me and the brethren) of the very holy our above-said Venerable and most blessed Master, the Martyr, to whom be honour and glory. Amen.

I, lastly, by the decree of the Supreme Assembly, by Supreme authority committed to me, will, say and order that the Scot-Templars deserters of the Order be blasted by an anathema, and that they and the brethren of St John of Jerusalem, spoilers of the demesnes of the Knighthood (on whom God have mercy), be outside the circle of the Temple, now and for the future.

I have appointed, therefore, signs unknown, and to be unknown to the false brethren, to be orally delivered to our fellow-knights, and in what manner I have already thought good to deliver them in the Supreme Assembly. But these signs must only be revealed after due profession and knightly consecration according to the Statutes, rights, and uses of the Order of fellow-knights of the Temple sent by me to the above-said eminent Commander, as I had them delivered into my hands by the Venerable and most holy Master the Martyr (to whom honour and glory). Be it, as I have said, so be it. Amen.

I John Mark Larmenius gave this Feb. 18, 1324.

I Theobald have received the Supreme Mastership, with the help of God, in the year of Christ 1324.

I Arnald de Braque have received the Supreme Mastership with the help of God A.D. 1340.

I John de Clermont have received the Supreme Mastership with the help of God A.D. 1349.

I Bertrand Gueselin &e. in the year of Christ, 1357.

I Brother John of L'Armagnac &e. in the year of Xt. 1381.

I humble Brother Bernard of L'Armagnac &e. in the yr. of Xt. 1392.

I John of L'Armagnac &c. in the yr. of Xt. 1418.

I John Croviacensis [of Croy] &c. in the yr. of Xt. 1451.

I Robert de Lenoncoud &c. A.D, 1478.

I Galeas Salazar a most humble Brother of the Temple &c. in the year of Christ 1496.

I Philip de Chabot . . . A.C. 1516.

I Gaspard Cesinia [?] Salsis de Chobaune &c. A.D. 1544.

I Henry Montmorency [?] . . . A.C. 1574.

I Charles Valasius [de Valois] . . . Anno 1615.

I James Rufelius [de] Grancey . . . Anno 1651.

I John de Durfort of Thonass . . . Anno 1681.

I Philip of Orleans . . . A.D. 1705.

I Louis Auguste Bourbon of Maine . . . Anno 1724.

I Bourbon-Conde . . . A.D. l787. [There are several places called Condate.]

I Louis Francois Bourbon-Conty . . . A.D. 1741.

I de Cosse-Brissac (Louis Hercules Timoleon) . . . A.D. 1776.

I Cla[u]de Matthew Radix-de-Chevillon, senior Vicar-Master of the Temple, being attacked by severe disease, in the presence of Brothers Prosper Michael Charpentier of Saintot, Bernard Raymond Fabre Vicar-Masters of the Temple, and Jean-Baptiste Auguste de Courchant, Supreme Preceptor, have delivered [these] Decretal letters, deposited with me in unhappy times by Louis Timoleon of Cosse-Brissac, Supreme Master of the Temple, to Brother Jacque Philippe Ledru, Senior Vicar-Master of the Temple of Messines [? Misseniacum], that these letters in a suitable time may thrive to the perpetual memory of our Order according to the Oriental rite. June 10th, 1804.

I Bernard Raymond Fabre Cardoal of Albi, in agreement with the vote of my Colleagues the Vicar-Masters and brethren the Fellow-Knights, have accepted the Supreme Mastership on November 4th, 1804.

Appendix 3 The Process That Created the Image on the Shroud of Turin

We are grateful to Dr Alan Mills for giving us permission to quote from his recent paper that explains how the image on the Shroud could have occurred.[1] We hope that he will forgive us for rendering his thorough scientific explanation of the chemical process into a considerably lighter text for the benefit of our lay readers.

The characteristics of the image which Dr Mills felt needed to be explained were:

1. *The lack of gross distortions.*
If the image had been made by a contact of the linen on the blood- and sweat-covered body it should show the kind of distortion evident when we made a contact print of Chris's face (see page 153). The effect is of dramatically wider features because the image of the side of the face appears to be at the front. The Shroud does not exhibit such an effect. The features of the face on the Shroud are normal and it follows that it cannot have been created by the linen being in contact around the face.

2. *That image density is an inverse function of the distance of the cloth from the skin, with the process saturating at a distance of 4 centimetres.*
The closer to the skin of the victim that the linen of the Shroud came, the darker the image. There is a decreasing greyscale, until at 4 centimetres, there is no effect.

3. *That there are no brush marks detectable on the image.*
If the Shroud had been painted some brush marks should be detectable.

4. *That the process affects only the surface fibres and does not penetrate to the inverse side of the cloth.*
If the image had been made with any pigment (blood or paint) the fibres

---

[1] Dr A.A. Mills: 'Image formation on the Shroud of Turin', *Interdisciplinary Science Reviews*, 1995, vol. 20 No. 4, pp 319–26

would have absorbed it and passed some of the staining through to the other side.

5. That the variations in image density are produced by changes in the density of yellowed fibrils per unit area, not by changes in the degree of yellowing.

The image appears to have been created by a 'digital' process where the tonal scale is an illusion created by the number of discoloured dots per square centimetre.

6. That the bloodclots had protected the linen from the yellowing reactions.

Dr Mills had noticed that very old botanical specimens that have been kept dry produce faint yellow-brown markings on cellulose that show a remarkable amount of detail in a blue-filtered negative image. He found excellent examples of this effect on the paper mounts of samples stored in the herbarium of Leicester University since 1888. These markings, known as Volckringer patterns, were thought to be caused by a lactic acid reaction.

The other related phenomenon he had noticed was one that had caused problems for the manufacturers of photographic plates when they found that images could be produced in total darkness by the proximity of various materials such as newsprint, resinous woods, aluminium and vegetable oils. Known as the 'Russel Effect' it was generally accepted that the process was connected with the release of hydrogen peroxide. By the 1890s film manufacturers had discovered how to make emulsions which did not suffer from the effect and interest in this strange image-making process, that needed no light, died away.

Dr Mills found clear evidence that a naked man in still air will produce laminar (non-turbulent) convection air flows for a distance of 80 centimetres and from this he worked out that any image-forming particle would take about a second to travel the 4 centimetres from the surface of the body to the cloth. He described the key to the process as follows:

Only if the active principle is highly unstable would its smooth vertical transport give rise to a modulated image.

A possible unstable particle which could result in yellowing of linen fibrils is a type of free radical known as a reactive oxygen intermediate.

A free radical is an atom which has extra electrons, which are not matched by positively charged particles in the nucleus. These extra electrons are referred to as being unpaired and give the molecule a negative charge. The most commonly occurring molecular oxygen has two outer or valance electrons (two oxygen atoms combine to make a single oxygen molecule referred to as O_2 to show it is made up of two atoms). These electrons can take in energy to cause them to form an unstable molecule which can, under certain circumstances, give out its energy. It is rather like charging up a nicad battery and then shorting it out to give a sudden surge of power. The longest-lived of these unstable oxygen molecules, known as singlet oxygen, carries no charge, but does have energy stored in its electrons. It cannot exist for very long in this 'excited' state and will quickly collapse back to its normal state, giving up the extra energy as it does so.

When this singlet oxygen is created as a gas, it lasts for quite a long time, in chemical terms. The way the decay rate back to normal oxygen is measured is to take a large number of singlet oxygen molecules and to work out the time it will take for half of them to have decayed back to their normal state; this is then called the 'half life'. Dr Mills calculated the half life for singlet oxygen as 80 milliseconds (one eighty-thousandth of a second) and showed that the acidosis shock or oxidative stress resulting from the build-up of lactic acid during the trauma of crucifixion would result in the surface body cells of the victim giving off singlet oxygen.

These atoms of oxygen would be carried in a straight line to the covering shroud by the laminar convection currents and they would all decay back to their natural state by the time they had travelled a maximum of 4 centimetres. The nearer to the cloth the body was then the greater the concentration of singlet oxygen reaching the surface of the cloth at that point.

This type of release of stored energy from reactive oxygen intermediates will cause yellowing to cellulose fibres and the process has been a continual problem for museum curators, solved only by exhibiting sensitive exhibits in very low light levels. Dr Mills showed that the process of singlet oxygen release under particular conditions would cause the yellowing of any linen fibrils that were struck by these unstable oxygen molecules. The molecules are so unstable that they will be quickly absorbed once they have hit the cloth surface, so forming a true image of the subject below. The closer the traumatised skin was to the cloth the more fibrils would be discoloured and the darker the mark would be.

A very interesting point is that the discoloration would not occur instantaneously. Once the singlet oxygen molecule gives up its energy to the linen thread, the yellowing will continue for a very long time. This energy release acts as a catalyst which starts a process which is very like extremely slow scorching. If the cloth was kept in a dry dark place with a good supply of oxygen, the darkening of the image would continue until the chain reaction had used up all the affected fibrils. This process, known as auto-oxidation, is a very slow reaction taking many years to reach saturation, after which the image will decline very slowly.

Dr Mills' theory predicts that the image on the Shroud will slowly become fainter and eventually disappear. It has been recently reported that the image on the Shroud of Turin is mysteriously fading away.

His conclusions were fascinating:

Although images of this nature associated with botanical specimens pressed on paper are not uncommon, that on the Shroud of Turin appears to be unique because of the need for a highly unlikely combination of circumstances that are not individually demanding, namely:

- *a long shroud woven from fine linen*
- *its hurried draping over the recently deceased (unwashed?) body of a tortured man in a sealed, thermally stable place*
- *removal after some 30 hours*
- *storage in a dry, dark place for decades or centuries.*[2]

1. The bloodstains on the Shroud have been shown to be methaemoglobin particles bound to the fibres by a proteinaceous film derived from serum. When some of this material was removed it was found that the bloodclot had protected the linen beneath from the yellowing process, exactly as Dr Mills' theory predicts (see page 159).

2. Dr Mills' range of circumstances 'that are not individually demanding' (see page 161) can be shown to be likely to have occurred under the scenario we described in Chapter 8.

- *a long shroud woven from fine linen*. The Templars used the same resur-

[2] Dr A.A. Mills: 'Image formation on the Shroud of Turin', *Interdisciplinary Science Reviews*, 1995, Vol. 20 No. 4 p. 325

rection ceremony which is still used by Freemasons today and this ceremony still uses a long shroud woven from fine linen, so there would have been a ceremonial shroud in the Paris Temple.

• *its hurried draping over the recently deceased (unwashed?) body of a tortured man in a sealed, thermally stable place.* The draping of the shroud over Molay's body was a last ironic touch by Imbert after Molay had collapsed unconscious and been placed in a bed to recover.

• *removal after some 30 hours.* He was left in a coma for some considerable time, perhaps until the Sunday morning, when he was roused and brought before the University of Paris to hear his guilt proclaimed.[3]

• *storage in a dry, dark place for decades or centuries.* The Shroud was produced by Geoffrey de Charney's descendants some fifty years after Molay had been tortured. The image may have continued to strengthen right up to the time when it was first photographed, in 1898.

We have provided the first full explanation of the creation of the Shroud which explains all the factors known about its creation and agrees with the carbon-dating results exactly.

3. Dr Mills' work provided the final piece of the jigsaw. The image had slowly developed over the fifty years it had remained stored away and it was only Jeanne's desperate search for a source of funds which finally brought it to light. Dr Mills' report explains how the image was created.

Although oxygen is an element, individual atoms do not normally exist in an unpaired state. The oxygen we breathe has twin atoms and is called O_2 (see figure 1).

The lactic acid layer on the skin causes the two atoms to split and the individual atoms absorb a packet of energy from the process. They then rise up on the smooth convection airflow from the hot body. This lone-atom condition is unstable and each atom will unify with the first other oxygen atom it comes across so that as they move upwards an increasing number return to a normal paired state. By the time they have travelled 4 centimetres, almost all of them will have stabilised (see figure 2).

[3] Anon: *Secret Societies of the Middle Ages*

As the lone atoms re-merge with oxygen atoms on the surface of the fibrils of the linen, the packet of energy that they absorbed on parting is given up and the fibre changes colour. It is effectively scorched to a depth of one molecule (see figure 3).

As the single oxygen atom takes another atom to pair up with, it steals the partner of another oxygen atom, which leaves another atom 'widowed', which in turn takes the next oxygen atom available, setting up a chain reaction which does not stop until the supply of oxygen runs out. At every transfer of an atom, another packet of energy is transferred, causing a further scorch to the cloth (see figure 4).

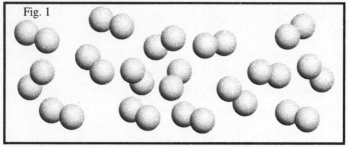

Oxygen atoms naturally occur only in pairs, called O_2

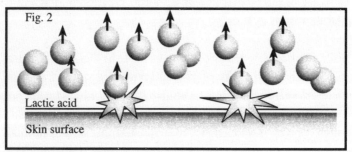

Contact with lactic acid adds energy to split pairs into singlets

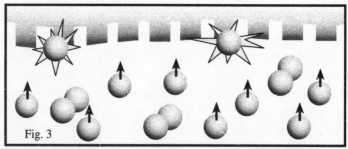

Some oxygen singlets reach shroud fibres and give up their energy as they re-unite causing singeing to fibres

The number of unstable 'widowed' atoms decreases with distance as more and more of them find a new partner. Therefore at 4 centimetres most atoms have paired up again and there will be relatively few energy packets hitting the surface of the fibrils, making less discoloration and therefore creating a lighter tone. Because the atoms are moving in a non-turbulent or laminar flow, the scorching that occurs on the fibrils of the Shroud gives what is in effect a digital picture of the subject underneath (a fibril is either completely discoloured or it is not affected at all), with darkness on the points close to the skin and lighter tones the further away the Shroud gets. This will produce a 'photograph' made with unstable oxygen atoms, rather than light photons (see figure 5).

Fig. 4

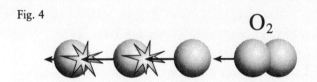

O_2

As one oxygen atom steals a new partner from another pair of atoms it leaves another unattached atom which takes one from the next pair, setting up a slow chain reaction.

Fig. 5

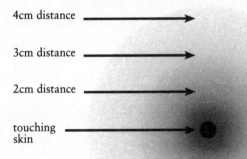

4cm distance

3cm distance

2cm distance

touching
skin

This process gives a negative image, just as we find on the Shroud.

Bibliography

Allegro, J.M., *The Treasure of the Copper Scroll*, Routledge & Kegan Paul Ltd, 1960

Allegro, J.M., *The Dead Sea Scrolls*, Pelican, 1964

Anon, *Secret Societies of the Middle Ages*, private publication, 1846

Anon, *The Lectures of the Three Degrees of Craft Masonry*, A. Lewis, 1891

Anon, *The Complete Workings of Craft Freemasonry*, A. Lewis, 1891

Anon, *Text Book of Freemasonry*, W.M. Reeves, 1902

Anon, *Text Book of Advanced Freemasonry*, W.M. Reeves, 1906

Anon, *The Perfect Ceremonies of the Holy Royal Arch*, A. Lewis, 1915

Anon, *The Lectures of the Three Degrees of Craft Masonry*, A. Lewis, 1954

Ashe, Geoffrey, *The Quest for Arthur's Britain*, HarperCollins, 1993

Bailey, Cyril, *The Legacy of Rome*, Clarendon Press, 1923

Barbour, Malcolm, *The Trial of the Templars*, Canto, 1978

Barbour, Malcolm, *The New Knighthood*, Canto, 1994

Bowman, Sheridan, *Interpreting the Past, Radiocarbon Dating*, British Museum Press, 1990

Brandon, S.G.F., *The Fall of Jerusalem and the Christian Church*, SPCK, London, 1951

Burman, E., *The Inquisition, The Hammer of Heresy*, The Aquarian Press, 1984

Burman, E., *Supremely Abominable Crimes*, Allison & Busby, 1994

Bussell: F.W., *Religious Thought and Heresy in the Middle Ages*, Robert Scott, 1918

Castells, F.P., *English Freemasonry*, Ryder & Co, London, 1931

Cawthorne, Nigel, *Sex Lives of the Popes*, Prion, 1996

Chadwick, Nora, *The Celts*, Pelican, 1971

Charpentier, Louis, *The Mysteries of Chartres Cathedral*, Thorsons, 1966

Clifton, Chas S., *Encyclopedia of Heresies and Heretics*, ABC-Clio, 1992

Curzon, Henri de, *La Maison du Temple de Paris*, Librairie Hachette et Cie, 1888

Powel Davies, A., *The Meaning of the Dead Sea Scrolls*, Mentor, 1956

Douglas, A., *The Tarot*, Penguin

Drower, E.S., *The Mandaeans of Iraq and Iran*, E.J. Brill, Leiden, 1962

Duncan, Anthony, *The Elements of Celtic Christianity*, Element Books, 1992

Eisenman, R. & Wise, M., *The Dead Sea Scrolls Uncovered*, Element, 1992

Eisler, R., *The Messiah Jesus and John the Baptist*, A.H. Krappe, London, 1931

Ellis, Peter Berresford, *Celtic Inheritance*, Constable, 1992

Fellows, John, *Mysteries of Freemasonry*, W.M. Reeves, 1906

Edward A. Freeman, *History and Conquests of the Saracens*, Macmillan & Co, 1876

Furneaux, R., *The Other Side of the Story*, Cassell and Company Ltd, London

Gerald of Wales, *The History and Topography of Ireland*, Penguin Classics, 1951

Goodwin, M., *The Holy Grail*, Labyrinth, 1994

Gould, Robert Freke, *History of Freemasonry*

Grand Lodge of Scotland, *Year Book 1996*

Guignebert, *Le Monde Juif vers le Temps de Jesus* (Colt, *L'Evolution de l'Humanite*), Paris, 1935

Hallam, Elizabeth M., *Capetian France 987–1328*, Longmans, 1980

Hancock, Graham, *Sign and the Seal*, Mandarin, 1992

Hodder, Edwin, *On Holy Ground*, William P. Nimmo, 1878

Horne, Alexander, *King Solomon's Temple in the Masonic Tradition*, The Aquarian Press, 1972

How, Jeremiah, *Freemason's Manual*, A. Lewis, 1881

Jones, Gwyn & Thomas, *The Mabinogion*, Everyman, 1949

Kenyon, K.M., *Digging up Jerusalem*, Ernest Benn Limited

Kitson, Annabella, *History and Astrology*, Unwin Hyman, 1989

Klausner, J., *Jesus of Nazareth* (English translation), London, 1929

Knight, Christopher & Lomas, Robert, *The Hiram Key*, Century, 1996

Knox, W.L., *Some Hellenistic Elements in Primitive Christianity* (Schweich Lectures, 1942), London, 1944

Landay, Jerry M., *Dome of the Rock*, Newsweek Book Division, 1972

Loomis, Roger Sherman, *Grail From Celtic Myth to Christian Symbol*, Constable, 1963

Maccabee, H., *The Mythmaker*, Element Books

Mack, Burton L., *The Lost Gospel*, Element Books, 1993

Marsden, John, *The Tombs of the Kings*, Llannerch, 1994

Pagels, E., *The Gnostic Gospels*, Weidenfeld and Nicolson, 1980

Peake, *Commentary on the Bible*, Thomas Nelson and Sons, 1962

Phillips, Graham & Keatman, Martin, *King Arthur: The True Story*, Arrow, 1992

Ravenscroft, Trevor, *The Cup of Destiny, The Quest for the Grail*, Samuel Weiser Inc, 1982

Rigby, Andrew, *Initiation and Initiative*, East European Monographs, 1984

Robinson, John J., *Born in Blood*, Century, 1989

Roderick, A.J., *Wales through the Ages*, Christopher Davies, 1959

Rolleston, T.W., *Myths and Legends of the Celtic Race*, Constable, 1911

Rose, Algernon, *The Director of Ceremonies*, Kenning and Son, 1932

Schlatter, D.A., *Geschichte Israels von Alexander dem Grossen bis Hadrian*, Stuttgart, 1925

Schonfield, H., *The Passover Plot*, Element Books, 1993

Schott, C.J., *The Tradition of The Old York Rite*, private publication, 1911

Scott, George Riley, *A History of Torture*, Werner Laurie, 1940

Spong, J.S., *Born of a Woman*, Harper, San Francisco

Springett, Bernard H., *The Mark Degree*, A. Lewis, 1931

Stebbing, George, *The Story of the Catholic Church*, Sands and Co, 1915

Stevens, J., *The Evolution of Symbolic Masonry*, Spottiswode & Co, London, 1892

Thompson, David, *The End of Time*, Sinclair-Stevenson, 1996

United Grand Lodge of England, *Book of Constitutions*

United Grand Lodge of England, *Masonic Year Book 1995–96*

Waite, Arthur Edward, *The Real History of the Rosicrucians*, Rebman, 1887

Arthur Edward Waite, *The Secret Tradition of Freemasonry*, Rebman, 1911

Walker, B.G., *The Secrets of the Tarot*, Harper, San Francisco, 1984

Wallace-Murphy, Tim, *An Illustrated Guide to Rosslyn Chapel*, Friends of Rosslyn, 1990

Walsh, John, *The Shroud*, W.H. Allen, 1964

Ward, J.S.M., *Freemasonry and the Ancient Gods*, Simpkin, Marshall, Hamilton, Kent & Co, 1921

Weston, Jessie L., *From Ritual to Romance*, Doubleday, 1920

Williams, A.L., *The Hebrew-Christian Messiah*, London, 1916

Wilmshurst, W.L., *The Masonic Initiation*, William Rider & Sons Ltd, 1924

Wilson, Edmund, *The Dead Sea Scrolls 1947–1969*, W.H. Allen, 1969

Wilson, Ian, *The Turin Shroud*, Victor Gollancz, 1978

Wilson, Ian, *Holy Faces, Secret Places*, Victor Gollancz, 1990

Zilva, Joan F. & Pannall, P.R., *Clinical Chemistry in Diagnosis and Treatment*, Lloyd-Luke (Medical Books) Ltd, 1984

INDEX